Essay Index

H. G. WELLS
and
MODERN SCIENCE FICTION

OTHER BOOKS BY DARKO SUVIN:

Dva vida dramaturgije (Two Aspects of Dramaturgy), Zagreb, 1965.
Od Lukijana do Lunjika (From Lucian to the Lunik: An Outline of Science Fiction Literature), Zagreb, 1965.
Bertolt Brecht: Dijalektika u Teatru (Dialectics in the Theatre), Belgrade, 1966.
Uvod u Brechta (An Introduction to Brecht), Zagreb, 1970.
Other Worlds, Other Seas: Science Fiction From Socialist Countries, New York 1970 and 1972 (also trans. Munich, 1972 and 1975, Paris, 1973, The Netherlands, 1976 and Tokyo in print for 1976).
A Production Notebook to Brecht's "St. Joan of the Stockyards," Montreal, 1973 (with Michael D. Bristol).
Science-Fiction Studies: Selected Articles, Boston, 1976 (with R. D. Mullen).
Russian Science Fiction 1956–1974, Boston, 1976.
Pour une poétique de la science-fiction, Montréal 1977.

OTHER BOOKS BY ROBERT M. PHILMUS:

Into the Unknown: The Evolution of Science Fiction from Francis Godwin to H. G. Wells, Berkeley and Los Angeles, 1970.
H. G. Wells: Early Writings in Science and Science Fiction, Berkeley and Los Angeles, 1975 (with the collaboration of David Y. Hughes).

H. G. WELLS
and
Modern
Science Fiction

Edited by
DARKO SUVIN
with
ROBERT M. PHILMUS
Associate Editor

LEWISBURG
BUCKNELL UNIVERSITY PRESS
LONDON: ASSOCIATED UNIVERSITY PRESSES

Associated University Presses, Inc.
Cranbury, New Jersey 08512

Associated University Presses
Magdalen House
136-148 Tooley Street
London SE1 2TT, England

Library of Congress Cataloging in Publication Data

Main entry under title:

H. G. Wells and modern science fiction.

Revised papers from an international symposium
held at McGill University in 1971.
  Bibliography: p.
  Includes index.
  1. Wells, Herbert George, 1866–1946—Congresses.
2. Science fiction—Congresses. I. Suvin, Darko,
1930–   II. Philmus, Robert M.
PR5777.H25 1976   823'.9'12   75–18696
ISBN 0–8387–1773–X

Contents

Acknowledgments

The international symposium "Wells and Modern Science Fiction" from which this volume resulted would not have happened but for the support from McGill University, in particular the then Chairman of the Department of English, Dr. Donald F. Theall, and Academic Vice-Principal, Dr. Michael Oliver, both science-fiction buffs. Financial assistance was provided by the McGill Department of English and the McGill Sesquicentennial Committee, chaired by Mr. David Bourke, whose staff helped in organizing the sessions. My sincere thanks are due to all of them. I also wish to acknowledge the financial support of the Canada Council for the research that resulted in my own essay, and of the Committee on Research and Resources, Humanities Division, McGill University, for partially defraying the costs of editorial work.

My special thanks go to Dr. Robert M. Philmus, who not only efficiently took over the ungrateful task of administrative correspondence during my leave year but also brought to the final editing a fresh energy and a critical glance. Ms. Mary E. Papke combined secretarial and editorial assistance with unusual precision and cheerfulness.

Earlier and somewhat different versions of some contributions have appeared in the following periodicals, to which acknowledgment is made for permission to reprint copyrighted material: to *Comparative Literature Studies*, for the essay by Darko Suvin; to *Science-Fiction Studies*, for the essays by Patrick Parrinder and Robert M. Philmus, and the bibliographies by R. D. Mullen, and David Y. Hughes-Robert M. Philmus; to *Strumenti critici*, for the essay by Darko Suvin; and to *Studies in the Literary Imagination*, for the essay by Howard Fink.

To quote material from the following volumes by George Orwell: *Collected Essays, Journalism and Letters* (4 vols.); *Coming Up for Air; Nineteen Eighty-Four; The Road to Wigan Pier*; published in U.K. by Secker and Warburg and in U.S.A. by Harcourt Brace Jovanovich, Professor Fink gratefully acknowledges the permission of Sonia Brownell Orwell and A. M. Heath & Co.

To quote material from Jorge Luis Borges's works, Professor Philmus gratefully acknowledges the permissions: for *Labyrinths,* of New Directions Publishing Corp. and their U.K. affiliate Lawrence P. Pollinger Ltd.; for *Other Inquisitions 1937–1952*, of the University of Texas Press and Señor Borges.

                                                                    D. S.

Introduction

by **DARKO SUVIN**

1

This book is the result of the eponymous international symposium "H. G. Wells and Modern Science Fiction," which I had the honor of organizing and presiding over at McGill University, Montreal, as part of that university's sesquicentennial celebrations in 1971. Participants from Canadian and American universities, joined by Sakyo Komatsu (Japan) and J.-P. Vernier (France), read their papers during three days (11 to 13 October), of sessions, which were open to the public and included discussions between participants and audience as well as among the participants themselves. Professor Chernysheva and Dr. Parrinder could not attend the symposium but submitted their contributions to this volume later. The two annotated bibliographies, also compiled subsequently, originated from public and private exchanges during the symposium itself.

The genre of the symposium—if I may call it that—has certain characteristics peculiar to it. It attempts to outline crucial areas of a given field in some detail, yet it includes different—hopefully congruent—approaches and can not claim to represent all conceivable methodologies and theories. Ideally, it is a forum for the critical exploration of new ideas as well as a kind of provisional atlas of the current state of research in the field.

The present volume is no exception. The contributors to it deal with some of the central *topoi* and patterns of Wells's science fiction in its relations with the writings of others. But admittedly much more remains to be said, on the one hand, about Wells's connections with older traditions—ranging from those in which Lucian, Plato, More, Verne (also Dickens), and, especially, Swift and Morris can be located, to others represented by the subliterature of the nineteenth century—and, on the other hand, about the influence of his science fiction and the models it embodies on practically all subsequent writers in the genre, from Jack London, G. K. Chesterton, Conan Doyle, Rosny the Elder, Aleksandr Bogdanov, Karel Capek, and Olaf Stapledon, through the "pulp" magazine writers after the 1930s (from—alphabetically, as it were—Asimov to Wyndham), right up to the newest science fiction of Lem, the Strugatsky brothers, Le Guin, Delany, Dick, Disch, and so on, with its attempt at synthesizing "highbrow" and "lowbrow" literature.

The essays here do, however, open up or extend inquiry into these large areas of Wells's affinities and influences. Adding to the investigations of Ian Clarke and Julius Kagarlitski on the place of Wells's science fiction vis-à-vis previous literary and subliterary tradition, Tatyana Chernysheva focuses on the folktale and the fairy tale; while David Y. Hughes, J.-P. Vernier, and I seek a way into his system by starting from Wells's sine-qua-non attachment to Darwinism as expounded by the teacher who made the most lasting impression on him, Thomas Huxley. Patrick Parrinder, Howard Fink, Robert Philmus, and Sakyo

Komatsu widen the area of exploration pioneered by Mark Hillegas in his study of Wells's influence: they discuss the instructive analogies—or no less instructive responses—to Wells in writers as geographically, and sometimes culturally, far apart yet as representative in world literature as Evgeny Zamyatin, George Orwell, J. L. Borges, and contemporary Japanese exponents of science fiction. While Parrinder points out not only the indebtedness to Wells of Zamyatin's *We,* but also these two writers' alternative models for science fiction, and Fink takes up the little-explored connection between Wells and Orwell's non science fiction (namely, *Coming Up for Air*), Philmus and Komatsu outline new areas of Wells's impact—either specifically, on the great Argentine writer Borges's "labyrinths of time," or generally, on an entire cultural milieu. Similarly, Hughes and I try to take a new look at Wells's early science fiction, which has already had a fair share of attention; while Vernier and, more extensively, R. D. Mullen, reopen the question of the value of Wells's later works, which Mullen argues deserve more attention than they have got since the beginning of a "revival" of Wells some fifteen years ago.

The contributors to this anthology (not excepting Komatsu, though he is also a practicing writer of science fiction) are literary scholars and critics. Though based in their own national—mainly British and American—tradition, they are interested in theoretical problems not only of comparative studies between one national literature and another, but also of the nexus between literature and philosophy, sociology, and cultural studies generally. It is perhaps not the least strength of science fiction that its writers, Wells in particular, are refractory to the treatment of literature as a semantically empty game. This literary genre uses its seeming estrangement from everyday space and time as a vantage point from which to see man's historical quandaries and existential anxieties more clearly than might be otherwise possible and, to appropriate a Shakespearean phrase, "by indirection find direction out."

Whatever differences may exist among their various approaches, the contributors hold certain premises in common regarding science fiction and regarding Wells. The first, and most obvious, is that there is sense in taking the genre of science fiction and Wells's fiction seriously, and talking seriously about it. Such a position is today not so paradoxical as it might have been considered to be only a relatively short time ago. The rapid spread of the teaching of science fiction in North American universities and, now, high schools (inaugurated by Mark Hillegas's course in the early 1950s, and followed by H. Bruce Franklin's first graduate course at Stanford and mine at McGill) preceded a slower, though steady, similar development in Britain, France, and the U.S.S.R. The parallel emergence of scholarly and critical writing on science fiction has added two new periodicals to the pioneering effort of *Extrapolation* (College of Wooster), both devoted exclusively to the genre: *Science-Fiction Studies* (Indiana State University) and *Foundation* (N.E. London Polytechnic). Critical journals not devoted exclusively to science fiction—*PMLA* and *College English*, for example—are giving more attention to the genre than used to be the case; and critics of the stature of C. S. Lewis, Stanislaw Lem, Leslie Fiedler, Fredric Jameson, Raymond Williams, and Robert Scholes—as well as the appearance of a number of books by lesser knowns— indicate the increasing attention that science fiction is getting. As for Wells, two biographies and almost a dozen critical studies—all of them published in the last ten years—speak for themselves.

If the first premise could be expected to meet with far less resistance than heretofore, the same can probably not be said of the second matter which contributors to this volume are fairly well agreed upon: that the famous battle between Wells and Henry James about "pure" versus "impure" art resulted in a stand-off draw rather than a Jamesian victory. True, Wells proceeded then to lose the war by his increasing impatience, in the latter part of his career, with the craft of writing—an impatience that aggravated and prolonged the normal recoil against his reputation by the generation of "sons" (and "daughters") from Virginia Woolf to George Orwell. Yet it should be clear by now that the attack by the Orwell-Leavis generation against the optimistic "crass Wellsianism" is as one-sided and distorting as the defense, by Anthony West and Bernard Bergonzi, that Wells was really a crass pessimist all the time. Both sides to the quarrel have made some valid points: the first reminded readers—as did Christopher Caudwell—of the haste or downright vapidity of some of Wells's transitory enthusiasms; the second uncovered a deep gloomy strain in his character to which several essays here (for instance, Vernier's) also refer. But perhaps writers can by this time strive toward the dialectical synthesis of saying that the interest of Wells's writings lies precisely in the ambiguities and tensions between his awareness of the possible or perhaps even probable doom of the human species and his humanistic commitment to intelligent collective action against such a catastrophe. Indeed, those writings of his where such a tension is largely absent—whether they be overwhelmed by optimism, as *In the Days of the Comet*, or by pessimism, as in *Mind at the End of Its Tether*—are his poorest. Fortunately, enough of his (probably too) voluminous output remains to justify a serious interest.

Having a predilection for collective (though not faceless) work in the *sciences humaines*, I am gratified to see a number of signs of mutual learning and help arising from the McGill symposium. From one of the two bibliographies already mentioned as an instance of this has come an anthology of Wells's early uncollected writings, edited with critical commentary and notes, by Philmus and Hughes (*H. G. Wells:*

Early Writings in Science and Science Fiction, published by the University of California Press). More pervasively, virtually all the essays here, though basically the same as were presented at the symposium, have been changed in a number of details, partly in response to the editor's (and later the associate editor's) nagging questions, but also as an outcome of scholarly osmosis and the rubbing of intellectual elbows. I know for certain that my own contribution has profited from the rest, including the bibliographical notes and discoveries. At any rate, it is my opinion, shared by my associate editor, that the essays here have a greater unity than is usual in publications arising from symposia.

2

Though the theme of the symposium did not call for a reappraisal of Wells's entire opus—that is, of the interrelations among his science fiction, his "mimetic," "naturalistic," or (as R. D. Mullen engagingly terms it) "mundane" fiction, and his nonfiction—an overview of Wells from a partly new perspective does, it seems to me, emerge from the contributions to this volume. The logical starting point for such an overview is Mullen's "Annotated Survey," which disguises under its modest title what is in fact an exhaustive essay in bibliographic form, outlining, by means of its useful and provocative categorizations and cross-references, a number of significant correlations among the various works in Wells's opus. Only formal reasons have prevented me, after much hesitation, from placing this bibliography at the beginning of the book, but I would still recommend that it be read first of all. The other bibliography, by Hughes and Philmus, complements Mullen's by offering an outline of the corpus of Wells's early science journalism, selected, annotated, and augmented by a number of articles not previously identified as belonging to

Wells. The discoveries of Hughes and Philmus indicate how further unattributed writings by Wells that could, no doubt, be found in various periodicals and newspapers, may provide materials for new bearings on his development. They remind one that a complete edition of Wells's collected works—which would finally allow scholars and critics to see his stature steadily and see it whole—is by now due, if not overdue. The researches of Hughes and Philmus have already brought to light not only new textual data (for example the review of Kidd's *Social Evolution*), but also new configurations of those data (for example Wells's revealing hesitations and reservations about Weismannism). The overview of his science journalism as embracing science popularization and education, science on its wonderful own as an intellectual game, and finally science as the basis for ideologically subversive speculation reveals much about Wells in his formative years, before 1900, and implies that it would be equally revealing to have a comprehensive account of his other reviewing activities and of his profound interest in education generally, not only science education. An indication of just how crucial it is—even for a purist literary analysis of Wells's fiction—to know the degree and direction of his scientific and educational bent is given in the essays of Hughes, Vernier, and myself, especially in the treatment of Wells's connection with T. H. Huxley. Indeed, the cognitive and educational pathos shared by the twofold subject of these essays, the literary genre of science fiction and the creative personality of H. G. Wells, is perhaps (paradoxically) never more clear than when didactics and scientific schematics are transmuted into poetry.

Yet, whatever overall bearings on Wells this book may offer, the focus is primarily on his science fiction and its relation to the genre as a whole. From the various discussions of Wells's science fiction, including his utopian fiction (which, more evidently in his case than in most others, is a subgenre of science fiction, or is, precisely, social science

fiction), this portion of his opus seems amenable to division
into three groups and periods. His *first* and most significant
science-fiction phase (roughly up to 1904) is based on the
vision of the Horrifying Novelty, the disruptive "Unique"
(in the extended Wellsian sense) as the long-range
sociobiological prospect for mankind. (I shall have more to
say about this first phase presently.) The *second* group
chronologically in part overlaps the first: two works belonging to it, *When the Sleeper Wakes* and its companion piece, "A
Story of the Days to Come," had already been published
(1899) before it came into its own, from 1904 to 1914, with:
*The Food of the Gods; A Modern Utopia; In the Days of the Comet;
The War in the Air;* and *The World Set Free.* It is based on
short-range sociopolitical extrapolation incorporating
some technological novelties such as the airplane and the
atom bomb, but it is centrally concerned with the utopian
organization of mankind as the sole alternative to the
criminal waste and muddle of Victorian bourgeois society
that will inevitably lead to world wars. Though history has
proved how very right Wells's diagnosis was, this group of
his science-fiction works is clearly inferior to the first one.
His first attempt in this phase, *When the Sleeper Wakes*,
remains the most interesting of the group. Its picture of a
future megalopolis with mass social struggles exploited by
demagogic leaders— "a nightmare of capitalism
triumphant"—is uncomfortably close to a number of developments in the twentieth century. But Wells's imaginative energy was beginning to flag: the observer-hero, waking
(like Bellamy's Western apostate, Julian West) in the new
social climate after two centuries, behaves alternatively and
incongruously like a Saviour (suffering his final Passion on
an aeroplane instead of a cross) and like a vacillating liberal
intellectual. The inconclusive plot makes for an adventure
of a beautiful soul in, rather than for a cognitive view of, the
future. Generically, as Mullen rightly reminds the reader in
his bibliographical entry, the novel is important as the

model of megalopolitan (and, as a rule, antiutopian) science fiction, from Zamyatin and von Harbou to Asimov, Orwell, and Pohl; and Parrinder's essay explores one particular case of action and reaction to this model (but that one, given the literary eminence of Zamyatin's *We*, is perhaps the most fruitful and paradigmatic of all). However, *When the Sleeper Wakes* (and Wells's second phase as a whole) is coresponsible not only for the persuasive "new maps of hell" but also for a spate of inferior science fiction, albeit with more rugged heroes, more wonderful weapons, and more sentimental entanglements than are found in Wells. Even his own later works of this phase are less convincing, in spite of interesting ideas and arresting passages. The lowest point is reached with *The Food of the Gods*, where the fundamental equation of moral and material greatness is never worked out, and with *In the Days of the Comet*, which is more perfunctory yet. The *third* group of Wells's science fiction is quite disjointed, transposing as it does his momentary political peeves and enthusiasms: it comprises the novels: *Men Like Gods, The Shape of Things to Come, The Holy Terror,* and possibly the more or less science-fictional *Mr. Blettsworthy on Rampole Island, The Croquet Player,* and *Star Begotten.*

Wells's whole sequence of programmatic utopias has interesting moments, especially when he is describing a new psychology of power and responsibility such as that of the "Samurai" in *A Modern Utopia* or of the dictator in *The Holy Terror.* This culminates in *Men Like Gods,* where Wells, impressed even while recalcitrant after his visit to young Soviet Russia, transiently returns to a Morris-like brightness. But his search for a caste of technocratic managers as "competent receivers" for a bankrupt capitalist society oscillates wildly from enlightened monarchs or dictators not too dissimilar from those of his great rival G. B. Shaw, through Fabian-like artists and engineers, to airmen and Keynesians (in *The Shape of Things to Come*). Wells's position "in the middle," wishing a plague on both the upper and the lower classes while trying to bypass history by conjuring up—as it were, single-handedly—a refurbished new upper class, proved singularly fruitless. Even this position and this third phase of his has, however, been extremely influential in subsequent Anglo-American science fiction, whose writers and readers mostly come from exactly those "new middle classes" or cadres Wells was putting forward as the hope of the future (I try to touch on this briefly in my essay). But in this later, less organized phase of his writing it might be more useful to proceed, as Mullen's essay does, by trying to cut across increasingly tenuous generic barriers in order to deal with Wells's general horizons. I think Mullen's essay succeeds in showing that from this point of view Wells's writing between the wars should not be simply written off, but on the contrary studied in all its surprising ups and downs.

3

Yet in the final analysis—as this book confirms—Wells's first phase, the cycle of evolutionary science fiction, is his lasting contribution to the genre (and—together with a few other "mundane" novels, culminating in *Tono-Bungay*—to fiction in general). Its basic situation is that of a destructive newness encroaching upon the tranquillity of the Victorian environment. Often, this is managed as a contrast between an outer framework and a story within the story. The framework is set in as staid and familiar Dickensian surroundings as possible, such as the cozy study of *The Time Machine,* the old curiosity shop of "The Crystal Egg," or the small towns and villages of southern England in *The War of the Worlds* and *The First Men in the Moon.* With the exception of the protagonist, who also participates in the inner story, the characters in the outer frame, representing the almost invincible inertia and banality of prosperous, bourgeois England, are reluctant to credit the strange newness. By contrast, the inner story details the observation of and the gradual, hesitant coming to grips with an alien, superindividual force that menaces such life and its certainties by behaving exactly as bourgeois progress did in world history—as a quite ruthless but technologically superior mode of life wedded to an imperial civilization.

As Wells himself observed, the element of newness is "the strange property or the strange world." The strange property can be an invention like the one that renders Griffin invisible. Or, obversely, it can be a new way of seeing: literally, as in "The Crystal Egg," "The Story of Davidson's Eyes," and "The New Accelerator"; indirectly, by rendering sensible what Vernier rightly calls *evolution by mutations*—radical changes subverting a prior state of affairs—as the Time Machine does; or fusing the "fields of view" of both the space-lens and what is in cinematography called the *time-lens* (speeded-up film), as in the spectacle of a wondrous new life seen through the Cavorite sphere. The new invention or way of seeing is always cloaked in a pseudoscientific explanation, the possibility of which turns out upon closer inspection to be no more than a conjuring trick by the deft writer, with "precision in the unessential and vagueness in the essential," as one critic put it—the best example being the Time Machine itself. The strange world is "elsewhen" or elsewhere. It is reached by means of a strange invention, or erupts directly into the Victorian world in the guise of the invading Martians or the Invisible Man. But even when Wells's own bourgeois world is not so explicitly assaulted, the strange New always reflects back on its illusions, its "false security and vain self-satisfaction."

The strange is menacing because it looms in the future of man. Wells masterfully translates some of the oldest folktale terrors of man (*see* Chernysheva)—the fear of darkness, monstrous beasts, giants and ogres, creepy crawly insects, and "things" outside the light of his campfire, outside tamed nature—into an evolutionary perspective validated by Darwinian biology, evolutionary cosmology, and the fin-de-siècle sense of a historical epoch ending. Wells, the student of Huxley, eagerly used alien and powerful biological species as a rod to chastise Victorian man, thus setting up the model for all the bug-eyed monsters of later chauvinistic science fiction. But the most memorable of those aliens, the octopuslike Martians and the antlike Selenites, are identical to "The Man of the Year Million" in an early article of Wells's (alluded to in *The War of the Worlds*): they are emotionless higher products of evolution judging men as men would insects. In the final analysis, since the aliens are a scary, alternative human future, Wellsian space travel is a trick, a variation on his seminal model of *The Time Machine*. The function of his interplanetary contacts is quite different from Verne's liberal interest in the mechanics of locomotion within a safely homogeneous space. Wells is interested exclusively in the opposition between the bourgeois reader's expectations and the strange relationships found at the other end: that is why his men land on the Moon and his Martians on Earth.

Science is the true, demonic master of all the sorcerer's apprentices in Wells, who have—like Frankenstein or some fairy-tale characters—revealed or brought about destructive powers and monsters. From the Time Traveller through Moreau and Griffin to Cavor, the prime character in his science fiction is the scientist-adventurer as searcher for the New, disregarding common sense and received opinion. Though powerful since it brings about the future, science is a hard master. Like Moreau, it is indifferent to human suffering; like the Martians, it blows up human pretensions of lording it over the universe:

> Science is a match that man has just got alight. He thought he was in a room—in moments of devotion, a temple—and that his

light would be reflected from and display walls inscribed with wonderful secrets and pillars carved with philosophical systems wrought into harmony [wrote the young Wells characterizing well nineteenth-century optimism, liberal or socialist]. It is a curious sensation, now that the preliminary splutter is over and the flame burns up clear, to see his hands and just a glimpse of himself and the patch he stands on visible, and around him, in place of all that human comfort and beauty he anticipated— darkness still. ("The Rediscovery of the Unique")

This science is no longer, as it was for Verne, the bright noonday certainty of Newtonian physics. Verne protested after *The First Men in the Moon*: "I make use of physics. He invents . . . he constructs . . . a metal which does away with the law of gravitation . . . but show me this metal." For Wells, human evolution is an open question with two possible answers, bright and dark; and in his first science-fiction cycle darkness is the basic tonality. The cognitive "match" by whose small light he determines his stance is Darwinian evolution, a flame that fitfully illumines man, his hands (by the interaction of which with the brain and the eye he evolved from ape), and the "patch he stands on." Thus Wells could much later even the score with Verne by talking about "the anticipatory inventions of the great Frenchman" who "told that this and that thing could be done, which was not at that time done"—in fact, by defining Verne as a short-term technological popularizer. From the point of view of a votary of physics, Wells "invents" in the sense of inventing objective untruths. From the point of view of the evolutionist, who does not believe in objects but in processes (which science has only begun to elucidate), Verne is the one who "invents" in the sense of inventing banal gadgets. For the evolutionist, Nemo's submarine is in itself of no importance; what matters is whether intelligent life exists on the ocean floor—thence "In the Abyss" and "The Sea Raiders." Accordingly, Wells's physical and technical motivations can and do remain quite superficial where not faked. Reacting against a mechanical view of the world, he is ready to approach again the imaginative, analogic veracity of Lucian's and Swift's storytelling centered on strange creatures, and to call his works "romances." Though the differences between Wellsian and folktale mutations are as significant as the similarities, Cavorite or the Invisible Man partake more of the flying carpet or the invisibility cap (*see* Chernysheva again) than of metallurgy or optics. Equally, the various aliens in Wells represent a vigorous refashioning of the talking and symbolic animals of fairytale, bestiary, and fable lore into Swiftian grotesque mirrors to man, with Wells's finishing touch of setting them in an evolutionary context. Since that context is temporal rather than spatial, Wells's science fiction presents itself as much more immediate and urgent than the earlier science fiction located in a safe, absolute time and far-off spaces that allowed even Swift to control his disgust. Thus, a note of fairly malicious hysteria is not absent from the ever-present violence—fires, explosions, fights, killings, and large-scale devastations—that in Wells's science fiction accompanies the sudden jumps in Darwinian time.

4

Having outlined the three groupings that Wells's science fiction as a whole seems susceptible to, I would like to focus on what I take to be his two best science-fiction tales of book length, *The Time Machine* and (with due respect to Bergonzi and also the excellent argument—in this volume—of Hughes, from whom I respectfully but firmly beg to differ in this judgment) *The First Men in the Moon*. These two works of Wells's first phase deserve special attention both because of their character as paradigms of science fiction and because they permit certain questions about Wells's outlook and its limitations to be clearly formulated.

The Time Machine, except for the mawkish business with Weena, is Wells's most economical work, and also his most programmatic: it shows his way of proceeding and its ultimate horizon. The horizon of sociobiological regression leading to cosmic extinction, simplified from Darwinism into a series of vivid pictures in the "Eloi," the "giant crabs," and the "eclipse" episodes, is established by the Time Traveller's narration as a stark contrast to the Victorian after-dinner discussions in his comfortable residence. The Time Machine itself is validated by an efficient forestalling of possible objections, put into the mouth of stereotypic, none-too-bright, and reluctantly persuaded listeners, rather than by the bogus theory of the fourth dimension or any explanation of the gleaming bars glimpsed in the machine. Similarly, the sequence of narrated episodes gains much of its impact from the careful foreshortening of ever larger perspectives in an ever more breathless rhythm. Also, the narrator-observer's gradually deepening involvement in the Eloi episode is marked by cognitive hypotheses that run the whole logical gamut of sociological science fiction. From a parodied Morrisite model ("Communism," says the Time Traveller at first sight), through the discovery of degeneration and of the persistence of class divisions, he arrives at the antiutopian form most horrifying to the Victorians—a run-down class society ruled by a grotesque equivalent of the nineteenth-century industrial proletariat. Characteristically, the sociological perspective then blends into biology. The laboring and upper classes are envisioned as having developed into different races or indeed species, with the Morlocks raising the Eloi as cattle to be eaten. In spite of a certain contempt for their effeteness, the Time Traveller quickly identifies with the butterflylike upper-class Eloi and so far forsakes his neutral-observer position as to engage in bloody and fiery carnage at the expense of the repugnant spider-monkeylike Morlocks, on the model of the most sensationalist, exotic adventure stories. His commitment is never logically argued, so that there is a strong suggestion it flows from the social consciousness of Wells himself, who came from the lower-middle class that lives on the edge of the "proletarian abyss" and thus "looks upon the proletariat as being something disgusting and evil and dangerous" (Christopher Caudwell). In lieu of logical or scientific consistency, the Time Traveller's attitude is powerfully supported by the prevailing imagery—both by animal parallels, and by the pervasive open-air green and bright colors of the almost Edenic garden (associated with the Eloi) opposed to the subterranean blackness and the dim reddish glow (associated with the Morlocks and the struggle against them). Later in the story these menacing, untamed colors lead to the reddish black eclipse, symbolizing the end of the Earth and of the solar system. The bright pastoral of the Eloi is gradually submerged by the encroaching night of the Morlocks, and the Time Traveller's matches sputter out in their oppressive abyss. At the end, the unforgettable picture of the dead world is validated by the disappearance of the Time Traveller in the opaque depths of time.

Many of these devices from *The Time Machine* reappear in other major works of Wells. The technique of domesticating the improbable by previews on a smaller scale, employed in the vivid vanishing of the model time machine, is repeated in the brutal struggles in the microcosms of the life boat and the ship *Ipecacuanha* that anticipate Moreau's island of beast people, or in the raising of the roof caused by the creation of Cavorite that prepares for the flight of the actual sphere, or in the description of a whole series of Selenites up to and including Phi-oo that culminates in the introduction of the Grand Lunar. The loss of the narrator's vehicle and the ensuing panic of being a castaway under alien rule (in *The War of the Worlds* this is inverted as hiding in a trap with dwindling supplies) recurs time and again as an effective cliff-hanger. Above all, the whole first cycle is a reversal of the popular concept by which the lower social and biological classes were considered as "natural" prey in the struggle for survival. In their turn, they become the predators: as laborers turn into Morlocks, so insects, arthropods, or colonial peoples turn into Martians, Selenites, and the like. This exalting of the humble into horrible masters supplies a subversive shock to the bourgeois believer in Social Darwinism; at the same time, Wells vividly testified that such a predatory belief was, to his mind, the only even fantastically imaginable alternative to things as they are. At the end, the bourgeois framework is shaken, but neither destroyed nor replaced by any livable alternative. What remains is a very ambiguous attack on liberalism from the position of "the lower middle class which will either turn to socialism or fascism" (*Pritchett).

Except for the superb late parable of, "The Country of the Blind," Wells's sociobiological and cosmological science-fiction phase culminated in *The First Men in the Moon*. It has the merit of summarizing and explicating openly his main motifs and devices. The usual two narrators have grown into the contrasting characters of Bedford, the Social-Darwinist speculator-adventurer, and Cavor, the selfless scientist in whom Wells manages for once to fuse the cliché of absentmindedness with open-mindedness and a final suffering glimpsed through cosmic vistas. The sharply focused space- and time-lens through which the travelers observe the miraculous growth of lunar vegetation is the most striking rendering of the precise-yet-wondering scientific observation often associated with the observatories and observation posts of Wells's stories. The Selenites not only possess the Aesopian fable background and an endearing grotesqueness worthy of Edward Lear's creatures, but they are also a profound image of sociopolitical overspecialization and of an absolute caste- or race-State, readily translatable from insect biology back into some of the most menacing tendencies of modern

political power concentration. Most Swiftian among Wells's
aliens, they serve a double-edged satire, giving an authentic
tone of savage and cognitive indignation:

> I came upon a number of young Selenites, confined in jars
> from which only the fore limbs protruded, who were being
> compressed to become machine-minders of a special sort. . . .
> These glimpses of the educational methods of these beings
> have affected me disagreeably. I hope, however, that may pass
> off and I may be able to see more of this aspect of this
> wonderful social order. That wretched-looking hand sticking
> out of its jar seemed to appeal for lost possibilities; it haunts me
> still, although, of course, it is really in the end a far more
> humane proceeding than our earthly method of leaving
> children to grow into human beings, and then making
> machines of them. (The First Men in the Moon)

The usual final estrangement fuses biological and social
disgust into Bedford's schizophrenic cosmic vision of himself "not only as an ass, but as the son of many generations
of asses." Parallel to that, Cavor articulates most clearly the
uselessness of cosmic as well as of earthly imperialism, and a
refusal to let science go on serving them (had this been
heeded, readers would have been spared the Galactic-
Empire politics and swashbuckling of later science fiction).
Finally, Bedford's narration, in its guise as a literary
manuscript with pretenses to scientific veracity, and the
complementary narration of Cavor's in the guise of interplanetary telegraphic reports, render explicit Wells's
ubiquitous mimicry of the journalistic style from that
heyday of early mass communication—the style, as one
critic remarked, of "an Associated Press dispatch, describing a universal nightmare."

Yet such successes can not mask the fundamental ambiguity that constitutes both the richness and the weakness
of Wells. Is he horrified or grimly elated by the high price of
evolution (Island of Dr. Moreau)? Does he condemn class

divisions or simply the existence of a menacing lower class
(The Time Machine)? Does he condemn imperialism *(First
Men in the Moon)* or only dislike being at the receiving end of
it *(War of the Worlds)*? In brief, are his insights into violence
and alienation those of a diagnostician or of a fan? Both of
these stances coexist in his works in a shifting and often
unclear balance: Wells's science fiction makes an aesthetic
form out of hesitations, intimations, and glimpses of an
ambiguously disquieting strangeness. The strange newness
is useful as a sensational scare thrown into the bourgeois
reader, but its values are finally held at arm's length. In
admitting their possibility he went beyond Verne; in
identifying them as horrible he opposed Morris. Wells's
works of science fiction are clearly "ideological fables"
(Parrinder), yet he is a virtuoso in having it ideologically
both ways. His satisfaction at the destruction of the false
bourgeois idyll is matched by his horror of the alien forces
destroying it. He resolutely clung to his insight that such
forces must be portrayed, but he portrayed them within the
framework of sensationalism, which neutralizes most of the
genuine newness. Except in his brightest moments, such
conflicts are therefore transferred—following the Social-
Darwinist model—from society to biology. This is a risky
proceeding, which can lead to some striking analogies but
scarcely to any resolution. His basic question about the
human future thus remains open; his science fiction can
present the future only as highly menacing yet finally
inoperative—the connection with its bearers (Time Traveller, Moreau, Griffin, Martians, Selenites, or Cavor) is always
broken off. Formally, this explains Wells's troubles with
writings of novel length. Except for the *First Men in the
Moon*, his most successful form is not the novel but either
the short story or the novelette. He therewith set the pace
for commercial norms of later science fiction—which adds
insult to injury by calling such works *novels,* which Wells did
not.

5

With all his strengths and weaknesses, Wells remains the central writer and nodal point in the tradition of modern science fiction. He collected, as it were, all the main influences of earlier writings—from Lucian and Swift to Kepler and Verne, from folktale, Plato, Bellamy, and Morris to Mary Shelley and the English, French, and American subliterature of planetary and subterranean voyages, future wars, and the like—and transformed them in his own image, whereupon they entered the treasury of subsequent science fiction. He invented a new thing under the sun in the story of time traveling without the help of dreams. He codified, for better or worse, the notions of invasion from space and cosmic catastrophe ("The Star"), of social and biological degeneration, of the fourth dimension, of the future megalopolis. Together with Verne's "scientific novel," his "scientific romances" and short stories became the privileged form in which science fiction was admitted into the official culture that rejected socialist utopianism. True, of his twenty-odd books that could be considered science fiction, perhaps only eight or nine are still of living interest, but those contain unforgettable visions (all in the five "romances" and the short stories of the early sociobiological-cum-cosmic cycle): the solar eclipse at the end of time, the faded flowers from the future, the invincible obtuseness of southern England and the Country of the Blind confronted with the New, the Saying of the Law on Moreau's island, the last Martian's lugubrious ululations in Regent's Park, the frozen world of "The New Accelerator," the springing to life of the Moon vegetation, the Lunar society. These summits of Wells's are a demonstration of what is possible in science fiction, of the cognitive shudder peculiar to it. Their poetry is based on transmuting scientific cognition, and poets from Eliot to Borges have paid tribute to it. It is a grim caricature of bestial bondage and a poetry of liberation achieved by means of knowledge. Wells was the first significant writer who started to write science fiction from within the world of science, and not merely facing it. For all his vacillations, his fundamental historical lesson is that the stifling bourgeois society is but a short moment in a menacing but also open-ended human evolution under the stars. Thus, he endowed later science fiction with a basically materialistic look backward at human life. For such reasons (further elaborated in my subsequent essay), all significant science fiction since Wells can be said to have come out of his *Time Machine*.

In the final analysis, then, whatever Wells's shortcomings, his achievement in science fiction is central to this genre's further course. The essays that follow accordingly attempt to define that achievement—its sources and affinities, its meaning, and its relation to Wells's successors and imitators in modern science fiction.

Zagreb and Montreal

NOTE:

It seems useful to append here selective book lists of both Wells's early science fiction and the secondary literature most pertinent to a further discussion of it.

A. A Book List of Wells's Early Science Fiction

Wells's fiction is cited throughout this volume by the first—that is, U.K.—edition; furthermore, in the case of his science fiction, citations are to chapter numbers rather than to page numbers. This decision was arrived at as the most practical one among the imperfect choices the contributors and editors were faced with and tried out. It rests on three main considerations. First, most of Wells's work from 1927 until his death in 1946 is unavailable except in first editions. Second, although the Atlantic Edition of 1924–27 contains what are presumably the final authorized texts of most of Wells's science fiction up to that time, it does not include his entire output even up to 1924 (*see* Mullen's bibliography at the end of this volume), and being a limited edition it is not readily available. Third, the problem is aggravated by the fact that the Atlantic Edition differs textually from most of the numerous subsequent publications of Wells's science fiction, which are readily available; on the other hand, these popular editions now in print vary in pagination and may go out of print without warning. Thus, the use of the first editions of Wells's science fiction ensures accurate, complete, and consistent documentation. However, since these first editions are very rare in the U.S.A., a corollary to their use is that references in this volume to Wells's science fiction denote chapter numbers, which as a rule do not vary from edition to edition. (*The Time Machine* is a special case: the sixteen chapters and epilogue of the first, Heinemann edition were divided into twelve chapters and epilogue in later editions. The following are the equivalents, with the Heinemann chapter numbers in each case at the left:

$1+2=1$; $3=2$; $4=3$; $5+6=4$; $7+8=5$; $9=6$; $10=7$; $11=8$; $12=9$; $13=10$; $14=11$; $15+16=12$; epilogue=epilogue.)

The Time Machine. London: Heinemann, 1895.
The Stolen Bacillus and Other Incidents. London: Methuen, 1895.
The Island of Dr. Moreau. London: Heinemann, 1896.
The Plattner Story and Others. London: Methuen, 1897.
The Invisible Man. London: Pearson, 1897.
The War of the Worlds. London: Heinemann, 1898.
When the Sleeper Wakes. London: Harper & Bros., 1899.

Tales of Space and Time. London and New York: Harper & Bros., 1900 [1899].
The First Men in the Moon. London: Newnes, 1901.

B. A Selective Book List of Secondary Literature

The following titles (here adduced by short title and latest full edition) will, when cited in this volume, be identified only by the asterisked name of the author:

Bailey, J. O. *Pilgrims Through Space and Time*. Westport, Conn.: Greenwood, 1972.

Bellamy, William. *The Novels of Wells, Bennett and Galsworthy: 1890-1910*. London: Routledge & Kegan Paul, 1971.

Bergonzi, Bernard. *The Early H. G. Wells*. Manchester, England: Manchester University Press, 1961.

Brooks, Van Wyck. *The World of H. G. Wells*. St. Clair Shores, Mich.: Scholarly Press, 1970.

Caudwell, Christopher. *Studies and Further Studies in a Dying Culture*. New York: Monthly Review Press, 1971.

Clarke, I. F. *Voices Prophesying War 1763–1984*. London, New York, and Toronto: Oxford University Press, 1966.

Hillegas, Mark R. *The Future as Nightmare*. New York: Oxford University Press, 1967.

Kagarlitski, Julius. *The Life and Thought of H. G. Wells*. London: Sidgwick & Jackson, 1966. Augmented edition *H. G. Wells: La vita e le opere*. Milan: Mursia, 1974.

MacKenzie, Norman and Jeanne. *The Time Traveller*. London: Weidenfeld & Nicolson, 1973. In U. S. as *H. G. Wells: A Biography*. New York: Simon & Schuster, n.d. [1973].

Nicolson, Marjorie H. *Voyages to the Moon*. Havertown, Pa.: R. West, 1973.

Parrinder, Patrick. *H. G. Wells*. Edinburgh: Oliver & Boyd, 1970—as *Parrinder.

————, ed. *H. G. Wells: The Critical Heritage*. London and Boston: Routledge and Kegan Paul, 1972—as *Parrinder, ed.

Philmus, Robert M. *Into the Unknown*. Berkeley and Los Angeles: University of California Press, 1970.

Pritchett, V. S. *The Living Novel*. London: Arrow, 1960.

Vernier, Jean-Pierre. *H. G. Wells et son temps*. Rouen: Université de Rouen/Didier, 1971.

Wagar, W. Warren. *H. G. Wells and the World State*. Freeport, N. Y.: Books for Libraries Press, 1971.

West, Geoffrey. *H. G. Wells*. London: Howe, 1930.

The important insights into Wells by Evgeny Zamyatin and Jorge Luis Borges are referred to in the essays of Parrinder and Philmus in this volume. Hadley Cantril, *The Invasion From Mars* (Princeton, New Jersey: Princeton University Press, 1940), offers a first insight into the mass-communications' transmission of Wells.

Finally, the works of Darwin, T. H. Huxley, Wells's autobiographical and critical writings (for example, prefaces to some of his works), and some bibliographies are also indispensable. In this volume, the following books will be cited as marked:

Huxley, Thomas H. *Evolution and Ethics and Other Essays*. New York: Appleton, 1896—as *Huxley.

Wells, Geoffrey H. *The Works of H. G. Wells 1887–1925*. London: Routledge, 1926—as *G. H. Wells.

Wells, H. G. *Certain Personal Matters*. London: Lawrence & Bullen, 1898 [1897]—as *Wells, *C.P.M.*

————. *Experiment in Autobiography*. New York: Macmillan, 1934—as *Wells, *Exp.*

H. G. WELLS
and
MODERN SCIENCE FICTION

The Folktale, Wells, and Modern Science Fiction

by TATYANA CHERNYSHEVA

Translated by Darko Suvin*

1

There was a time when mentioning the folktale and science fiction in one breath would have seemed silly, or even blasphemous. Jules Verne, the positivist taken with scientific fact, exiled the folktale from his "scientific novels." In Soviet science fiction, too, there was a time when the worst accusation a writer could face was a reproach for "baseless" ideas and hypotheses, which were then called *folktale-like*. However, the folktale is so deeply embedded into the history of art and folk culture that its powerful influence was inescapable in this tradition, too.

The first writer who opened wide the doors to folktale in the genre that later came to be called *science fiction* was H. G. Wells. The strong influence of Romanticism on Wells shows clearly in the imagery and the narrative manner of novels such as *The Island of Dr. Moreau* and *The Invisible Man*, and

---

*Note: Asterisked footnotes are from the translator.

35

especially in the *small forms** in his earlier stories. Like the Romantics, Wells plays a sui generis game of "possible-impossible" with the reader, suggesting to him a plausible explanation of strange, almost miraculous events, which is then immediately retracted (for example, in "The Magic Shop," "The Door in the Wall," "The Temptation of Harringay").

But Wells's romanticism did not only stem from literary traditions and associations. Wells came into science and literature at a time when the old model of the world, whose seeming permanence and stability had attracted and inspired Jules Verne, was breaking down. In Wells's time, as at the beginning of the nineteenth century, the world was again felt to be full of paradoxes and mysteries, unsolved riddles and the most unexpected possibilities. In such an intellectual atmosphere, a renaissance of interest in folktale motifs and images was not only possible but perhaps inevitable as well.

In the early work of Wells the folktale can appear directly, without masks. Thus, "Mr. Skelmersdale in Fairyland" is a true romantic fairytale, with a miraculous kiss and a moralizing conclusion befitting a proper individualistic literary offshoot of the folktale. In "The Man Who Could Work Miracles," Wells stuns the reader with a whole cascade of miraculous transformations of an openly folktale type. But a funny thing happens in that story; in it Wells tries the impossible: to reconcile in his artistic system—if not in life—the folktale miracle and the determinism of scientific thought. He makes his protagonists consider how and why those wonders become possible. Of course, the lucubrations of his protagonists, one of whom is interested in occultism, should not be taken too seriously, but the readers may nonetheless wish to listen carefully to them. In their discussion, a miracle is defined as a phenomenon that goes counter to natural laws and that can

---

*The Russian Formalists' term for short prose forms, such as the short story.

come about only by a great effort of the will. In this way, Wells tried to salvage the folktale miracle that still attracted him, but at the same time provide it with a new motivation, befitting the new times: human will is here postulated in place of the magic wand.

But this path led to a dead end. The good old folktale wonders in their direct meaning could not be restored— such a return to the sources was obviously artificial.

The point is that the folktale represents an almost closed world, with certain stable possibilities of plot and other elements. The particular, unique charm of the magical folktale lies in the fact that there are no miracles in it at all, if one regards a miracle as something contrary to the norm. Miracles are common and usual in that reality which the folktale relates. That is why it does not require any fairies and wizards. The wizards emerged in the individualistic, literary fairy tale when it became necessary to somehow motivate the wonders, if only aesthetically; they then became a symbolic sign, a key opening the door into the land of various miracles and transformations that are undoubtedly impossible in a real life.

However, Wells was at that time attracted precisely by the idea of creating a link between folktale and reality. If modern science had discovered the bottomless ocean of the still unknown, there may have been room for folktale wonders in it, too. Such a hope can be found in Wells's early stories, even though hidden by irony and humor. But the link forged by Wells turned out to be too weak. The folktale could not be made to harmonize with empirical reality, and Mr. Fotheringay's willpower was of little help here. It was as stylized as the interference of fairy and wizard; it explained nothing but required further explanations. In his later work, Wells would resort neither to willpower nor to a balancing at the limits of the possible and the impossible borrowed from the Romantics. He would found his artistic system firmly on determinism, and always do his best to give the events full verisimilitude.

This is not to say that Wells wholly refused the folktale. The degree of folktale influence on Wells, as well as on many more recent science-fiction writers, is rarely determined by their direct use of conventional folktale themes or characters; for example, of the Baba Yaga witch of Russian tales. The folktale created distinct conventions of its own, which were extremely important for the development of literary art through many centuries. Verne's fundamental creative approach and style were alien to the folktale imagery and convention, and could not draw sustenance from them. When Verne dreamed of conquering the underwater kingdom, he thought of the *Nautilus* submarine, but he did not dare to let man settle under water; when he dreamed of conquering space, he thought of an ultraperfect balloon or "battleship in the sky," but he could not bring himself to make men simply fly (as was later done by Aleksandr Belyaev). The unbound creative imagination of Wells allowed him to draw sustenance from all the riches of human thought, not only from the newest achievements of science and from its near future. Wells's links with literary traditions were much richer than Verne's. Conventional images and forms stemming ultimately from folktales often guided his imagination and shaped its ends.

In the complex symbols and allegories of *The Island of Dr. Moreau,* apparently nothing reminds one of the folktale. Nonetheless, the very thought of man's transformation into animal, or vice versa, stems not only from Darwin's theory of evolution, but also from the most ancient folktale metamorphoses. True, at first such metamorphoses are hardly recognizable, because they are very carefully dressed out in scientific terms. Dr. Moreau is not a wizard, though his appearance is unusual and his actions mysterious; he is a scientist acting in the laboratory atmosphere normal for a scientist. And the metamorphoses he brings about do not happen with folktale ease and simplicity: they are difficult, they are not instantaneous. The great surgeon works at creating human beings from animals by a series of operations, and the chance visitor to his island can hear the cries of an operated-upon puma gradually growing into the voice of a human being suffering from unbearable pain.

Similarly, the folktalelike transformation of normal-sized people, animals, and insects into giants in *The Food of the Gods* is shown as the result of a scientific experiment. The author is at great pains to prove that all such metamorphoses are in no way contrary to natural laws; only in that case could Wells count on a relative belief by the reader.

Even more interesting in this connection is *The Invisible Man*. Here, too, there is no folktale accessory such as an "invisibility cap" or a magic ring whose turning renders the hero invisible to his foes. However, it is clear that the idea of invisibility hails from the folktale. Science supplies in this instance only a new means and motivation of the wonderful, but on strictly scientific grounds the Wellsian protagonist is simply impossible: even assuming that invisibility could be attained, the invisible man would immediately have been blinded and all his normal contacts with the world blocked. Wells here does not follow science but the folktale, where the man with the invisibility cap retains the faculty of seeing and acting, just as the man who is turned into an animal or thing does not lose his human perception of the environment.

In these novels, the folktale tradition proved artistically more valuable for Wells than scientific cognitions. Wells's use of the folktale amounts to founding a new tradition. His significance lies in a liberation of the imagination, in the widening of boundaries imposed by natural science, and in making it again possible to turn to the folktale.

After Wells, folktale themes, motifs, and images enter increasingly into science fiction, even into the work of those authors who took much from Verne and developed within his tradition. In this connection the opus of Aleksandr Belyaev is important. His first significant work was published in 1926, and from then to his death in World War II he kept an eye on all the advances of science. He took after his teacher Verne in being sensitive to all scientific novelties and capable of seeing their further prospects and horizons. But as soon as he left pedestrian, scientific popularization (and in those years this was often all that there was to science fiction), he was captivated by the folktale, which clearly guided his imagination in the literary use of scientific discoveries.

This is especially noticeable in Belyaev's cycle of stories about the discoveries of Professor Wagner, where his imagination roamed with almost complete freedom. In one of those stories, "Hoity-Toity,"* the brain of a man named Ring is transplanted into an elephant; then follow the adventures of an animal aware of being a man. Scientific knowledge about transplanting organs from dying people was at that time limited, and insufficient for his theme; in this case, the folktale steered the writer's imagination far more than science, pointing out the fantastic possibilities of scientific experience. In particular, the story uses one of the most widespread folktale motifs, the transformation of a man into an animal (as Ring himself is fully aware). Again, in Belyaev's *The Devil's Mill,* the hand of a dead man helps to turn the millstones. This image, too, was brought about not merely by scientific knowledge about muscular physiology but also by the tradition of Russian folktales, where two magic hands often did the hard work for the hero.

Belyaev's flying man (in *Ariel*) and Ichthyander (in *Chelovek-amfibiia—The Amphibian***) did not come about without regard for folktale metamorphoses of men into fish and birds. True, in these two novels of his there are no direct transformations but only a similitude (the "amphibian man" has gills, for example): but the science of the time

---

*Available in an English translation in *A Visitor From Outer Space* (Moscow: Foreign Languages Publ. House, 1961), and in *Soviet Science Fiction* (New York: Collier, 1962).

**Available in an English translation published by Foreign Languages Publishing House (Moscow, 1959).

could not have produced such a similitude, and the writer asked from science in this case only a new justification for a folktale motif.

The folktale is alive and well in other modern science fiction, too: a tree blooms with dollars (Clifford Simak's *All Flesh Is Grass*), or an ancient pike-that-talks pokes its head out of a well (Arkady and Boris Strugatsky's *Ponedel'nik nachinaetsia v subbotu—Monday Begins on Saturday*). But the point is not, as I should like to stress, merely in playing with folktale motifs, which can be found in the work of many modern authors as in the already mentioned Strugatsky brothers. Such a play has been known to satirists and wits of past centuries, also. The point is primarily that in modern science fiction, as in Wells, the folktale is an indispensable constructive element for creating new science-fictional imagery. In modern science fiction, science does not replace the folktale; they interact in still imperfectly known ways. The ideas and figures of science fiction are created by a complex fusion of newest scientific and technical knowledge, fabulous wonders, and sometimes even medieval mysticism. These old image-clusters and associations, well known from childhood days, have not lost their power: they direct the writer's imagination, so that he willy-nilly tries on the new scientific discovery for congruity with them—will it give a new effect?

Such an orientation—not always a conscious one—toward folktale and older fantasy is also present in the work of the modern science-fiction writers. It is a witness to unbroken links between all periods of culture and human history. Human thought in each new stage of its development tries to conserve and save what was accumulated in the earlier cultural epochs, to find a way of inserting the old imagery into a new world view. As ancient gods and heroes have turned into alien visitors to Earth, so the fixed motifs of folktales, sometimes unrecognizably altered, turn into no less fixed motifs of modern science fiction: men go through walls, changing the structure of their bodies; they transform themselves into animals through skillful surgery; they learn to live under water; and the like. And though far-off galaxies do not much resemble the "thirtieth empire" of the folktale, the hero who is using "zero-transportation" or a "space warp" gets there as instantaneously as the hero of the magical folktale is transported beyond the ocean sea.

In brief, after H. G. Wells the folktale—in a sometimes indistinguishable conglomerate with antique and Christian myths as well as with later literary layers and associations—is actively present in modern science fiction. Together with science, such a use of the folktale organizes the imagery of science fiction. Thus, Wells's union of scientific explanations with folktale motifs, which are deeply embedded at the core of his fantastic ideas, considerably broadened the imagistic and thematic possibilities of science fiction. This gave a new impetus to its development.

2

However, the influence of the folktale can of late be found in aspects of science fiction other than its imagery. At this point, it might be useful to turn to some gnoseological roots of folktale imagery.

The folktale figures carry an echo of that plastic ancient world, where the mind of man did not accept impassable boundaries between things and phenomena, where any of them could transform itself into any other. That time has passed and its ethos can not be retrieved, but in many formulae, motifs, and situations of the magical tale its traces have been preserved.

This applies with particular force to one of the most characteristic folktale motifs—to the *motif of transformation* present in very many folktales. The transformations or metamorphoses can be very different—a man may turn into any animal or thing (needle, well, apple, bed, and so on). Two properties of folktale metamorphoses are especially interesting: (1) they always proceed easily, painlessly, and matter-of-factly, since for the folktale—or more precisely, for the ancient sensibility whose echoes it conveys—this is the normal state of the world; and (2) they are always material and literal: a man does, indeed, turn into a mouse, needle, well, and the like, with a subsequent return to the original shape.

However, in the folktale such transformations had become fixed poetic formulae, with no immediate relationship to the ancient transformational world feeling or sensibility. In the individualistic writings of the later epochs this became a literary device, a convention, an allegory, in which the transformation divested itself of any material character. Such a tendency is to be found in the fairytales of Charles Perrault and of his numerous followers and imitators. It is even more evident in the work of the Romantics, who constantly appealed to fairy-tale motifs and images.

Now, modern science fiction seems to be reinstating the original sense of the ancient transformation motif. Returning to it, science-fiction writers surprisingly seem to find a basis for it and for other folktale miracles in present-day science. Modern cognition—though, of course, on quite different grounds and levels of understanding than those assumed by the transformational mythology—again sees the world as flowing, changeable, and plastic. Present-day science does not acknowledge an impassable barrier between elements and states of matter. Other barriers also have silently begun to break down. The boundaries between life and death, reason and instinct have turned out to be relative and movable. Certainly, none of this is resuscitating the naive transformationalism of the folktale nor can man turn into a mouse or a needle. This natural plasticity of the universe exists by and in itself, it is not under man's domination. Thus the transformations of animals into people in Wells's *Island of Dr. Moreau* are excruciating, painful, and dreadful: there is no trace of folktale lightness in them. And yet even such a concept of a plastic and changeable world provides a new gnoseological basis for fantastic transformations. Modern scientific concepts are not wholly alien to the artists' and writers' return to depicting "flowing" worlds, without clear boundaries between phenomena and things. Brian Aldiss's novel *The Long Afternoon of Earth*, for example, mingles vegetation and animals, showing a world in which all realms of life are blended. In the story "Shape" by Robert Sheckley (in his collection *Untouched by Human Hands*) a world is drawn without stable forms: any shape may be assumed and altered almost endlessly. This world is perhaps even more flowing and changeable than the one envisaged in the ancient mythologies.

The renaissance of interest in transformations in modern science fiction is not to be explained only by the writers' playful imagination and the new opportunities for making up the most whimsical fantastic worlds, but also by far more serious reasons. Envisaged is the possibility of controlling matter, since most often the new transformations dealt with in science fiction are not natural to the state of the world, as they are in the ancient transformational consciousness, but a directed remodeling, which—as Wells had it—is a result of an effort of will and reason.

Most often, such a power over matter is depicted as a common feature of everyday life and belongs to an indistinct far future, when human civilization has significantly altered the very nature of man. In A. E. Van Vogt's story "Resurrection" (in his collection *Science Fiction Monsters*), for example, such a future man controls the nuclear processes merely by the power of thought. Even more frequently, perhaps, the wonderful possibility, which is nevertheless felt as natural and reasonable, is ascribed to super-civilizations. Their members can do practically anything: they can recreate their environment—time, space, matter—as they wish, and transform themselves into anything and any being. Such are the purple flowers in Clifford Simak's novel *All Flesh Is Grass*, and the "bowling balls" in his novel *They Walked Like Men*: they turn into men, houses, cars, money. As in the folktale, Simak does not try to explain how and why these transformations are possible, since in the world from which the "bowling balls" came this is simple, usual, and natural, although strange to a man. Vladimir Savchenko assumes that for such transformations the mind must gain full control of body metabolism. This makes it possible to change the human shape and become a different-looking person at will. The hero of his novel *Otkrytie sebia (Discovery of Oneself)*, Krivoshein–2, demonstrates his powers before an examining judge by showing several such transformations: "And suddenly his face started to change swiftly, the nose jutted out, thickened, grew purple, and hung slack, the eyes widened and turned from green into black, the hairs faded back from the forehead, forming a bald spot, and went gray, on the upper lip a gray moustache burgeoned, the jaw shortened. . . . In a minute the shaken Matvey Apollonovich was facing the Georgian face of Professor Androsiashvilli—with red-veined eyeballs, a heavy nose with angrily inflated nostrils, and bluish afternoon-stubble cheeks."[1] This is very similar to a miracle but the author strongly stresses its scientific materiality, so that the reader should not take it for a fantastic illusion. After such physical proceedings Krivoshein feels very tired: "The muscles of his body and face ache strongly. Inside, the painful itching of glands was slowly dying away. 'Well, three transformations in a few minutes—that's an overload. It did me in!' "[2]

For all their differences, transformations play a central part in the above-mentioned works. I would like to stress again that they are not simply the fruit of the writer's playful fantasy sustained by a new scientific grounding.

Such transformations belong to a wide range of themes and motifs in modern science fiction, connected with the search for new relationships between men—and intelligent life in general—and their environment. Intelligence peopling the universe, organizing and gradually changing its environment, must learn to adjust to any physical condition of existence. This is one of the main problems of modern science fiction, and it is exactly how Savchenko's Krivoshein–2 explains his endeavors: "The present environment changes from year to year: of what help here is the lesson of a million-year past, the repeating of old experience? Man has left the path of natural evolution, now he has to think for himself."[3] Transformations, suggested by the ancient folktale, are one possible aspect of such a cognitive adjustability. Properly, Savchenko treats transformations as a side effect, not as something central or basic. The final aim is to master all the powers of the body, to control all unconditioned reflexes by reason, which will bring about totally new relationships between man and his environment. The science-fiction writers who endow imaginary supercivilizations with such heretofore unknown powers suggest thereby that these new relationships are a norm of development of civilization and a result of long cultivation of reason. Igor Rosokhovatsky even tries to generalize this condition. In his story "Na Dal'nei" ("On Dalneya"), a Dalneyan explains his likeness to Earthmen in the following way: "The form of an intelligent being must change in accordance to his ends. It is the form of wind, not of rock."[4]

Transformations in modern science fiction often are neither a convention nor a graceful allegory, but the witness to a search for a novel, plastic world, where man could advance without painfully bumping into sharp corners and hard walls. Because of that, in modern science fiction transformations are, as in the ancient folktale, again becoming material and literal, and gradually losing their extraordinary character.

Thus the ancient folktale images and motifs are being reborn in twentieth-century science fiction, and it was Wells who ushered in this new life for the folktale. The Romantics dreamed about the marvelous, but they did not believe it could exist in reality. They regarded the world of the fairy tale as a beautiful land where all wishes come true, but it was an imaginary world opposed to and not connected with empirical reality. Wells was the first to see in a new changeable world the possibility for wonders similar to folktale miracles, but he still regarded them as miracles, for which it was very difficult to find a believable rationale. Such a rationale was found later: it appeared with the idea of supercivilizations.

The very notion of alien visitors to Earth as representatives of a supercivilization can explain everything and requires no further complicated motivations. Aliens and supercivilizations are as sufficient a motivation for the marvelous in present-day science-fictional thought as fairies and wizards were in the folktale. But there is little reason to regard the parallel ironically: it does not point to a simple substitution. A supercivilization is by itself almost a miracle; however, this miracle is presented as occurring in empirical reality. It is a miracle that is not only some dreamer's fancy, but also the subject of scientists' debates. Thanks to the concept of supercivlizations, ancient folktale wonders could be connected in modern science fiction with scientific possibilities after all—if not with what is now the case, then at least what could be. This is what gave new life to the old folktale.

NOTES

1. V. Savchenko, *Otkrytie sebia (Discovery of Oneself)* (Moscow, 1967), pp. 76-77.
2. Ibid.
3. Ibid., p. 87.
4. I. Rosokhovatskii, *Vitok istorii (The Spiral of History)* (Moscow, 1966), p. 213.

The Garden in Wells's Early Science Fiction

by DAVID Y. HUGHES

Since H. G. Wells considered his study of Darwinian biology under T. H. Huxley to be the foundation of his world view,[1] I shall here assume that influence as a fact and merely attempt to indicate the shape it takes in the cycle of Wells's imaginative works wherein the biological paradigm most clearly inheres, namely, his early science-fiction stories. Wells called them his *scientific romances*, a convenient term that I retain as distinguishing them both from his utopias and forecasts and from his later science fantasies. In the scientific romances, the presiding metaphor is biological: a garden; the self-ordering garden of nature, with or without a niche for man therein. It is a metaphor as significant for Darwin[2] and T. H. Huxley as for Wells: a scientific and didactic metaphor. But since it conveys the sweep and complexity of processes as large as life itself—uniform processes despite the diversity of their end products—it becomes associated with a grand design and is therefore aesthetically satisfying. Didactic and aesthetic motives variously intermingle in the garden metaphor, whether in Darwin, Huxley, or Wells.

The garden need not involve man. It may be thought of as a spectacle and man as the observer. Of the "spectacular" view of the garden, I shall take up three famous instances: the ending of *The Origin of Species*, the opening of "Evolution and Ethics," and a key passage from *The First Men in the Moon*. On the other hand, a vision of man's involvement is usually uppermost with Huxley and Wells (with Darwin less often). Of this naturalized view of man—whether as a life form generated by the garden or as himself the gardener—I take Huxley's "Prolegomena" to "Evolution and Ethics" as the discursive model and then turn to its imaginative uses in *The First Men in the Moon* (man-as-gardener) and in *The Time Machine, The War of the Worlds*, and *The Island of Dr. Moreau* (man-as-gardened).[3]

At the end of *The Origin of Species*, Darwin gives final expression to his perception of nature as ordered garden by means of the specific memorable image of the "tangled bank." "It is interesting to contemplate a tangled bank," he says, concluding that if one does so attentively, "there is grandeur in this view of life": for he envisions in the tangled bank—it might be any natural bank—an interpenetrating dynamism of birds, bushes, insects, worms in the mold, and so on, and therein he sees a scenic metaphor for the whole evolutionary drama, which, "from the war of nature, from famine and death, [has produced] the most exalted object which we are capable of conceiving, namely, . . . the higher animals." He invites enjoyment of the grandly ordered panorama as if it were a play, and at least in later editions he identifies the gardener with God, the Creator, who originally "breathed life into a few forms or into one," before the long ascent of evolution was brought about by secondary powers and causes.[4]

In "Evolution and Ethics," the emblem of nature—of the

"cosmopoietic energy," as Huxley calls it—is a bean. Jack reached wonderland by a beanstalk, and by a beanstalk Huxley promises to transport his audience to a world with powers that "do not excite our wonder as much as those which meet us in legendary history, merely because they are to be seen every day." Then, with swift strokes, he describes the "inert-looking" bean and how, planted and warmed by the sun, it generates "root, stem, leaves, flowers, and fruit," in accord with a "complex but, at the same time, minutely defined pattern," and how "no sooner has the edifice . . . attained completeness, than it begins to crumble," leaving only "apparently inert and simple bodies, just like the bean from which it sprang." Then he generalizes: "neither the poetic nor the scientific imagination" is at a loss for "analogies with this process of going forth and, as it were, returning to the starting point." He likens the cycle of the bean to the arc of a flung stone or arrow, to an upward and a downward road, to an unfolding fan, to a widening stream. Such, he says, is the "Sisyphaean process" of passing from a "seed to the full epiphany of a highly differentiated type, thence to fall back to simplicity and potentiality" (*E.E.*: 46–50).

Like the tangled bank, the bean is a scenic life metaphor, its cycles universal; and Huxley, like Darwin, joins didactic and aesthetic qualities in contemplating the economy of nature. On the other hand, Huxley specially stresses the death of the individual in the life cycle, and—in view of the comparison to the toil of Sisyphus—one gathers the bean would be in hell if it could feel at all. To contemplate the cosmopoietic energy is edifying and beautiful. To be sentiently involved in it—as in fact man is—may well be a nightmare of pain and suffering. Also in fact, such figures as those of the unfolding fan and the widening stream reflect what Frank Kermode calls *end-dominated* thought—a sort of musing on the astronomical end of time common in the fin de siècle.[5]

Cousin to the tangled bank and the bean is Wells's lunar vegetation. On the surface of Wells's Moon, the frozen air vaporizes at sunrise, revealing "these round bodies, these little oval bodies" like "very small pebbles"; and out of these bodies, there steadily arises on the bare moonscape—as if in a speeded-up film—"a bristling beard of spiky and fleshy vegetation" hurrying in the blaze of the sun to bud, flower, fruit, and seed again before night and death. And all this is seen through the spherical glass hull of the spacecraft, "distorted [as if] by a lens" (ch. 7), a spectacle "out there,"[6] miraculous, beautiful, yet ruled by natural law. But for Wells, as for Huxley, the upward course entails the downward. As the lunar twilight draws on, "dimly through the steaming glass" of the spacecraft are seen "the blazing red streamers of the sinking sun, dancing and flickering through the snowstorm and the black forms of the scrub thickening and bending and breaking beneath the accumulating snow"; for the air is condensing, "thinning out as it thins under an air pump" (ch. 18), and losing the power of supporting life.

Here, one may generalize on the end-dominated quality both of the lunar cycle and of corresponding elements in the other scientific romances. On Wells's Moon, the periodicity of the imagined vegetation approaches to a recapitulation of phylogeny by ontogeny: a working out of evolution and devolution, *not in the womb but in the life cycle.* Moreover, in a life cycle so immediately subject to the sun, nightfall is an apocalypse no different in kind from the final heat-death of the solar system, an event anticipated by nineteenth-century physicists within a relatively near future and likened by Lord Kelvin, in a popular figure, to "the winding up of a clock and letting it go till it stops."[7] In similar end-stopped fashion, the cyclic pattern of nature enters into the other romances also. Concluding *The Time Machine* comes the image of the crepuscular seashore of the year thirty million, while in *The War of the Worlds,* a similar though somewhat less advanced aging of Mars forces the Martians to flee sunward and invade Earth. On Moreau's island too, there is compressed in space and time an evolutionary arc rising with the painful manufacture of beasts into people and then falling with their reversion to animality.

Futhermore, Bedford and Cavor are not to remain spectators. In Wells's early science fiction, whether scientific romances or short stories, the protagonists are likely to become unexpectedly and ironically entangled[8] in their environments. To give a few examples out of many, in "The Flowering of the Strange Orchid," the aesthetic sense of Winter-Wedderburn is utilized to have him all but eaten alive by an orchid in his greenhouse; in "The Sea Raiders," Fison's sense of security and curiosity puts him within an ace of the tentacles of certain cephalopods that raid the English beaches; or, in "Through a Window," the avidity of an invalid looking through an open window for vicarious excitement is more than met when through the window comes a fugitive Malay servant run amok with a kris.[9] So, too, though the phases of the lunar garden in *The First Men in the Moon* make a fine show framed in the lenslike glass of the spacecraft, Bedford and Cavor soon cease to be mere observers. Venturing outside, they eat part of the environment, get drunk, go sailing about in the light lunar gravity, lose themselves, and, with fear and violent exertion, grope their way back to safety—Bedford at any rate does—just as the vacuum of night reclaims the scene. Thus, where Huxley condemns the cosmic process, so beautiful as a mechanism, because it produces pain, Wells renders that pain and its conditions imaginatively.

In order to mitigate the painfulness of the garden of nature, man himself gardens. Later, the messages of Cavor from within the Moon are about that. But the explication of the metaphor of man-the-gardener first involves another look at Huxley. In the "Prolegomena," Huxley anatomizes the shortcomings of both pleasure and utility as the proper objects of life, doing so in terms of gardening. The gardener manages the flowers and weeds in his garden according to some conscious design. Certain plants or plant arrangements are useful or pleasurable. He supports them in contradistinction to the state of nature. If he ceases his labors, the indigenously fittest weeds move in. On the other hand, he systematically "rogues" the poorer specimens of the very varieties he prizes. In this, he emulates natural selection. If an administrator of a human society acted in the same fashion, he would protect his colony both from external encroachments and from the survival of its own "weaker" members. Therefore, Huxley concludes, neither the cosmic process nor the pigeon-fancier's criterion of beauty or utility is a fit ethical model for human society, and "the gardening of men by themselves" must be limited to "facilitating the free expansion of the innate faculties of the citizen, so far as it is consistent with the general good" (*Pr.*:43), "until the evolution of our globe shall have entered so far upon its downward course that . . . once more, the State of Nature prevails over the surface of our planet" (*Pr.*:45).

These are familiar Victorian sentiments. One finds them, for example, in John Stuart Mill's "Nature" and in Tennyson's exhortation to "Move upward, working out the beast,/And let the ape and tiger die."[10] That last fine phrase Huxley quotes and elaborates throughout; and he ends by quoting the quest of "Ulysses": "strong in will/To strive, to seek, to find, and not to yield" in doing still "some work of noble note." No life more than Huxley's had exemplified that creed.

On the other hand, Huxley is an epiphenomenalist. To him, man's place in nature is really a settled affair. A garden is a subsystem of that very state of nature it opposes—like an eddy in a current—for the gardener himself is a product of evolution. Gardens—and "every other work of man's art"—arise by means of "the cosmic process working through and by human energy and intelligence" (*Pr.*:12). This is reductionism. It follows that a beehive is "a work of apiarian art, brought about by the cosmic process, working through the organization of the hymenopterous type" (*Pr.*:24). Analogously—it would be fair to conclude—the "full epiphany" and "Sisyphaean process" manifested in a bean are as much the will of the bean as the hive is of the bee or the garden is of man. One thinks by contrast of Camus's Sisyphus. Through his recurrent flashes of consciousness just at the pause before the rock crashes down again, Sisyphus "teaches the higher fidelity that negates the gods and raises rocks."[11] For Huxley, however, as he elsewhere states, consciousness need not be more than a coloring to neural activity, "as the steam-whistle which accompanies the work of a locomotive-engine is without influence upon its machinery."[12] Moreover, since pain accompanies consciousness, it would be easy to infer a biological advantage in the negative consciousness of the beehive.

Despite an advanced civilization and nominally superhuman intelligences, Wells's Selenites suggest this negative consciousness. The habitat within the Moon—honeycombed in part naturally, in great part artificially—is an ordered world-state safe from "waves and winds and all the chances of space" (ch. 24). Cavor is assigned a "hexagonal apartment" (ch. 23), as if with bees (or it may be with ants), and, among many standard functional types of Selenite, he recognizes two basic classes: "heads" and "hands." The "heads" are mere brain sacs on puny bodies, and the Grand Lunar lacks even a face, except eyes. Unindividuated, too, are the multiform "hands," each existing as the basis of some hypertrophied organ: a nose, a set of eyes, a forelimb. To the natural differentiae of social insects, the Selenites add surgical and psychological reinforcements and revisions. "In the moon," says Cavor, "every citizen knows his place," possesses "neither ideas nor organs for any purpose beyond it" and so "attains his end" as a "perfect unit in a world machine" (ch. 23).

What Bergonzi terms "uncertainly directed irony"[13] makes *The First Men in the Moon* the least satisfactory of the romances. But it is seemingly without irony at all that big heads are equated with brains and morality. Cavor calls the Selenites "colossally, in intelligence, morality, and social wisdom, higher than man" (ch. 23). As a biologist, Wells should have known better. Huxley pauses to spoof a "philosopher bee," who calls himself "an intuitive moralist," whereas to a biologist a hive is "an automatic mechanism, hammered out by the blows of the struggle for existence" on organisms each so constructed that if each had desires, it "could desire to perform none but those offices for which its organization specially fits it" (*Pr.*:25, 26). In ignoring the natural automatism of the hive, Wells forfeits rich satiric possibilities.

Advanced as they are, the Selenites do draw Wells's sporadic satire, aimed at Herbert Spencer's dogma of inevitable moral progress. "As surely as there is any meaning in such terms as habit, custom, practice," says Spencer, "so surely must the human faculties be moulded into complete fitness for the social state";[14] evil and immorality disappear and man becomes perfect. Here, "molding" is Spencer's equivalent for "gardening." Treating the figure of speech literally, Wells depicts Selenite machine-"hands" being "molded" in jars with the forelimb protruding and growing outside the vessel while the body within it is dwarfed. Wells's literary source is important here as showing that by "Selenites" human beings may be meant. The source is a passage (cited by Dr. Moreau in explaining his plastic surgery) from Victor Hugo's *L'Homme qui rit* on supposed Chinese practices of "molding" men in quaintly shaped vases by confining the child therein until it fills up "the embossments of the vase with its compressed flesh and twisted bones," enabling one, conveniently, to "order one's dwarf beforehand, of any desired shape."[15]

Cavor claims colossal moral superiority for the Selenites. Evidently, he prefers stability to freedom. Though affected "disagreeably" by the "hand" sticking out of the jar and seeming to "appeal for lost possibilities," he concludes "it is really in the end a far more humane proceeding than our earthly method of leaving children to grow into human beings, and then making machines of them" (ch. 23). Similarly, upon seeing scores of "hands" stored under opiates till their services shall again be required, he dispels an "unpleasant sensation" with the reflection: "To drug the worker one does not want and toss him aside is surely far better than to expel him from his factory to wander starving in the streets" (ch. 23). This surely is not the committed satire Wells might have written, surely not the uncompromising indictment that Zamyatin actually read into it:

> And suddenly, to your astonishment, you find that our own terrestrial social ills exist on the moon as well. The same division into classes, the rulers and the ruled. But here the workers have already turned into some sort of humpbacked spiders, and during periods when they do not work they are simply put to sleep and stacked in the lunar caverns like firewood, until they are needed again.[16]

Wells's use of Cavor as narrator is equivocal and temporizing. Bedford calls the Selenites "ants on their hind legs" (ch. 12) and escapes, but Cavor, a scientist, lingers and makes contact. Pointedly, Cavor's decision is a scientist's decision, and it is as a scientist that he becomes sole chronicler of the Selenites. Should his encomiums of the scientific Selenite state be discounted? Is he a mere foil? Readers' responses are now conditioned against utopia by Zamyatin and later antiutopists and the lessons of recent history. One easily forgets that *Looking Backward*, for example, invites another sort of irony: that of looking back at man's barbaric bourgeois pieties from the year 2000. Under this light—to whatever extent Cavor may appear to sympathize with the Selenites—it is notable that he becomes indisputably deluded only when he falls into glorifying terrestrial institutions. Like Gulliver facing the Brobdingnag king, he naively reveals the violence, chanciness, and irrationality of human life and, with true Gulliverian madness, assures the court of the Grand Lunar that "men of my race considered battle the most glorious experience of life, at which the whole assembly was stricken with amazement" (ch. 24). True, it is a discrepant fact that the Grand Lunar—unlike Swift's king—is not a compassionate ruler but only a reasoning machine; yet the Grand Lunar fills that king's role, functionally. The dilemma thus posed is the one Aldous Huxley said he intended in *Brave New World*: the necessity of choosing either the lunacy of scientific rationalism or the insanity of the old instinctual life.[17] Neither Huxley nor Wells explicitly states a preference, but no reader is in real doubt that Aldous Huxley leans to the instinctual life or that Wells in *The First Men in the Moon* leans to the rationalized, futuristic machine model as social ideal.

This was in 1901. By hindsight, *The First Men in the Moon* emerges as a rather fragile union of elements of Wells's earlier scientific romances with elements of the utopias and forecasts to come. Thus, the metaphor of the cosmic garden (on the lunar surface) counterpoints the metaphor of the gardening or molding of man by men (within the Moon). In turning now to the earlier scientific romances, therefore, the remainder of this discussion will in the main be restricted to biological man and his place in nature. That is, it will concern the Darwinian garden, not the Comtean or Spencerian one.

Wells's classic invention of an ironic and nonutopian automatism is in *The Time Machine,* and to it the garden is fundamental. As on the Moon, there are two gardens (but here they turn out to be one): the flowered upper world of the Eloi and the functional underworld of the Morlocks; and, as with the Moon, the existence of the underworld at first is unsuspected. Into these environs drops the Time Traveller, a believer in progress, whose preconceptions blind him to the significance of the facts his activism uncovers until, despite himself, he—and the reader—become entangled in the truth. In eight days' stay in the year 802,701, the evidence at first suggests a decadent humanity sustained by automatic underground machinery and turning its waning energies into aesthetic channels. The Eloi enjoy a life freed of toil and cured of weeds, fungi, gnats, even disease bacteria, and a land filled with "fruits and sweet and delightful flowers", broken by "no hedges, no signs of proprietary rights, no evidences of agriculture; the whole earth had become a garden" (ch. 6). The Time Traveller concludes that what T. H. Huxley called the *horticultural process* (*Pr.*:13) has eventuated in the aesthetic automatism of a garden of flowers and butterflies wherein consciousness is no longer a necessary presence.

In fact, the Eloi have forgotten fire and writing and they eat no meat. But, as Bergonzi remarks, one expects herds and herdsmen in Arcadia.[18] Yet here are neither flocks nor herders, it seems, and no wolves, either. Later, the Time Traveller becomes aware of the Morlocks. Since they run the machinery, he infers they are the descendants of the working classes, whose underground habitat accounts for their lemurlike divergent evolution; and he concludes they attend to the "habitual needs" of the Eloi "through the survival of an old habit of service," "as a standing horse paws with his foot . . . because ancient and departed necessities have impressed it on the organism" (ch. 10). Thus, he envisages a functional automatism of the Morlocks complementary to the aesthetic automatism of the Eloi. But even this stops short of the truth. When, elsewhere, the Time Traveller mentions "human spider[s]," "a monstrous spider's web," "the Morlocks on their anthill" (chs. 8, 12, 10), he prefigures his final, reluctant perception of the relationship of symbiotic cannibalism between Morlocks and Eloi. "These Eloi," he realizes, "were mere fatted cattle, which the antlike Morlocks preserved and preyed upon—probably saw to the breeding of" (ch. 10). In such fashion, then, does this self-adjusting eco-system of the Thames Valley perpetuate itself, preserved by a world-wide preventive equilibrium devised by the human intellect in a former age.

Thus, though the dials of the Time Machine register a specific year, 802,701, the time in reality is posthistoric and posthuman. Eloi and Morlocks are entangled in an evolutionary mechanism that, ironically, is the residual force in the garden that man built hoping to stop the evolutionary clock. Instead, he succeeded only in institutionalizing the aggressive and gregarious—predatory and herd—instincts he had inherited from his apelike ancestors of the prehuman world, and in passing them forward into a posthuman age. (And beyond that in the cosmopoietic process lies the Time Traveller's further vision of the dead Earth of the year thirty million.)

The automatism of *The Time Machine*, taken as a behavioral account, approximates to Cavor's notes on the natural history of the Selenites, who behave like ants—with an enslaved working class and a bloated aristocracy (still in command in the lunar society)—and who even pasture "mooncalves" on the lunar surface, as the Morlocks do the Eloi. But the accommodating note of intellectual playfulness in the later book reflects the beginnings of Wells's shift in outlook, mentioned earlier, away from biology and the condition of man over to sociology and the conditioning of man.

For the early Wells and for T. H. Huxley, "Eden would have its serpent" (*Pr.* :20). There would be a fall. Huxley's serpent is the Malthusian mechanism. Oversuccess at the horticultural process generates a backlash in the form of a population explosion, which, in turn, brings about a reversion to the brute struggle for existence. Thus, horticulture (in the sense of improving the living arrangements) taken by itself is merely self-defeating. Wells's serpent—also nourished by peace and plenty—is not overpopulation but simply the indwelling feral instincts themselves (and, to a lesser degree, the slavish instincts). Into the garden the Eloi and Morlocks have inherited, their ancestors built not only the technology to achieve a long-term stability, but also, inevitably, a value system based not on stability but on the struggle for existence. The local variant institutionalizing the struggle for existence in nineteenth-century England was the capitalist class structure. Accordingly, the Eloi and Morlocks perpetuate the shell of that structure. However, the intelligence and the will that created the garden have disappeared because, in the garden, they are disused and "nature never appeals to intelligence until habit and instinct are useless" (ch. 13). The garden has reverted to the state of nature, ruled by the instincts. Let the instincts rule, and the feral man will win out. Besides, the aggressive values of the struggle for existence were built into the garden originally through class inequities. There is a vicious cycle. Thus, functionally, Wells's and Huxley's serpents accomplish the same result of reducing the edifice of a materially advanced civilization to barbarism by boring from within at the biological compulsions.

The metaphor of the garden, though reaching a natural conclusion in *The Time Machine*, is by no means exhausted. By a logical extension it may include the idea of colonization. With this in view, Huxley suggests, as a likely state of nature, a country such as the Tasmania of a century before. He must have intended this sardonically, since the English settlers treated the Tasmanians like animals—for example, setting out poisoned meat for them to eat.[19] Anyway, starting with a primitive locale like the island of Tasmania, the colonizing process involves the clearing or extirpation of the local life forms, and, Huxley continues:

> In their place, [the colonists] introduce English grain and fruit trees; English dogs, sheep, cattle, horses; and English men; in fact, they set up a new Flora and Fauna and a new variety of mankind, within the old state of nature. Their farms and pastures represent a garden on a great scale, and themselves the gardeners who have to keep it up, in watchful antagonism to the old *régime*. Considered as a whole, the colony is a composite unit introduced into the old state of nature; and, thenceforward, a competitor in the struggle for existence, to conquer or be vanquished. (*Pr.* :16–17)

If one reads "Martian" for "English," this is a plot outline of *The War of the Worlds*, a work that is largely an allegory of the conquest of a primitive society by technologically sophisticated colonists with no respect for native values or culture. England falls to the imperialist Martian war machines. Yet, in the end, it is the Martians who perish because their organisms possess no antibodies against terrestrial microbes.

Thus, England (England as symbolic referent for modern mankind) is the Tasmania of Wells's story, the primitive state of nature. The scene in practice is localized still further, partly to London but mostly to the outlying courses of the Thames and its tributaries. The setting is pastoral. There is a slight resemblance to the Thames Valley of *The Time Machine*, and, like the Morlocks, the Martians keep cattle, at first using manlike creatures brought from Mars, and later the English. But the fundamental use of landscape in *The War of the Worlds* is in terms of an allegory of the world's body. According to Huxley, the colony "is a composite unit introduced into the old state of nature," there to conquer or succumb in the struggle for existence. In Wells's version, Mother Earth plays host to an alien body (the theme of entanglement again), but then rejects it. But by "Mother Earth" I mean not only the watercourses of the Thames but also the whole industrial and communications net of the region (and, by extension, of the world).

A useful way of viewing the Martians is as the disseminators of the technology through which they conquer. Wells finds various ways of representing this technology organically or quasi-organically, then setting it to interpenetrate with the familiar landscape. Early on, for example, the Woking Common is described as follows:

> In the centre, sticking into the skin of our old planet Earth like a poisoned dart, was this cylinder. But the poison was scarcely working yet. Around it was a patch of silent common, smouldering in places, and with a few dark, dimly seen objects lying in contorted attitudes here and there. Here and there was a burning bush or tree. Beyond was a fringe of excitement, and further than that fringe the inflammation had not crept as yet. (bk. I, ch. 8)

The stuck skin, the smoldering common, the burning tree, the fringe of excitement: such images—animate or inanimate, but all accessory to that "inflammation"—have the effect of personifying the fabric of the scene.[20] Thus, the fringe of excitement takes fire from the burning tree, as it were, then embraces several sightseers, then affects the number of lights looking toward the common that night from Woking. Wells's language groups the works of man and nature as a single organism, barely alerted or affrighted or inflamed as yet by the "poisoned dart."

From within the pits made by the impact of such cylinders, the Martians erect their tripod fighting machines, forty or fifty feet high. These machines look startlingly alive, with well-articulated limbs governed by a sham musculature. They may be seen to bowl along "with a rolling motion and as fast as flying birds" (bk. I, ch. 12), blending with the landscape while dominating it through their size and mobility. From the pits, too, spreads the metallic red weed that grows with prodigious fecundity, choking the rivers and then following the floodwaters until, at times, not a terrestrial growth is in sight (bk. II, ch. 6).

Thus, the poison spreads through the circulatory system to the heart, the city of London:

> So you understand the roaring wave of fear that swept through the greatest city in the world . . . , the stream of flight rising swiftly to a torrent, lashing in a foaming tumult round the railway stations, banked up into a horrible struggle about the shipping in the Thames, and hurrying by every available channel northward and eastward. By ten o'clock the police organization, and by mid-day even the railway organizations, were losing coherency, losing shape and efficiency, guttering, softening, running at last in that swift liquefaction of the social body. (bk. I, ch. 16)

Afterwards, Wells carries through the metaphor of dissolution with powerful descriptions of the clogging of the north roads, the coast roads, and the Thames estuary far out into the English Channel. Yet, dictated by the logic of the guiding metaphor of colonization and struggle for existence, the rejection of the aliens by the host body comes as the inevitable finishing stroke—one that has been constantly implied by the language of personification. Nature brings in her revenges.

Turning last to *The Island of Dr. Moreau,* where Wells's didacticism comes most clearly into focus, again Huxley provides the appropriate starting point for discussion. Continuing the colonial-garden metaphor, Huxley writes:

> Let us now imagine that some administrative authority, as far superior in power and intelligence to men, as men are to their cattle, is set over the colony, charged to deal with its human elements in such a manner as to assure the victory of the settlement over the antagonistic influences of the state of nature in which it is set down. (*Pr.*:17)[21]

Huxley follows this train of thought to the conclusion that the administrator's task is self-defeating since the Malthusian "serpent" will unleash the feral instincts the administrator above all wishes to suppress. Thus, Huxley's true protagonist is not the godlike administrator but, as always, the biological imperatives. With all his powers, the administrator bows to the forces of nature within and outside of man, and these are unadulteratedly Manichaean forces. Huxley was forbidden by the rules of the Romanes Lecture to mention religion. Privately, he called the lecture, "really an effort to put the Christian doctrine that Satan is the Prince of this world upon a scientific foundation."[22]

The setting of *The Island of Dr. Moreau* is a remote island governed by Dr. Moreau, a man of commanding physical and intellectual presence, a skillful biological researcher; in short, a good likeness of Huxley's superior "administrative authority." On the island, Moreau maintains a colony to whom his wishes are undisputed commands. As it is in the other romances, Wells bypasses Malthus, though, and the feral instincts of the colonists emerge without need of population pressures to trigger them. Moreau is a vivisectionist. Aided by hypnosis and chemical alteration of the blood, he makes animals into men surgically. These creatures have an unfinished look. Moreau is always hopeful of his next experiment, but the old ones he turns off and allows to wander into the settlement of the Beast Folk, where they are subject to the injunctions not to go on all fours or suck up drink, and where they chant the litany:

> "*His* is the House of Pain."
> "*His* is the Hand that makes."
> "*His* is the Hand that wounds."
> "*His* is the Hand that heals." (ch. 12)

The work of Wells's scientific administrator, in other words, is directly addressed to and threatened by the very slight hold of acquired civilized characteristics over "the ape and tiger" within.

For obvious reasons, Wells called *The Island of Dr. Moreau* "a theological grotesque."[23] Moreau seeks to avoid the pitfalls that beset him in his likeness to Huxley's "administrative authority" by installing himself as God and hedging his enterprise with religious sanctions. He is impatient of pain—"simply our intrinsic medical adviser to warn us and stimulate us"—because what counts is the "intellectual passion" of attempting "to find out the extreme limit of plasticity in a living shape" (ch. 14). That is, Moreau consciously emulates the evolutionary laboratory of the world, for "the study of Nature makes a man at last as remorseless as Nature" (ch. 14). Not surprisingly, he dies, like Frankenstein, at the hands of one of his own creations, one that has reverted. His is thus a figure of satanic pride. The way to the Beast Folk's village, described by the narrator, Prendick, might be the way down to hell. After traversing a copse, "all charred and brown," leading to "a bare place covered with a yellow white incrustation" and obscured by "a drifting smoke, pungent in whiffs to nose and eyes," "the path coiled down abruptly into a narrow ravine between two tumbled and knotty masses of blackish scoriae," into which he "plunged" (ch. 11). Later, Moreau convenes the Beast Folk by means of a Miltonic trumpet blast, calling them to a steaming and smoking natural amphitheater reported by Prendick to be "covered over with a thick powdery yellow substance which I believe was sulphur" (ch. 16).

Moreau plays at Huxley's "Satan, Prince of this world," standing in the same relation to the Beast Folk as Nature, he feels, stands to the evolutionary creation. He also plays the role of Huxley's administrator—"as far superior in power and intelligence to men, as men are to their cattle"—who scientifically molds and selects colonists, only to be thwarted by their instinctual drives. On Moreau's island, Prendick, comfortable amateur of biology and former student of Huxley's, comes to feel the whole game of life may be a mere matter of the chance interplay of irrational constraints and compulsions: "A blind fate, a vast pitiless mechanism, seemed to cut and shape the fabric of existence, and I, Moreau (by his passion for research), Montgomery (by his passion for drink), the Beast People, with their instincts and mental restrictions, were torn and crushed, ruthlessly, inevitably, amid the infinite complexity of its incessant wheels" (ch. 16).

From the microcosm of Moreau's island, Prendick at last escapes to find what solace he can, not in "the confusion of cities and multitudes" and "the daily cares and sins and troubles of men," but in the unspoiled countryside and the "infinite peace and protection in the glittering hosts of heaven" (ch. 22). Fittingly, insofar as his sanity is restored, in a measure, it is by the "little stars"[24]—as it were by the astrophysical constancies of nature illuminating the Sisyphaean darkness of biological life.

Wells in the scientific romances is never an explicit moralizer. Yet, since his plot outlines approximate to extreme limiting cases of the possibilities of evolution, the stories emerge as elaborations and realizations of the aesthetic and didactic potentialities of T. H. Huxley's and Darwin's garden. One might say that as the aesthetic quality of such presentations increases, so does their didactic power. To perceive life in terms of the metaphor of the garden is to advance a metaphysical proposition with clear implications for ethics. Huxley appears not to have fully grasped the fact that to the degree "the ape and tiger" within man is in evidence, ethical considerations go out the window. Aware that "Eden would have its serpent" when he speaks of an administrator's "garden," he yet has hope of combating the beast on the high ground of an act of ethical repudiation. He seems less than conscious that "Satan, the

Prince of this world," holds sway over the only empire Huxley, the agnostic, publicly admitted of. Wells, on the other hand, does not raise the image of ethical man. In the scientific romances, Wells keeps to the image of biological man and holds true to its implications. Man, vulgar and stoic and opportunistic (like Bedford, who escapes with the Moon gold), may best survive by means of his adaptability, in its quality neither bestial nor simply rational but human—as long as man survives at all.

Darwin and Huxley placed man firmly inside of nature and nature firmly inside of man, and that is the human condition so far as biology knows it. But the recognizing of the condition was a process unfolding itself in Darwin for half his life and long continuing to unfold in the consciousness of the age. Wells's scientific romances have the form of quests (or would-be conquests) where the revelation of the limits of the human condition—expressed in terms of the garden—is brought about heuristically through the eye-opening of initially blinded narrators. This is not only effective literary form but also a viable transliteration into poetic-imaginative terms of the didactic method of science itself.

NOTES

1. *See,* for example, *Wells, Exp.,* pp. 161–63, passim.

2. It is the thesis of Stanley Edgar Hyman—*The Tangled Bank* (New York, 1962), p. x—that Darwin's books are "art, . . . the work of the moral imagination, imposing order and form on disorderly and anarchic experience. That this vision of order and form is primarily metaphoric makes it no less real." And Theodore Baird—"Darwin and the Tangled Bank," *American Scholar* 15 (1946): 486—contrasts metaphor in, say, Carlyle ("revelations of his own inner self") with metaphor in Darwin ("pointers to actions outside the observer") and shows that Darwin's metaphors both define and are defined by what goes on "out there" upon the stage of nature.

3. *Huxley, cited further in the text as *Pr.* (for "Prolegomena") and

E.E. (for "Evolution and Ethics") with page number; H. G. Wells, *The First Men in the Moon, The Time Machine, The War of the Worlds,* and *The Island of Dr. Moreau,* cited further in the text by chapter numbers. Omitted for reasons of space are *The Wonderful Visit, The Food of the Gods,* and many early short stories; in Wells's early science fiction, the only longer works that fall outside the garden cycle are *The Invisible Man* and parts of *When the Sleeper Wakes.*

4. *The Origin of Species by Charles Darwin,* ed. Morse Peckham (Philadelphia, 1959), pp. 758–59: from the 2d ed. on, the words "breathed into a few forms" became "breathed by the Creator into a few forms."

5. Frank Kermode, *The Sense of an Ending* (New York, 1967), pp. 11, 96–98, passim; *see also* *Bergonzi, pp. 3–14, on the myth of fin de siècle = fin du globe.

6. *See* note 2.

7. William Thomson, Lord Kelvin, "On the Sun's Heat," in *Popular Lectures and Addresses* (London, 1897), 1: 422; he estimates in future "five or six million years of sunlight" (p. 397); H. G. Wells—Preface, *The Time Machine* (New York, 1931), pp. ix-x—recalls that "geologists and astronomers of that time told us dreadful lies about the 'inevitable' freezing up of the world—and of life and mankind with it. There was no escape it seemed. The whole game of life would be over in a million years or less. They impressed this upon us with the full weight of their authority."

8. Robert P. Weeks—"Disentanglement as a Theme in H. G. Wells's Fiction," *Papers of the Michigan Academy of Science, Arts, and Letters* 39 (1954): 440—shows how Wells's heroes characteristically (and in the end unavailingly) "desire to escape" from "a world enclosed by a network of limitations."

9. "The Sea Raiders," in H. G. Wells, *The Plattner Story and Others*; the other two, in his *The Stolen Bacillus and Other Incidents.*

10. *In Memoriam,* sec. 118; "the ape and tiger die" is a phrase Huxley quotes (*E.E.*: 52) and harks back to repeatedly; Tennyson, he felt, especially in *In Memoriam*—Leonard Huxley, *Life and Letters of Thomas Henry Huxley,* 2 vols. (New York, 1900), 2: 358–59—"was the only modern poet . . . who has taken the trouble to understand the work and tendency of the men of science."

11. Albert Camus, *The Myth of Sisyphus,* trans. Justin O'Brien (New York, 1955), p. 123.

12. "On the Hypothesis that Animals Are Automata," in Thomas H. Huxley, *Method and Results* (New York, 1893), p. 244.

13. *Bergonzi, p. 163.

14. Herbert Spencer, *Social Statics, together with Man Versus the State* (New York, 1910), p. 32.

15. Victor Hugo, *The Man Who Laughs*, trans. William Young (New York, 1885), p. 17; in *Moreau*, ch. 14.

16. "H. G. Wells," in *A Soviet Heretic*, ed. and trans. Mirra Ginsburg (Chicago, 1970), p. 267.

17. Aldous Huxley, Foreword to *Brave New World* (New York, 1946), p. viii.

18. *Bergonzi, p. 58.

19. H. G. Wells, *The Outline of History*, New Republic Edition, 2 vols. (New York, 1920), 2: 189; in *The War of the Worlds* (bk. I, ch. 1), Wells remarks, "The Tasmanians . . . were entirely swept out of existence . . . by European immigrants, in the space of fifty years. Are we such apostles of mercy as to complain if the Martians warred in the same spirit?"

20. David Lodge—*Language of Fiction* (New York, 1966), pp. 214–42—convincingly demonstrates Wells's mastery of landscape-and-architectural metaphor in *Tono-Bungay*; this technique is prefigured in *The War of the Worlds*.

21. Quoted by Jack Williamson—*H. G. Wells* (Baltimore, Maryland, 1973), pp. 75–76—who notes that *Moreau* "dramatizes Huxley's metaphor of the garden"; Williamson briefly discusses the metaphor in connection with *Moreau* only.

22. In Leonard Huxley, 2: 381; *also* 2: 322, 379; the devil, says T. H. Huxley, is " 'Prince' (note the distinction—not 'king') of the Cosmos" (2: 406), and the "king," or "Providence," is at this juncture barely emerging, "operating through men" (2: 321), and otherwise absent from the universe.

23. *The Works of H. G. Wells*, Atlantic Edition (London, 1924), 2: ix.

24. *Time Machine*, ch. 12; quoted by *Parrinder, p. 22, who remarks that to Wells's heroes "the stars may seem to offer shadowy emotional alternatives to earthbound frailty and fear; the human spirit can be affirmed and identified with the whole cosmic process" (*see also* pp. 21, 28).

Evolution As a Literary Theme

in

H. G. Wells's Science Fiction

by J. P. VERNIER

It is interesting to notice that although Wells, throughout his life, was concerned with the future of mankind—that is, with the outcome of evolution—the main body of his science fiction was spread over a relatively small number of years at the turn of the century.

The impact of the theory of natural evolution on his mind is well known: it was first felt when he attended the lectures of T. H. Huxley, at South Kensington, in 1884 and 1885, and, ten years later, evolution was to provide him with the fundamental theme of his "scientific romances" and of many of his short stories. In the 1890s the concept of evolution had lost whatever polemical value it may have possessed; it had become fairly generally recognized and accepted, and T. H. Huxley was pointing out the moral implications of this situation. Against the many muddled attempts at "Social Darwinism," he asserted the necessity of diverting the evolutionary process into channels devised by man, if the human species was to survive:

> Social progress [he wrote in his classic book on the subject: *Evolution and Ethics*] means a checking of the cosmic process at every step, and the substitution for it of another, which may be called the *ethical process*; the end of which is not the survival of those why may happen to be the fittest, in respect of the whole of the conditions which exist, but of those who are ethically the best.[1]

This is the lesson Wells kept on repeating right to the end of his life, with varying emphasis. There does not seem to be sufficient evidence to support the view that, in the last years of the nineteenth century, Wells was already intent on saving the world from impending catastrophe. On the contrary, he had just embarked upon a literary career, was writing short stories, and was moving away from the ponderous reflections that he later considered as "serious writing." His failure to get anything along the lines of his "The Rediscovery of the Unique" printed certainly led him to abandon for a time the field of abstract speculation. At the same time as he was writing his science fiction, he contributed book reviews to the *Saturday Review*, and these clearly show that he was then more concerned with literary problems than with political ones.

This leads me to the question I should like to discuss here. Undoubtedly his imagination was kindled by the theory of evolution, as expounded by Huxley, but evolution is a scientific notion implying far-reaching consequences in the realm of ethics and social organization; it had to be translated into the particular language of fiction. It had to be imparted to the reader by means of characters caught in the web of a fictional structure, and deriving "life" from the language they used and the situations in which they were placed. Many of the later "discussion novels" expound almost the same views on evolution as the "scientific romances"; and yet they are now forgotten and often rightly so, while the latter retain today the fascination exerted by the great literary works. Is it not therefore reasonable to assume that, in these, Wells achieved an artistic unity that is sadly wanting in the former?

If one also assumes that nowadays the concept of evolution has become so much a part of the intellectual background that it has lost whatever originality it possessed in Wells's day, can one not suppose that Wells's treatment of evolution led him to illustrate some of the themes that recur in present-day science fiction and that this accounts for the modernity of his fantasies?

Wells himself was aware of the problem involved in the creation of credible stories from material based on extrapolations of scientific possiblities and took pride in the way he managed to hold his reader's attention:

> The technical interest of a story like *The War of the Worlds* [he asserted in 1920] lies in the attempt to keep everything within the bounds of possibility. And the value of the story to me lies in this, that from first to last there is nothing in it that is impossible.[2]

With qualifications, this could probably be said of most of his science fiction, and it is fairly easy to point out the simple but effective devices Wells relied upon to create this impression. His use of well-defined, familiar geographical locations, concrete details, pseudo–objective scientific accounts of the phenomena described, all come within the province of realism, but the theme of evolution that is illustrated in most of these books implies a number of facts that have a direct bearing on the literary treatment: firstly, the emphasis falls on man, not as a individual character defined through his relationship with other individuals, but on man as a representative of his species at the turn of the century, sharing a number of assumptions with his contemporaries and confronted with extraordinary circumstances due to the passing of time or to the practical application of some unheard-of scientific discovery. Thus the individual characters are subservient to the species.[3] One may notice, for example, the frequent description of Prendick as *The Man*, in *The Island of Dr. Moreau*, which stresses the representative quality of the character and the opposition with the Beast Folk. Here are the titles of some of the chapters: "The Man who was going Nowhere," "The Man who had Nowhere to go," "The Crying of the Man," "The Hunting of the Man," "The Man Alone."

Second, evolution implies the passage of man, or rather of a living being, from a familiar state to one that is usually so extraordinary that the shock of recognition hits the reader with great strength. What matters essentially is this change from one state to another, so that *evolution* is, in fact, the equivalent of *mutation*. The passage of time is not conveyed to the reader by means of narrative devices; when it becomes necessary for readers to know, they are simply told the amount of time that has elapsed. The newly acquired invisibility of Griffin makes him as much of an oddity to the rest of the world as the 800,000-odd years that have gone into the making of the Eloi and the Morlocks. This evolution may stress not only the biological change but also the social one, as in *When the Sleeper Wakes* or "A Story of Days to Come," although it is remarkable that, when Wells devoted his attention only to this aspect of evolution, he usually failed to create a convincing vision.

Finally, evolution being, as I have just said, practically synonymous with mutation, it follows that the problem of the linear representation of time hardly ever arises. In fact, one can say that natural evolution is spread over such a vast span of time that no ordinary reader can be expected to grasp such vastness.

"There is no difference between Time and any of the three dimensions of Space except that our consciousness moves along it,"[4] the Time Traveller asserts, but nowhere are readers made to witness, through literary means, the movement of this consciousness along time. Indeed, the Time Traveller finds himself confronted with the world at various stages of its evolution, but evolution must become imperceptible for him to be able to take in its consequences. In other words, the important factor is *change* and not the cause of this change. This means that the narrative is usually connected with events on a human scale, while descriptive chapters are interspersed in it to explain why things were what they were. In fact, except for *The Time Machine*, in which readers are shown several moments in the evolution of the Earth toward its destruction, almost all of Wells's "scientific romances" deal with the *results* of a change: the Martians and Selenites are the outcome of centuries and centuries of evolution; the Beast Folk are the result of Moreau's experiments; the Eloi and the Morlocks and the giant crabs are also the consequence of natural evolution.

This insistence not on the evolutionary process but on the mutations it brings about creates a clear parallelism between science and nature: Moreau and Griffin both turn living creatures into something different, just as nature has created Martians and Selenites from humanlike beings. In their own imperfect way they duplicate the natural process. They illustrate views that Wells had stated earlier in the article that was to provide him with the material for chapter 14 of *The Island of Dr. Moreau:*

> Now the suggestion this little article would advance is this: that there is in science, and perhaps even more so in history, some sanction for the belief that a living thing might be taken in hand

and so moulded and modified that at best it would retain scarcely anything of its inherent form and disposition; that the thread of life might be preserved unimpaired while shape and mental super-structure were so extensively recast as even to justify our regarding the result as a new variety of being.[5]

Thus change, whether due to science or to nature, is presented as leading to horrifying results: the Martians and the Beast Folk were certainly meant to produce in the reader the same kind of reaction. The ethical inference seems clear: neither nature nor science must be left uncontrolled and unchecked if man wants to avoid catastrophes, but the emphasis, in Wells's science fiction, is hardly on the moral and social consequences, as stressed by T. H. Huxley. The Wells of the 1890s was certainly less interested in conveying an explicit message than in shocking his readers out of their complacence, and this meant resorting to literary devices and offering a homogenous vision of the future. In fact, all the ethical points raised by Huxley are present, but translated into a vision.

The pattern of Wells's "scientific romances" is usually extremely simple: one man—sometimes two, but hardly ever more—finds himself confronted with a situation resulting from an unexpected change, as though he had been gifted with the power of abolishing time, and had to face the results, not the actual process, of evolution. This leads to the establishment of a number of relationships between this main character and the new environment in which he is suddenly placed. This character, because he is the only one endowed with values the reader can understand, tends to assume the part of a representative of the species. In all of Wells's science fiction these relationships take the shape of conflicts in which violence is rife. This means that, in most cases, the narrator is also an actor taking an active part in these conflicts and deeply involved in their outcome: the Time Traveller's narrative depends on his escaping from the Morlocks, the story of the Martian invasion is told by a narrator who is constantly threatened by death and barely escapes it, Prendick's flight from Moreau's island is the condition of one's learning his story; even Griffin must resort to a first-person narrative and tell a friend how he succeeded in making himself invisible. Thus the narrator, who is frequently identified with the reader by means of a simple device of telling his story in the first person—yet with variations in the distance between the narrator and the reader due to differences of values within a common framework—is in a position of constant instability. Only in *The First Men in the Moon* does Bedford, the narrator, present a more complex picture, since his lack of idealism and of disinterestedness is what ultimately enables him to escape from the Selenites. Even here Cavor is left to utter the final words in his messages that are again a form of first-person narrative. Everywhere these narrators find themselves in hostile environments in which their lives are constantly threatened; the only possible exception is *When the Sleeper Wakes* in which, significantly enough, Wells was far more concerned with the social and political evolution than with the biological.

One can therefore say that evolution means sudden change and that this change is always hostile to contemporary man. Danger and pain await man in the future, but they also have a positive value because they act as a stimulus for human intelligence. This is what the Time Traveller makes clear:

> It is a law of nature we overlook, that intellectual versatility is the compensation for change, danger, and trouble. An animal perfectly in harmony with its environment is a perfect mechanism. Nature never appeals to intelligence until habit and instinct are useless. There is no intelligence where there is no change and no need of change. Only those animals partake of intelligence that have to meet a huge variety of needs and dangers. (ch. 13)

It was undoubtedly part of Wells's purpose to emphasize

the dangers lurking in the future in order to fight a general complacence he found unbearable. This is a notion that keeps recurring throughout the the articles he wrote at that time:

> No; man's complacent assumption of the future is too confident. We think, because things have been easy for mankind as a whole for a generation or so, we are going on to perfect comfort and security in the future. . . . Even now, for all we can tell, the coming terror may be crouching for its spring and the fall of humanity be at hand. In the case of every other predominant animal the world has ever seen, I repeat, the hour of its complete ascendancy has been the eve of its entire overthrow.[6]

However, there remains a certain amount of ambiguity in the values extolled by Wells: if, as he says, "intellectual versatility is the compensation for change, danger, and trouble," are readers to infer from this statement that an increase in man's intellectual faculties would necessarily lead to progress? That is, does Nature, by imposing painful forms of evolution on man, and thus making it necessary for him to become more intelligent in order to adapt himself to a constantly changing situation, provide him, at the same time, with the elements that will enable him to improve his condition while retaining his human characteristics? The examples found in his fiction are hardly convincing: the Time Traveller yields to the fascination exerted by a dying world; the attack of the Martians leaves a world in ruin but hardly the wiser for all that; Prendick's experience leads him to complete despair, and Cavor disappears on the Moon with his secret, unknown and lost forever. The intellect is constantly shown as leading to inhuman behavior: Griffin and Moreau are both endowed with more than ordinary intellectual faculties; the Martians and Selenites are beings entirely governed by their brains and devoid of all feelings. The paradoxical situation seems to be that evolution leads to a dehumanization of man because the brain will tend to supersede the body, since it is the brain that enables man to strive toward harmony with nature, but, at the same time, man needs more developed intellectual faculties to avoid this dismal prospect. In his science fiction Wells was simply illustrating the dilemma clearly stated by Huxley:

> Cosmic evolution may teach us how the good and the evil tendencies of man may have come about; but, in itself, it is incompetent to furnish any better reason why what we call good is preferable to what we call evil than we had before.[7]

Or, to put things more concisely, in order to avoid becoming a monstrous creature led by its intellect and devoid of all ethical sense, man must develop his intellect and will, and fight evolution.

Yet this contradiction at the level of values, illustrated by the "scientific romances," is hardly apparent at first reading and does not impair the unity of these works. The reason for that is probably to be found in the quality of Wells's vision and in the recurrent imagery that, to my mind, transcend whatever contradictions may exist at the level of the ideas. Because of the fact that, through this imagery, he embodied some of the familiar patterns upon which modern science fiction rests, he can probably be regarded as one of the founders of the genre in its own right. The notion of evolution that provided him with a starting point for most of his stories fortunately appealed more to his imagination than to his intellect. His was the kind of mind that was kindled by the immense vistas that evolution opened out before him, and it is not surprising that a number of familiar patterns should keep recurring through these early works.

Two points seem to have struck his imagination with a particularly strong impact: the immensity of space and the fact that the world was bound to end one day; and I would suggest that this second point was probably the fundamental obsession underlying all of Wells's works.

Why he was particularly aware of the vastness of space is difficult to explain, but several influences must have been at work on him: when he came under the ascendancy of Huxley, Wells had been, for several years, trying to escape the notions of sin and redemption that were part of the education he had received from his mother. Although this is obviously an oversimplification, it is highly probable that he was then looking for some cosmology that would give the world a meaning. And evolution, with its emphasis on change brought about by aeons, and its insistence on immensity, came to him as a sort of revelation. The existence of countless worlds surrounding this Earth keeps reappearing in the "scientific romances" and many of the short stories. They exert a kind of fascination on his characters, and their influence on them ranges from downright hostility to a certain comforting reassurance. Coming from outer space, the Martians illustrate all the dangers that may suddenly spring upon men from the unknown; however, for Prendick, the same stars mean comfort after his ordeal among the Beast Folk:

> My days I devote to reading and to experiments in chemistry; and I spend many of the clear nights in the study of astronomy. There is, though I do not know how there is or why there is, a sense of infinite peace and protection in the glittering hosts of heaven. There it must be, I think, in the vast and eternal laws of matter, and not in the daily cares, and sins and troubles of men, that whatever is more than animal within us must find its solace and its hope. (ch. 22)

Here, hostility comes from man and from changes artificially brought about in the species, and the stars mean peace; but to the Time Traveller they bring consciousness of the coming death of the world:

Looking at these stars suddenly dwarfed my own troubles and all the gravities of terrestrial life. I thought of their unfathomable distance, and the slow inevitable drift of their movements out of the unknown past into the unknown future. I thought of the great precessional cycle that the pole of the earth describes. Only forty times had that silent revolution occurred during all the years that I had traversed. And during these few revolutions all the activity, all the traditions, the complex organizations, the nations, languages, literatures, had been swept out of existence. (ch. 10)

Thus space stands in various relationships to the human observer, but Wells always emphasizes its permanence: evolution will change man, the Earth will slowly become cooler and eventually die, but the cosmos will still be there, and it is the one reality men may apprehend. The stars are the unknown and, in Wells's science fiction, they constantly remind the characters of the vanity of human enterprises against the background of the cosmos. This is a theme that Wells used constantly at that time, both in his fiction and in his essays. Here is, for example, what he was writing in 1894:

And what then if *our* heavens were to open? Very thin indeed is the curtain between us and the unknown. There is a fear of the night that is begotten of ignorance and superstition, a nightmare fear, the fear of the impossible; and there is another fear of the night—of the starlit night—that comes with knowledge when we see in its true proportion this little life of ours with all its phantasmal environment of cities and stores and arsenals, and the habits, prejudices, and promises of men. Down there in the gaslit street such things are real and solid enough, the only real things, perhaps; but not up here, not under the midnight sky. Here, for a space, standing silently upon the dim, grey tower of the old observatory, we may clear our minds of instincts and illusions, and look out upon the real.[8]

Thus the stars are clearly linked with evolution in several ways: either they harbor hazards of which man is unaware, as they do in *The War of the Worlds* or the remarkable short

story called "The Star," or they provide man with an
element of permanence against which evolution can be
measured, and produce in the individual a sense of awe at
their infinite magnitude. This is an essential function
because, as Bernard Bergonzi showed very convincingly,[9]
one of the fundamental obsessions pervading Wells's science fiction is that of the end of the world. I would even say
that it appeared all through Wells's literary output; it can be
seen in the Samurais' pilgrimages and in Trafford's retire-
ment to Labrador, and it culminated in Wells's prophetic
announcement in *Mind at the End of Its Tether*. The fact that
evolution meant a constant progress toward death seems to
have struck Wells as something at once inescapable and
unacceptable. At the same time, the idea that death might
strike unexpectedly because some beings have already
developed far beyond the point reached by modern man
adds a new dimension to the theme. Man may be unable to
do anything to prevent the Earth from getting colder and
colder, but he can certainly do something to avoid being
ousted by inhuman species.

And yet, things are not quite so clear-cut because a sort of
death wish pervades these stories, creating a dialectic
movement between the urge to go on living and the wish to
destroy things as they are, probably in the hope of
re-creating them better. Very little hope is left to the
narrator of *The Time Machine* when he reflects upon the
disappearance of the Time Traveller:

> He, I know—for the question had been discussed among us
> long before the Time Machine was made—thought but cheer-
> lessly of the Advancement of Mankind, and saw in the growing
> pile of civilization only a foolish heaping that must inevitably
> fall back upon and destroy its makers in the end. If that is so, it
> remains for us to live as though it were not so. But to me the
> future is still black and blank—is a vast ignorance lit at a few
> casual places by the memory of his story. (Epilogue)

On the other hand, the artilleryman in *The War of the*

Worlds gives voice to the hope that the disaster brought about by the Martians will accelerate the process of evolution, thus giving rise to a new sort of natural selection under the pressure of circumstances. Here is part of the dialogue he has with the narrator, after learning that the Martians can fly:

> "It is all over with humanity," I said. "If they can do that they will simply go round the world. . . ."
>
> He nodded.
>
> "They will. But—It will relieve things over here a bit. And besides—" He looked at me. "Aren't you satisfied it *is* up with humanity? I am. We're down; we're beat. (bk. II, ch. 7)

This is in fact a form of death wish, for the reader learns that the artilleryman is quite incapable of carrying out any of his projects for the salvation and improvement of mankind.

Evolution is thus connected, at the level of the imagination, with the threat of death coming from outside the human universe, but it also implies the existence of suffering and violence. V. S. Pritchett's remark[10] about there being fires and fisticuffs in practically all the "scientific romances" is too well known to be quoted again. It certainly conveys the impression of violent conflict all these works give, and the use of fire clearly symbolizes a desire for purification through destruction. It represents the culmination of and release from pent-up tensions, the irrational destruction of the-thing-that-is through an exultation that is almost sexual in its intensity. At the same time, fighting is a manifestation of being and wanting to stay alive. It is a refusal to surrender to the blind laws of evolution and thus perfectly in keeping with Wells's attitude.

For evolution, particularly when artificially accelerated and taking the form of a rapid mutation entails pain. Change means suffering: Moreau achieves a godlike status through inflicting pain upon the Beast Folk, and each new change is preceded by a return to the House of Pain.

> Each time I dip a living creature into the bath of burning pain [Moreau declares] I say, This time I will burn out all the animal, this time I will make a rational creature of my own. (ch. 14)

The alliance of pain and fire is here particularly revealing. And Griffin becomes invisible only at the price of intense sufferings:

> I had not expected the suffering [he says]. A night of racking anguish, sickness and fainting. I set my teeth, though my skin was presently afire, all my body afire, but I lay there like grim death. (ch. 20)

Again there is a very significant cluster of images here, connecting pain with fire and death and illustrating the way themes are intermingled to produce a unified vision. These themes are all to be found at the level of the imagination and do not necessarily reflect personal experience. In fact, Wells did not become aware of the actual existence of pain and suffering as a cardinal component of man's plight before the Second World War, and, in the same way, his experience of fighting was entirely divorced from reality. This is a point that must be emphasized because it explains why Wells gave up writing science fiction fairly early in his career, when reality began to intrude upon and to supersede the world of his imagination, and it enables one to see more clearly the relationship between these romances and modern science fiction.

As I mentioned at the beginning, Huxley's teaching provided Wells with just the kind of incentive his imagination needed. Evolution, which he never questioned, was to be the ruling force in the universe his fancy was creating. But it was all a game played according to the laws of literary creation: the main problem he had to tackle was not the intellectual one of trying to solve the ethical dilemma

implied by evolution, it was to present a multifarious vision in
such a way as to make it acceptable to his readers. The
popular appeal of science at the time made it possible for
him to offer explanations that would be credible, but he was
not greatly interested in the technical details involved. The
main question for him was: What would happen under
given circumstances? It was not: Why should it happen
thus? Starting from a somewhat abstract proposition, he
would develop it concretely by creating characters, imagining settings, situations, incidents, thus making an overall
picture that would draw upon all the resources of his
creative mind. But this does not mean that he had any fixed
views on evolution, whether biological, social, or political.
What he wrote is a series of visions set in such a distant
future as to be almost entirely severed from the present; he
certainly used a fairly crude brand of Marxism to account
for the societies found in *The Time Machine, When the Sleeper
Wakes,* or "A Story of Days to Come," but I think he did so
simply because his mind was fascinated by the vistas that
this theory opened. And the same kind of attitude probably
applied to evolution, with one important difference, which
is that he did believe in it as the only possible alternative to
the Christian view of the world he had abandoned.

But, at the same time, he was also deeply interested in the
fictional representation of the social circles he knew: there
was, I think, no period in his life when he was working on
science fiction alone, and often the genres overlapped. *The
Invisible Man,* for example, uses science simply to provide
an explanation for Griffin's invisibility, but the book is
much closer to works like *The Wonderful Visit* or *The Sea
Lady,* in which a fantastic element plays a similar part, than
to *The War of the Worlds.*

As far as Wells's science fiction is concerned, evolution
was essentially a means of creating plausible visions of the
future. Only at the turn of the century did Wells begin to
conceive that he might possibly foresee the near future of

the world about him. *Anticipations* and the various utopias that followed all proceeded from the desire to imagine the shapes of future societies as a prelude to the actual changing of contemporary society. Science remained prominent in them, but the vision was gone, probably because the fictional element had become subservient to practical, political purposes. From playing with the idea of evolution as a means of giving birth to a vision, he had come to believe, probably largely under the pressure of popular response, in the possibility of initiating such a change in actual life. These two trends, the visionary one and the didactic one, are constantly mixed throughout his life, but before the turn of the century Wells was probably satisfied with the exhilaration arising out of literary creation. Inventing worlds, imagining the changes evolution would bring about provided him with sufficient release from the fetters of the world he lived in, and this may well be the reason why his science fiction has remained very modern.

One may indeed wonder at the sort of relationship it has with modern science fiction, and I think the answer lies in the choice of the themes found in them. Science fiction is admittedly almost impossible to define; readers all think they know what it is and yet no definition will cover all its various aspects. However, I would suggest that evolution, as presented by Wells, that is, as a kind of mutation resulting in the confrontation of man with different species, is one of the main themes of modern science fiction. The fascination exerted by strange worlds and beings, and the attendant fear are all there, as are the reflections on man's condition; and the reason for it may well be that today's circumstances are so similar to Wells's. Space travel does exist, and the spreading of nuclear weapons has turned mass killing and biological mutation from fantastic hypotheses into frightening possibilities. Modern man has at least equalled the Martians in destructive capability. The complacence out of which Wells wanted to shake his contemporaries is still part of everyone's daily life; and the sense of an age coming to its end and opening out into an unknown future, which Wells expressed in his fantasies, is an integral part of today's background. Modern consciousness seems to be particularly aware of the accelerating rhythm of change and is thus attuned to Wells's fantasies. In a world subjected to rapid change and constantly threatened by destruction, science fiction enables modern man to define his own position in relation to science and to the main trends of modern civilization. It also enables him to control his future, if not in reality, at least through the inalienable rights of the imagination.

The question has often been asked whether Wells had not in fact a pessimistic view of the future, and it seems highly probable that, in spite of his genuine admiration for the scientific turn of mind, he had serious misgivings about the ethical consequences of science; but, in these early works, he was far more concerned with visions of the future than with the actual evolutionary process. And change, which seems to be the fundamental theme of these books, is fraught with ambiguous implications. On the one hand it entails a fascination with death that is connected with the fin-du-monde myth, a fascination highly characteristic of a time when threats are felt to be constantly present, and yet the world is sufficiently stable for these threats to be perceived at the level of the imagination. On the other hand, there is a refusal of this very same death, often expressed through acts of violence. The consideration of the world as something finite makes it possible to find a meaning behind it, while, at the same time, it is a solution that remains unacceptable because it would make this process of understanding meaningless. It is true that, at this period of his life, Wells did not go so far as to imagine man as responsible for a change for the worse (as so many modern science-fiction writers have done): the threats to mankind always come from creatures that have reached a superior degree of development. Even Moreau, when creating the Beast Folk, takes upon himself the attributes and function of nature; but Wells did express the constant existence of mortal dangers and man's violent refusal of death. In his view, man's main fault lay not in any natural viciousness but in his inability to realize the fact that (as Huxley had pointed out) the survival of the fittest did not necessarily imply the survival of the best. In this early science fiction he was not yet concerned with the forms of social and political bodies, which was to be the stuff of later utopias, but with the more basic concepts of life and death. He saw man as a creature subjected to the blind forces of evolution and tried to imagine him confronted with the future. In so doing he foresaw with surprising clarity the malaise echoed by modern science fiction. For science fiction is, in fact, the manifestation of a very paradoxical attitude; by showing men the various consequences of change, however disastrous, it assumes willy-nilly the existence of a future. Even the Time Traveller, when witnessing the end of the cooling Earth, is able to survive conditions that have caused the death of the human species, and to come back and give an account of it. One may even wonder whether the very act of creating the future through an act of the imagination is not a way of exorcizing this future. Be that as it may, the fact remains that, in the few years about the turn of the century, Wells wrote science fiction tales that remain among the most original of his works. They represent only a very small proportion of his output, and he had but a rather indifferent opinion of them, considering them as so many potboilers, but they reflect a view of the future that remains modern.

In the first years of the twentieth century, Wells gradually abandoned science fiction to devote himself to the writing of "straight" novels and to political work. He seems to have been motivated by the impression that his works could help to check the natural bent of evolution and turn the tide in favor of man. But his "scientific romances," unburdened by propaganda for socialism, the world state, or the endowment of motherhood, expressed a vision of the future that had a deep unity at the level of underlying patterns. As I have tried to suggest, I think that this is mainly due to the fact that evolution was then for Wells a kind of revelation that appealed directly to his imagination and was expressed in literary terms. He had not yet begun to give precedence to ideas over vision, and could still think of his works, not in terms of their influence upon the world of reality, but in terms of achievement in the realm of creative imagination. In this achievement lay the source of the exhilaration that is such a striking feature of these romances. New vistas were opening out and, however bleak and full of hazards they might have seemed to him, they meant change. There is no denying that his story-telling smacks strongly of Victorianism, but the vision remains modern, essentially because it illustrates fictional patterns that still form the ideological basis of modern science fiction.

NOTES

1. *Huxley, p. 81.
2. *Strand Magazine* 59 (1920): 154.
3. It is interesting to notice that Wells's conception of his characters is perfectly in keeping with that expounded by Dr. Johnson in *Rasselas*, a book Wells had read at Up Park. *See* the following quotation: "The business of a poet," said Imlac, "is to examine not the individual but the species; to remark general properties and large appearances. . . ." *Rasselas* (London, 1967), p. 23.
4. *The Time Machine*, ch. 1; all further references to Wells's science-fiction novels will be cited in the text by chapter number.
5. "The Limits of Individual Plasticity," *Saturday Review* 79 (19 January 1895): 90.
6. "The Extinction of Man," *Pall Mall Gazette* (25 September 1894); reprinted in *Wells, C.P.M., pp. 178–79.
7. Huxley, p. 31.

8. "From an Observatory," *Saturday Review* 78 (1 December 1894); reprinted in *Wells, *C.P.M.* pp. 265–66.

9. In *Bergonzi, pp. 3–5, 11–12, passim.

10. *Pritchett, p. 122.

A Grammar of Form and a Criticism of Fact: *The Time Machine* as a Structural Model for Science Fiction

by DARKO SUVIN

Let me begin by stating that I am not an orthodox structuralist, if this catchword is taken to entail synchronic analysis opposed to cultural genetics, myth as synonymous with literature, and similar sectarianisms. I agree with the Goldmann-Piaget attempt to integrate structural approaches with genetic ones, and I would interpret structuralism not as an exclusive doctrine but as a synthesizing method. As such, it has a venerable, scholarly tradition from, say, medieval discussions to some of Lukács's analyses or Professor Kuhn's *Structure of Scientific Revolutions*. In that spirit, I shall try to show that H. G. Wells's *The Time Machine* is—to put it prudently, in the absence of further evidence—at least one of the basic historical models for subsequent science-fiction structuring.

A student of Wells[1] is emboldened in such an approach by the fact that comparative morphology was, in Wells's student days, one of the first great modern breakthroughs of the structural method. As Wells himself noted, biology was in T. H. Huxley's days establishing the phylogenetic tree or "family tree of life": "Our chief discipline was a rigorous analysis of vertebrate structure, vertebrate embryology, and *the succession of vertebrate forms in time. We felt our particular task was the determination of the relationships of groups by the acutest possible criticism of structure.*" Wells left no doubt of the indelible vistas the "sweepingly magnificent series" of zoological exercises imprinted on his eager imagination, leaving him under an urgency for "coherence and consistency": "*It was a grammar of form and a criticism of fact.* That year I spent in Huxley's class was, beyond all question, the most educational year of my life."[2] It should not, thus, be too surprising to find in *The Time Machine* (which has much to say about succession of zoological forms in time) an attempt at coherence and consistency—"a grammar of form and criticism of fact." Of course, this does not prejudice the particular grammar or criticism, the type of coherence and consistency that might be found in it.

I am proceeding upon the hypothesis that the basic device of *The Time Machine* is an opposition of the Time Traveller's visions of the future to the ideal reader's norm of complacent, bourgeois class consciousness with its belief in linear progress, Spencerian "Social-Darwinism," and the like.[3] The Victorian norm is set up in the framework of *The Time Machine* and supplemented by the Time Traveller's reactions. His visions are shaped by means of two basic and interlocking symbolic systems: that of biological regression, and that of color imagery polarized between light and darkness—both systems being allied with violence, pain, and the basic confrontation between Man and Death.

1. THE CONVERGING BIOLOGICAL SERIES

The one thing earlier drafts of *The Time Machine* have in common with the vastly different and superior final version is an opposition between the present and a different future. However, the narrative organization of the final version manifestly took its cue from Darwinism as expounded by Wells's teacher Huxley since 1860, and applied to "Evolution and Ethics" by Huxley's homonymous Romanes Lecture and the subsequent "Prolegomena" in the year preceding Wells's writing of the final version (1893–94).

In the "Prolegomena,"[4] Huxley tried to face the implications of evolution applying not only to "progressive development" but also to "retrogressive modification" (*Pr.* 4, note 1), not only to "gradual change from a condition of relative uniformity to one of relative complexity" but also to "the phenomena of retrogressive metamorphosis, that is, of progress from a condition of relative complexity to one of relative uniformity" (*Pr.* 6). Evidently, the connotations of progress in the bourgeois-liberal sense were being challenged by connotations that made it synonymous with any evolutionary change, for better or for worse; progress was being expanded to encompass the antonymic possibility of "retrogressive metamorphosis." Another variation of this ambiguity is the possibility of envisaging evolution in terms of devolution. Again in the "Prolegomena," setting up his basic exemplum or parable of English vegetation that might evolve from a primitive state of nature into a garden under purposeful, that is, ethical, human intervention, Huxley mused that "if every link in the ancestry of these humble indigenous plants had been preserved and were accessible to us, the whole would present *a converging series of forms of gradually diminishing complexity,* until, at some period in the history of the earth ... they would merge in those low groups among which the boundaries between animal and vegetable life become effaced" (*Pr.* 5, italics added).

Huxley was, of course, only indulging in the common evolutionist device of exalting even the humblest "indigenous plants" as wonderful products of an evolutionary chain,[5] here traversed backward into the past and functioning as a kind of double negation—since the reader is tacitly invited to reascend the evolutionary scale from the Protistae to the "humble" (now not so humble) indigenous plant in the direction of a diverging series of increasing complexity. But what if one were to take this formal exercise of Huxley's literally, and his sense of uneasiness about evolution and progress versus devolution and regress seriously, that is, without a rhetoric that descends into the deeps of the problem and of time in order to end with an upward flourish? All that would be needed is to suppress Huxley's second negation by inverting his vision from past to future, and to imagine a canonic sociobiological "converging series of forms of gradually diminishing complexity" unfolding as *de*volution that retraverses the path of evolution backward to a *fin du globe*. That is what Huxley's heretical student did in *The Time Machine*: a slip under the time telescope, to use a Wellsian phrase.[6]

"Canonic series," of course, begs the question "according to what type of canon?" An answer is to be found comparing the orthodox Darwinist and Huxleyan canon with the one actually used in *The Time Machine*. The orthodox seriation would, in rough outlines, look as follows (simplified and adapted from J. B. S. Haldane and Julian Huxley[7]):

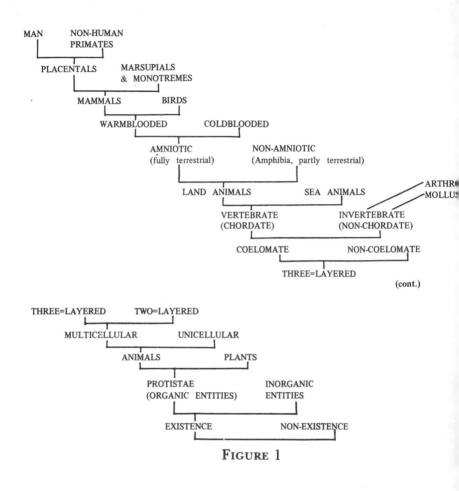

FIGURE 1

The final two levels are an extrapolation going beyond biology, but are present in Lyell, Darwin, and T. H. Huxley.

As distinct from this converging series, Wells not only used the symmetrically inverse time direction, changing the sign from plus to minus, but he also considerably foreshortened and regrouped the series, as follows:

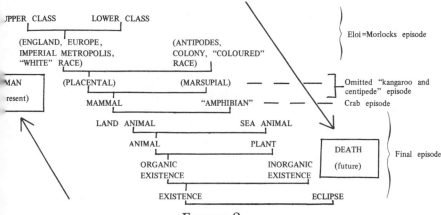

FIGURE 2

Comparing the two series, a number of significant divergencies obtrude:

1. Even the simplified Darwinist seriation (omitting the level of Chordates vs Nonchordates, the distinctions among Bony fish, Cartilaginous fish, and Cyclostomes, and so on) contains twelve levels beginning with Placentals vs Marsupials, whereas the corresponding Wellsian seriation contains six levels beginning with Placentals vs Marsupials, or five without this level that is omitted in the final (Heinemann) version. The levels Wells retained are those

that can be vividly represented by striking images. The differences between existence and eclipse, plant and animal, sea and land animal, "amphibian" crab and mammal, are readily understood without the Darwinian schematism. They are based on a "self-evident" or commonsensical, topical bestiary antedating Linnaeus and going back to the dawn of human imagination. Therefore, they are eminently usable for producing in the average nonscientific but science-believing reader effects of stark opposition, such as the revulsion felt by the Time Traveller when faced with the giant crabs or with the unnamed archetypal "thing" from the sea. Though Wells's task was, as far as lower rungs of the phylogenetic series are concerned, facilitated by the unsettled state of invertebrate phylogeny at the time (*see Exp.* 160), there is little reason to suppose scentific scruples carried significant weight with him. Indeed, when Wells had to choose between the ABC of Darwinian classification and a kind of folk biology, he unhesitatingly chose the latter, inventing—as the hero of his parable "The Triumphs of a Taxidermist" did—new taxonomic positions: the triumph of a quasi-taxonomist, indeed.[8] This is evident in the third episode of *The Time Machine,* where the crabs are—against all biological taxonomy—situated between the opposition Man vs Marsupial (in the omitted episode) and Man vs Sea Animal, that is, in the false, "folk-taxonomic" position of amphibian creatures because of their location or ecological niche. That ecological niche—the line where sea meets land—is easily represented and possesses rich literary overtones; the representation of a taxonomic amphibian (say Capek's giant salamanders) would lack the element of menace present in the insectoid antennae and claws, the alienness of eyes wriggling on stalks, and so on. Wells was to use this biologically collateral branch of arthropods for similar "creepy-crawly" effects in "The Empire of the Ants" and "The Valley of Spiders," just as he was to do with the taxonomically isotopic molluscs in

"The Sea Raiders." Incidentally, through the octopoid Martians from *The War of the Worlds,* the insectoid Selenites from *The First Men in the Moon,* and perhaps the vaguely reptilian bipeds of "In the Abyss," Wells set the xenobiological paradigm for science fiction's bug-eyed monsters and menaces from outer space right down to the supremely unscientific appellative of "the thing."

2. The beginning or top of Wells's devolutionary series stems from that curious hybrid of deterministic or Malthusian pseudo-Darwinism and bourgeois or indeed imperialist social theory (and practice) represented, for example, by the so-called Social-Darwinism of Spencer, and later by Carnegie, Rockefeller, Nietzsche, and fascists of various stripes, who translated differences in socioeconomic position into a biological terminology stressing the "survival of the fittest." T. H. Huxley's concern with the relationships of evolution and ethics is due to an uneasiness about such uses of Darwinism. However, the usual strategy of the Social-Darwinists was to use the more convenient and mystified vocabulary of racism, preaching social peace in the imperial metropolis and among "Whites" at the expense of colonial peoples or "lower races." [9] Wells's personal class experiences and acquaintance with Plato, Blake, Shelley, Morris, and Marx precluded at the moment of writing *The Time Machine* such a mystification, and induced him to put the problem in its basic terms of social class rather than in pseudobiological ones. He was to be followed on that level by some of the best social criticism in science fiction, from Jack London's fusion of Wells and utopianism in *The Iron Heel* to the antiutopia of Zamyatin, the political "new maps of hell" of American science fiction in the 1940s and 1950s, and the satirical science fiction from the Warsaw Pact countries (Lem, Dneprov, the Strugatskys).[10] Indeed, the sequence of the Time Traveller's hypotheses about the "Eloi episode"—(a) Communist classless society; (b) degenerated classless society; (c) de-

generated class society; (d) degenerated inverted class society—comprises the whole logical gamut of sociological science fiction, or of utopian and antiutopian fiction as the ideal poles of sociological science fiction, from More and Plato to the present day. Finally, with the Time Traveller's realization that the capitalists and workers have not only degenerated and inverted their power roles, but also differentiated into separate biological species one of which is the "cattle" of the other (*see* the identical and no doubt seminal metaphor in *Pr.* 17), Huxley's evolution that encompasses devolution comes true with a vengeance; at the same time, the ideological basis of such speculations in real class fears and hopes is uncovered. The resulting "race" level of oppositions was to be used by Wells, again inverted, in *The War of the Worlds* or stories such as "Lord of the Dynamos." Reverting to crude xenophobia and losing Wells's ambiguities, this became the model for a whole group of subsequent and inferior science-fiction narratives exporting social and national conflicts into outer space.

3. It also becomes clear why Wells felt he had to delete the "kangaroo and centipede" episode. While completely breaking up the narrative rhythm (as discussed in the next paragraph) by introducing at a still leisurely stage of narration two new phylogenetic levels in a single episode—of which, furthermore, the arthropod ("centipede") level is used again in the following "crab episode"—it added little to the basic opposition of the Time Traveller as mammal, land animal, and so forth, to nonanimals, sea animals, and so forth. On the contrary, it logically raised the dissonant question of using a full Darwino-Huxleyan converging series, beginning with the opposition of Man (Time Traveller) to Primates. With commendable tact, Wells was unwilling to venture onto grounds later annexed by Tarzan of the Apes, although he subsequently compromised under Kipling's influence to the point of exploring the opposition Man/(Mammalian) Beast, in *The*

Island of Dr. Moreau (where Kipling's serpent is necessarily omitted).

4. If one looks at the distribution of the seriation levels in the episodes of *The Time Machine*, it is possible to gain further insight about its basic narrative rhythm, also characterized by growing pace and compression as the reader is swept into the story, the motivations and justifications gradually dispensed with, and the levels cumulated in an exponential progression. *The Time Machine* consists of a framework and three fantasmagoric evolutionary futures that I have called the "Eloi," the "crab," and the "eclipse" episodes. In the first U.K. edition, their quantitative relationships are as follows:

A. Framework established, chapters 1–3, pp. 1–26
B. Eloi episode, chapters 4–13, pp. 27–133.
C. Crab episode, first half of chapter 14, pp. 134–39
D. Eclipse episode, second half of chapter 14, pp. 139–41
E. Framework reestablished, chapters 15–16 and Epilogue, pp. 142–52.

Or, taking into account only the inner narration of the Time Traveller's experiences:

Eloi episode, year 802,701—one seriation level (or two), 107 pages

(Omitted "kangaroo and centipede" episode, year?—two seriation levels, approximately 4 pages)

Crab episode, several million years hence—one seriation level, 5 pages

Eclipse episode, 30 million years hence—four seriation levels, 3 pages.

Taking the Eloi episode as two levels (first a class and then a "race" or species one[11]), there is in the above, four future episodes:

1. one level per 54 pages
2. (one level per approximately 2 pages—omitted)
3. one level per 5 pages
4. one level per 0.7 pages.

One could venture further into a discussion of such an exponentially regressing rhythm—which is certainly analogous on its own structural level to the whole regressive structure of *The Time Machine*—but I shall confine myself to one general observation. The rhythm starts as *lento,* with two sociobiological levels envisioned for 107 pages. It continues as *presto,* with one biological level (mammal vs "amphibian") for five pages, and ends in an abrupt *prestissimo* with four existential levels (land vs. sea animal; animal vs plant—lowest plant forms at that; organic existence vs sand, snow, rocks, and sea; and existence of Earth vs eclipse) all present pell-mell, outside of their proper taxonomic order, within approximately three pages. This telescoping and foreshortening powerfully contributes to and indeed shapes the effect of the logical or biological series. Also, this asymptotic series makes it imperative that the Traveller finally vanish: its final and validating member can only be zero or nonexistence, extinction.[12]

Thus, Wells's *Time Machine* has in the organization of its cognitive thematic material hit upon the law—inherited, as well as much else, from *Gulliver's Travels*—that seems to have remained unshaken in subsequent significant science fiction, according to which the cognitive nucleus of narration, or theme, can become a principle of narrative organization only by fitting into the storytelling parameters of pace, sequence, symbolic systematization, and so on. Wells knew of Haeckel's law that ontogenesis (development of any species' embryo) is a foreshortened recapitulation of phylogenesis (that species' evolution); in other words, that the new environment of individual embryonic gestation inflected and modified—though it did not change the general outline of—the evolutionary sequence. Consciously or not, he applied the same principle to the new narrative and aesthetic environment—an environment to which the cognitive evolutionary sequence of Darwinian seriation had to adapt by evolving or, perhaps, mutating. *The principle of a Wellsian structure of science fiction is mutation of scientific into aesthetic cognition.* It is oriented toward cognitive horizons that it shares with any good handbook of sociology, biology, or philosophy of science. But the orientation is achieved in its own way, following the autonomy of a narrative, fictional, aesthetic mode.

2. THE SYNOPTIC PARADIGM

Obviously, in order to account for Wellsian narrative strategies paradigmatic of later science fiction, one would have to analyze the symbolic system that is intertwined with this regressive biological seriation inflected toward "folk taxonomy." As a number of critics have noted, this symbolic system is based on violent oppositions of color, polarized between the Doomsday connotations of "eclipse black" and "fiery red" on one hand, and the green and bright colors of the utopian garden and sunlit, landscaped vegetation on the other. It is not too difficult to see in these poles a coloristic translation of the opposition between tamed and untamed, safe and menacing, evolutive and devolutive nature; Huxley's parable of the cultivated garden or evolutionary Eden is thus supplied with the missing black hues (though *see Pr.* 17 and further, for Huxley's Malthusian "serpent within the garden"). The scope of this study precludes such an analysis, which would go to the heart of Wells's anthropology and cosmology. Instead, I would like to further examine the temporal orientation of *The Time*

Machine, and the basic oppositions implicit in the annunciation of the bad, devolutionary, or black future in store for the bourgeois reader as a sociobiological entity, and for any reader as a cosmological entity.

The Time Traveller's futures are a geometrically progressive series of devolutions, which can—by explicating the implicit opposition between (1) Social-Darwinist Britain, and (2) the particular future vision—be tabulated using a Lévi-Straussian scheme. This would play upon the Social-Darwinist preconceptions of a "natural" order of power and of a safe evolutionary progress keeping each "lower" evolutionary rung in its place as the prey of the "higher" predator; Wells takes these preconceptions over wholesale and simply inverts them. What results is an inverse and symmetrical structure, which can be finally reduced to a general abstract scheme or paradigm:

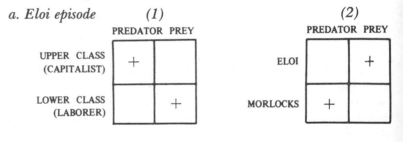

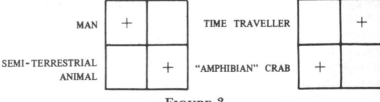

FIGURE 3

This cumulates the logical progression of MAN/MAMMAL and LAND ANIMAL/SEA ANIMAL—cf. the "kangaroo" episode left out.[13] (Clearly, the missing link in and paradigm behind *The Time Machine*, that is, the opposition between MAN and LAND ANIMAL, is to be found—as are many other aspects—in *Gulliver's Travels*.)

c. Eclipse episode

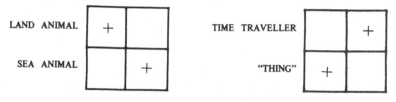

FIGURE 4

In the last episode, the tentacled "thing" does not attack the Time Traveller because he flees in time, but it is clearly the master of that situation. It is reinforced by the addition of liverwort and lichen, the only land survivors; of the desolate, inorganic landscape; and of the blood-red sun in eclipse, which suggests the nearing end of Earth and the whole solar system. The episode, as has been explained, telescopes the taxonomic progression of LAND ANIMAL/SEA ANIMAL, ANIMALS/PLANTS, ORGANIC/INORGANIC, EXISTENCE OF THE EARTH & SOLAR SYSTEM/DESTRUCTION OF SAME—the last being left to the by-now-conditioned extrapolative mechanism of the reader.

The progression is a "black" progression, or regression, also insofar as both parties of any preceding paradigm are subsumed as prey in the succeeding one. For example, all classes of man are—symbolically by way of the Time Traveller as Everyman—the prey of crabs in b); all land animals, even the "amphibious" crabs, have by c) succumbed to more vital and primitive sea animals, mosses, and lichens; and in the suggested extrapolation of a destruction of Earth and/or the solar system, all life would succumb or "become prey" to inorganic life, cosmic processes, or just entropy.

The general scheme of Wellsian science fiction, true of his whole early period of science-fiction novels and stories, is thus:

(1) SOCIAL-DARWINIST BRITAIN

FIGURE 5

It is logically, genetically, and genologically relevant to compare this to the basic opposition in More's *Utopia* or Morris's *News from Nowhere*—remember the first reaction of the Time Traveller was to suppose he had found a pastoral communism. The relevant oppositions are: England is empirically present, but axiologically empty or bad; utopia is empirically absent (*ou-topos,* nowhere) but its values are axiologically affirmed *(eu-topos)* or present. The opposi- tions Locus/Value and Present/Absent give rise to the following scheme, and it should be no surprise that it shows More's Utopia or Morris's Nowhere as (inverted) mirror images of England at Wells's time:

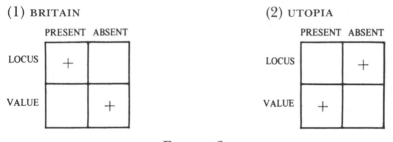

FIGURE 6

In More's *Utopia*, the analysis of space without value in Book I (England—"here") is opposed to an axiologically "full" space presented in Book II as Hythloday's revelation (Utopia—"out there," isomorphic with folktales of a just and abundant place beyond seven seas). This induces the logical and magical possibility of arriving at utopia in space or time, of finding or constructing a sociopolitical Earthly paradise. On the contrary, the general predatory paradigm of Wellsian science fiction is finally ambiguous. In its *inversion* of Social-Darwinism, it supplies a subversive shock to the bourgeois reader, it is critical and estranging; in its *use* of the parameters of Social-Darwinism, however in- verted—that is, of the anthropological vision dividing all life, including man, into predator and prey—it supplies a subversive shock to the humanist and socialist reader, it is antiutopian or black. Wells's seriation converges upon absence of value and existence, a lay hell:

FIGURE 7

as opposed to the utopian terrestrial paradise of More and Morris:

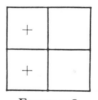

FIGURE 8

3. THE PROPORTIONS OF POWER, AND A RETURN INTO HISTORY

One final aspect of *The Time Machine*'s structure, which is again a methodological key for much science fiction, is the use of *proportion* or *rule of three* (A is to B as B is to C). Wells himself admitted he used this extrapolative method—arriving at C given the known increase from A to B—to depict the megalopolis in *When the Sleeper Wakes*, but lamented its arithmetic linearity and obviousness as "thoroughly wrong." [14] As often, he was unduly impatient with his preceding work and working methods, for proportion does not have to be used as a simple arithmetic rule of three or linear extrapolation—that is merely its more primitive variant. Indeed, proportion as a specific method for formalizing classification and seriation seems to be one of the basic approaches and inescapable epistemological tools of science fiction, since this literary genre is characterized by the estrangement inherent in radically different figures and/or a radically different formal framework of narration, where "radically different" means "belonging to another classifying category" (sociological, biological, anthropological, cosmological, and so on).

In both the Darwino-Huxleyan and the Wellsian biological series from section one of this essay, each subsequent term cumulates, as was noted in section two, the two preceding terms, setting up a new opposition on a more primitive evolutionary level. Thus, Placentals embraces both Man and Nonhuman Primates in opposition to Marsupials, Warmblooded subsumes Mammals and Birds in opposition to Coldblooded, and so forth. The peculiarity of this seriation, Wells saw, is that its two extremes, Man and Nonexistence, are privileged members. In both series, Man is the highest evolutionary category, and he is contained in all the left-hand members of both Huxley's and Wells's series. In the Darwino-Huxleyan series, Man is Placental, Mammal, Warmblooded, Amniotic, Land Animal, Vertebrate, and so on down to Organic Being. In the Wellsian series, Man is Mammal, Land Animal, Animal, Organic Being, and Existing Entity as against the respective negations. Any negation can come into play only when opposed to Man, that is, when the Time Traveller in the last two episodes beholds for himself—and for the human readers—the crabs, the "thing" from the sea, the lichen and liverwort, the desolate rocks and sea, and finally the eclipse. At those points, the Time Traveller is a generic representative of Homo sapiens, an Everyman defined in terms of biological rather than theological classification, as a species-creature and not a temporarily embodied soul. The medieval Everyman was an immortal soul in a mortal body; the principle of individuation was saved. Symmetrically but inversely, the Darwinist Everyman is a quasi-immortal species (germ plasm) in a mortal body; the principle of individuation is lost. But quasi-immortal is not immortal[15]: even the generic principle could get lost, and biology is full of cautionary tales about dominant species or whole orders (such as the giant reptiles, significantly absent in *The Time Machine*, though a staple of much science fiction since Jules Verne's *Voyage to the Centre of the Earth*) that disappeared in the depths of geological time. The mighty are humbled indeed in such perspectives, which Wells turned against Victorian complacency with zest and relish.

In the Eloi-Morlocks episode, however, the Time Traveller can not be simply a representative Man, since he is faced with creatures that are maybe no longer Homo sapiens but are certainly other races or species of the genus *Homo* (say *Homo eloii* and *Homo morlockius*).[16] What he can be, as against the unifunctional Hominidae of the year 802,701, is a complex Victorian gentleman-inventor who displays various fin-de-siècle attitudes when faced with shifting situations and interpretations of the Eloi and of the Eloi-Morlocks relationship. Christopher Caudwell's critique of the Time Traveller as occupying an intermediate position between the two new species, isotopic with the position of the petty bourgeois Wells disdainful of a decadent upper class but horrified and repelled by a crude lower class, seems to me, for all the nuances and elaborations it needs, to remain a key for interpreting the topographic and the color symbolism of that episode.[17] In the later episodes, the Time Traveller is placed in an ever-widening temporal perspective that corresponds to the descent down the phylogenetic series.

Returning to the proportions inherent in *The Time Machine*, it becomes clear that section two of this essay is a synchronic presentation of the devolutionary diachrony discussed in section one. On each devolutionary level in Wells's narration, there is a symmetrically inverted situation usually mediated by the Time Traveller, as:

A. Victorian upper class dominates over the Victorian working class, which is the inverse of the Eloi's position in respect to Morlocks: or, $VUC : VWE = [E : M]^{-1}$.

B. In the present geological epoch, Mammals are more powerful than "Amphibians," which is the inverse of what the Crabs are to the Time Traveller; or, $M : A = [TT : C]^{-1}$.

C. In the present geological epoch, Land Animals prevail in the mastery of the globe, which is the inverse of the panic flight the "thing" from the sea puts the Time Traveller to; or, $LA : SA = [TT : Th]^{-1}$. The "normal" hierarchical relation Animals:Plants is inverted in the survival of hardy lichen and liverwort after animals have died out (though there is a sleight-of-hand here because the sea "thing" has not died out, thence its first inanimate appearance), thus, $A : P = [TT : L\&L]^{-1}$. The same holds true for the relations Organic: Inorganic Existence, and finally for Existence : Entropy.

The unity of this series of proportions and of *The Time Machine*'s composition hinges on the full—though somewhat unmotivated, because ideologically mystified—sympathy the Time Traveller must, for all his cavils, feel for the Eloi. They occupy the same position, which is simultaneously characterized by functionally appertaining to the upper class and yet being powerless in relation to the "lower" Social-Darwinist class of Morlock, Crab, "Thing," and further into cosmological entropy. The series of proportions can be recapitulated as:

$$VUC : VWC = [E \quad : M]^{-1}$$
$$M \quad : A \quad = [TT : C]^{-1}$$
$$LA \quad : SA \quad = [TT : Th]^{-1}$$
$$A \quad : P \quad = [TT : L\&L]^{-1}$$

and so on.

Notice the isotopism of the Eloi and the Time Traveller. It springs from the fact that the horror of this inversion of basic *power norms* is predicated upon the Time Traveller's being also a mammal, a land animal, an animal, an organic being, and finally an existing entity; this is a continuation and validation of the Eloi and Morlocks being descended from, apparently corresponding to, and certainly being magically associated with the Victorian upper and lower class. The different sociological, biological, and cosmological oppositions in the Wellsian series have the final common denominator of dominant existence or power. Power is the arbiter, fate, or nemesis in science fiction.

As was suggested in section two, the paradigm for these proportions is undoubtedly supplied by the relationships in *Gulliver's Travels*, in particular the black, Swiftian variant of book 4:

Horse : Houynhnhnm = Man : X

"X" is the *animal rationale* Swift believed might perhaps be found in some individuals but not in mankind as a whole. Though there might be a few noble men *rationis capax*, such as Captain Mendez or Lord Munodi, there was no rational "Noble Man" corresponding *sub specie humanitatis* to the "Noble Horses," and the only fully consistent categorical alternative was that Mankind is Yahookind, *animal implume bipes*.[18] Beyond that, section two tried to show how Wells's paradigm leads back to More's *Utopia*. Between More's inversion from axiologically bad to good, and Wells's inversion of biologically dominant to dominated, Swift's absence of the "Noble Man" (synthesizing axiology and biology) provides the middle term. This section on proportion might fittingly conclude with noting the secular proportion—

Utopia : Gulliver's Travels = Gulliver's Travels : The Time Machine

In terms of ideological vision—though perhaps not in

terms of aesthetics—this is also a devolutionary series. Beside Man, Nonexistence or Death is the second privileged member of Wells's scale. Finally—as it is in the magnificent eclipse description—the two allegorical protagonists Everyman and Death meet again: and it is not Everyman who wins. Having adopted such horizons, modern Anglophone science fiction from Stapledon to Heinlein, Orwell, Asimov, Pohl or Aldiss had to concentrate on filling in Wells's paradigm and varying its surface. The only other course would have been to return, on a higher bend of the spiral, to the original Morean paradigm: a turn that it has so far been either unwilling or unable to take. For better or for worse (as Russian literature is said to have sprung from Gogol's "Overcoat"), all of this science fiction has sprung from *The Time Machine*. Furthermore, even the abandoning of science fiction in favor of futurology, popular punditry, and more prestigious literary genres is another case of Wells's paradigmatic position in relation to the sociology of science fiction (from Asimov and Pohl to Vonnegut and Ballard). And in Wells's concomitant utopian speculations—so much more muddled and less cognitive than his early science fiction—there can be found the reasons for and social roots of such unwillingness, inability, and abandonings.

NOTES

1. I have learned more than I could properly indicate by however copious footnotes from critics of Wells, even when I disagreed with some of their premises or details. At the very least, I should mention the books (or their relevant chapters or essays) by *Bergonzi, *Brooks, *Caudwell, *Hillegas, *Kagarlitski, *Parrinder, *Philmus, *Pritchett, *Wagar, and *West, as well as Mark R. Hillegas, "Cosmic Pessimism in H. G. Wells's Scientific Romances," *Papers of the Michigan Academy of Science, Arts, and Letters* 46 (1961): 655–63; and Bernard Bergonzi, "The Publication of *The Time Machine*, 1894–5," *Review of English Studies* 11 (1960): 42–51.

2. *Wells, *Exp.*, pp. 160–61 (italics added); cited further as *Exp.* with page number. Compare also Wells's explicit preoccupation with biologi-

cal "degradation" inherent in evolution under capitalism in the articles
"Zoological Retrogression," *The Gentleman's Magazine* (7 September
1891); "On Extinction," *Chambers's Journal* (30 September 1893); "The
Man of the Year Million," *Pall Mall Gazette* (9 November 1893); and "The
Extinction of Man," *Pall Mall Gazette* (23 September 1894)—the last two
reprinted in *Wells, *C.P.M.*; also his comment in *'42 to '44* (London,
1944), p. 9.

3. Wells referred to his type of science-fiction story as "the vivid
realization of some disregarded possibility in such a way as to comment
on the false securities and fatuous self-satisfaction of everyday life"—
quoted in *West, p. 112.

4. "Prolegomena," in *Huxley; cited further in the text as *Pr.* with
page number.

5. *See* as outstanding examples, the final paragraph of ch. 6 and ch. 21
in Darwin's *The Descent of Man* (London, 1874)—not to mention the
famous parable of the tangled bank that concludes *The Origin of Species*.
T. H. Huxley uses the same device at the end of ch. 2 ("On the Relations
of Man to the Lower Animals") of *Man's Place in Nature* (London, 1863).
The collocation of such passages at the climaxes of books or book
sections testifies both to the rhetorical effectiveness of the parable and to
the Darwinist sense of its importance as ethicoaesthetical justification of
evolution. The upward, "excelsior" course of the arrow of time provided
a new type of dynamic sublimity, analogical to the "per aspera ad astra"
("per evolutionem ad hominem"?) rise of the Victorian "self-made man."
For an approach to Darwin's aesthetics and rhetoric, *see* Stanley Edgar
Hyman, *The Tangled Bank* (New York, 1962); Walter F. Cannon,
"Darwin's Vision in *On the Origin of Species*," in *The Art of Victorian Prose*,
ed. George Levine and William Madden (New York, 1968), pp. 154–76,
who situates them convincingly in ideological time and place. On
Darwin's concept of the sublime *see* Donald Fleming's "Charles Darwin
the Anaesthetic Man," in *Darwin*, ed. Philip Appleman (New York, 1970),
pp. 573–89; Fleming speaks of Darwin's hidden "Carlylean self," p. 583,
but for differences between them *see* Theodore Baird, "Darwin and the
Tangled Bank," *American Scholar* 15 (1946).

6. This inversion of the Darwinian arrow of time seems to have been
one of Wells's basic intellectual, morphological, and visionary discoveries. His first work that transcends adolescent doodling (a student
debating address in 1885) was entitled *The Past and Future of the Human
Race*, the title of a key book in 1902 is *The Discovery of the Future*, and in
1936 it is (characteristically) the archaeologist in his *The Croquet Player*
who speaks of the abyss of the future bringing the ancestral savage beast
back (ch. 3). In *The Future in America* (London, 1906), p. 10, Wells
explicitly connects monstrous science-fictional projections with such
Darwinian anticipations.

Strictly speaking, Darwin's theory is neutral as far as prospects or the present state of mankind are concerned. He himself, although quite aware of biological retrogression, extinction, and similar facts, assumed that biological groups "which are now large and triumphant . . . will for a long period continue to increase," and stressed the ennobling aspects of evolution—*see* note 5, and *On the Origin of Species* (Cambridge, Mass., 1964), pp. 126 and 488–90. For philosophical implications of the Darwinian time-arrow, *see*, for example, Loren Eiseley, *Darwin's Century* (New York, 1958), pp. 330–31; for literary ones, the stimulating essay by A. Dwight Culler, "The Darwinian Revolution and Literary Form," in Levine and Madden, pp. 224–46. It was the opponents of Darwin's theory who first seized upon its malevolent aspect—cf. chapters 12–14 of Leo J. Henkin, *Darwinism in the English Novel 1860–1910* (New York, 1940). On the other extreme, Spencer's contention that evolution through struggle for life "can end only in the establishment of the greatest perfection and the most complete happiness"—*First Principles* (New York, 1900), p. 530—is the real villain of this ideological drama or *pièce à thèse*. The naive, capitalist Spencerians or Social Darwinists (in the U.S.A, for example, Rockefeller or Carnegie) wholeheartedly embraced trampling the "less fit" multitude; John D. Rockefeller's parable of the American Beauty rose, "produced . . . only by sacrificing the early buds," deserves to be as famous as Darwin's tangled bank or Menenius Agrippa's fable of the belly and the members. See Richard Hofstadter, *Social Darwinism in American Thought* (Boston, 1955), especially ch. 2.

7. J. B. S. Haldane and Julian Huxley, *Animal Biology* (Oxford, 1927), fig. 81 on pp. 258–59.

8. Faced with the divergent impulses of scientific classification and subdivision on one hand, and artistic vividness of individuation on the other—a pull that was to remain constant albeit with different outcomes throughout his life—Wells as early as 1891 satirized the deterministic rigidity in "The Universe Rigid," and then went on to find a first compromise in "The Rediscovery of the Unique" (also 1891) and its successive avatars in "The 'Cyclic' Delusion" (1893), "Scepticism of the Instrument" (1903), and *First and Last Things* (1908); for their publication, *see* the two bibliographies at the end of this volume. These texts, and the deep though unclear tension they tried to formulate, seem to give an account of the central morphological dilemma facing Wells in the years of his first and best science-fiction cycle, whose underlying paradigm is contained in *The Time Machine*. At his best, Wells solved this problem by opting for representativeness, for fusing individual and species into socially and/or biologically typical figures, like the Time Traveller. *See Exp.* for his references to "de-individualizing" and perceiving individuals in relation to a story and a thesis, on p. 175, p. 520, and particularly the "seriational" account of his creative imagination in the dispute with Conrad on p. 528.

9. *See*, for example, Wells's explicit comment on such an attitude,

which fused scientific progress and a sense of imperial mission in the fin-de-siècle Britain, in *Joan and Peter* (London, 1918), bk. I, ch. 3. In his admiration of Malthus, however, Wells himself was not always immune from it—say in *Anticipations* (New York and London, 1902), pp. 313–14, and the last three chapters generally. Such instances could be multiplied.

10. *See* some of their stories in (and also the Preface to) D. Suvin, ed., *Other Worlds, Other Seas* (New York, 1972).

11. Some evidence that Wells associated class and race as isomorphic antagonistic opositions in conflicts between oppressors and oppressed, such as those that presumably led to the development of the Eloi and Morlocks, can be found in a statement like, "the driving discontent has often appeared as a conflict between oppressors and oppressed, either as a class or as a race conflict. . ." (*Exp.* 626).

12. *See* Robert M. Philmus, "*The Time Machine*; or, the Fourth Dimension as Prophecy," *PMLA* 84 (1969): 530–35, for effects of this structural device.

13. Wells's 1894 essay, "The Extinction of Man" (*see* note 2), discusses this inversion of roles with man succumbing—among other possibilities, all later used in his science fiction—to *huge land-crabs* or *unknown sea monsters*: "In the case of every other predominant animal the world has ever seen, I repeat, the hour of its complete ascendency has been the eve of its complete overthrow," he concluded.

14. H. G. Wells, *The Future in America*, pp. 11–12.

15. *See*, for example, Wells's anonymous article "Death" in the *Saturday Review* (1895) (quoted in *West, p. 275), which makes exactly this point.

16. I shall tangentially remark that T. H. Huxley explained at length in his works—and no doubt in his lectures—the difference between physiological and morphological species, which is intricate and mainly resolvable by experimental crossbreeding; in Weena, the mawkish avatar of Dickens's Little Nell and other Victorian girl heroines, Wells supplied the Time Traveller with a somewhat imperfect subject for such experimentation. Wells's private and later literary efforts at sexual liberation prove, I think, that he passed up such clearly present considerations only out of deference to very strong social taboos. One can blame him the less since the taboo has been prudently respected in science fiction until these last years in the most ludicrous ways—for instance, in the Tarzan-Jane relationship, as shown by Professor R. D. Mullen the Elder in *Riverside Quarterly* 4 (June 1970). It almost goes without saying that the situation was different in French science fiction from its early masterpiece *L'Eve future* by Villiers de l'Isle Adam to a novel by the noted writer Vercors (published in the U.S. as *The Murder of the Missing Link*) having exactly this experiment in miscegenation—performed by a Daniel Ellsberg among zoologists to force a test trial for antigenocidal

purposes—to its theme. Still, it is surprising that Wells never really fused his sexual liberation novels and his scientific romances into xenoerotics of the Rosny Aîné. Alain Dorémieux or P. J. Farmer type; but here, too, he has at least provided an "empty" model.

17. For Wells's view of any historical "social edifice" as divided into a basic "labouring class" and a "superior class"—a view directly echoing *The Communist Manifesto*—see his *Anticipations*, pp. 75–83. That passage leads into a discussion on pp. 83–91 of the parasitic decadence of both the fin-de-siècle upper and lower classes, the "shareholders" and the "abyss" (the latter a metaphor that Jack London was to pick up in *The People of the Abyss* and *The Iron Heel*). That such a "future decadence" is the source of the Eloi-Morlocks episode is explicitly brought out in the conversation with Theodore Roosevelt at the end of *The Future in America*. However, the *Anticipations* passage continues with a long discussion, pp. 92 and further, of the rise of a new middle class of educated engineers and scientific managers that holds the only hope for the future. Wells's subsequent ideological career is, as Caudwell rightly remarked, a search for this third social force— for *"a competent receiver"* for society along Saint-Simonian rather than Marxist lines *(see Exp.* 206, passim*)*.

18. For a first approach to the complicated categories and proportions in book 4 of *Gulliver's Travels, see* the following books:

Frank Brady, ed. *Twentieth-Century Interpretations of "Gulliver's Travels"*. Englewood Cliffs, New Jersey, 1968.
Robert C. Elliott. *The Shape of Utopia*. Chicago and London, 1970.
Ernest Tuveson, ed. *Swift*. Englewood Cliffs, New Jersey, 1964.

The essays by R. S. Crane and Joseph Horell in the above collections seemed most useful for the purposes of this article. Professor Traugott in the Tuveson volume and also Professor Elliott address themselves directly to the evident connections between Swift and More.

Aristotle points out in *Poetics*, 1457 b, that any metaphor is either: (1) a relation of species to or within genus: or (2) an analogy that always presupposes the A:B=C:D proportion. In my essay, "On the Poetics of the Science-Fiction Genre," *College English* 34 (December 1972), I tried to demonstrate that significant science fiction operates on an analogical model. It is thus understandable that the clearest paradigm of science fiction is to be found in *Gulliver's Travels,* and that Wells closely followed it. He revived the paradigm by substituting Darwinist evolution for Swiftian or Christian-humanist ethics, and the classification methods of *arbor huxleiana* for those of *arbor porphyriana*—Huxley being to Darwin what Porphyry was to Aristotle (on the Porphyrian tree *see* Walter J. Ong, *Ramus, Method, and the Decay of Dialogue* [Cambridge, Mass., 1958], pp. 78–79, passim).

"I Told You So": Wells's Last Decade, 1936–1945

by R. D. MULLEN

In his Preface to the 1940 edition of *The War in the Air*, Wells stated that his epitaph, "when the time comes, will manifestly have to be: 'I told you so. You *damned* fools.' " In most if not all of the books written on Wells, only a few pages are devoted to the years in which he most emphatically and explicitly told the world so. In a sense, this is perhaps as it should be. Although I think that Wells wrote on of his best romances in *The Holy Terror* (1939), one of his best novels in *Apropos of Dolores* (1938), and the best of all possible introductions to his work in *The Anatomy of Frustration* (1936), I would not wish to contend that the books of his last decade have anything like the stature of those he wrote between 1895 and 1915. But that is not to say that Wells's last decade should be ignored altogether, as it all too often is. Contrary to what the "new orthodoxy" about him supposes, the late H. G. Wells is continuous with the early H. G. Wells: in his last decade Wells was voicing concerns

116

similar to those that preoccupied him at the start of his career. Chief among these is what might be called the *crisis of man's destiny*, which he focused on with a perspicacity that justifies him as much as, if not more than, anyone else in saying, "I told you so."

1

For the last ten years, what have been the most fashionable topics of conversation? Ecology? The conservation of resources? The sexual revolution? The youth rebellion? The black rebellion? The revolt of subject peoples? Continuing, unending, indecisive war? The possibility that men, being descended from killer apes, are inherently aggressive? The probability that men all take pleasure in cruelty and have an appetite for inflicting torture more powerful than lust itself? These are the subjects of Wells's work. These *were* his subjects at a time when they were not fashionable—not fashionable because the dreadful implications then seemed a mere cloud on the horizon, not fashionable because then there seemed to be time to deal with them if and when they actually became serious. In the thirty years since his death, the cloud has turned into a storm. These are fashionable subjects now. Now everybody is a Wellsian—at least in the sense that everybody is reading and discussing books of a kind that Wells was almost alone in writing in the last decade of his life.

Look first at the bulk and variety of the work of his last decade, and then consider the themes on which he plays variations.

The bibliography published by the Wells Society[1] lists thirty-three titles for the years 1936–1945, but these include four or five duplications and a number of brief pieces. If some of the briefer works were gathered into collections and others were appended to longer works, the whole would fill only about twelve average-sized volumes: five volumes of essays and articles on the world crisis, four novels of contemporary life, one book-length "scientific romance," one collection of shorter romances, and one book, *The Anatomy of Frustration*, of a rare kind that might be called *the imaginary review*, for it is a study of the work of an imaginary writer.

In this imagined set of twelve volumes there is a good deal of variety and a good deal that is repetitious. The repetition can be seen in perspective if two things are noted. First, that a number of the shorter works were published only as pamphlets or six-penny paperbacks; that is, were written for an audience presumed to be not overly familiar with the books published in more expensive editions.[2] Second, that when these are eliminated, the repetitious passages turn out to be brief statements of Wells's most basic concepts—concepts pertinent to all his work.

With the repetition accounted for, what is found is an amazing variety within an overall unity. The articles and essays[3] range over all the world and deal with men and movements of almost every conceivable kind. Although having a common subject, the romances[4] differ from each other in structure and approach. The four novels exhibit the greatest variety. *You Can't Be Too Careful* (1941) is comparable to the comic novels and *Babes in the Darkling Wood* (1940) to the prig novels of the earlier periods. *Apropos of Dolores* turns on a battle royal between man and wife that, if dramatized, could well rival *Who's Afraid of Virginia Woolf*. *Brynhild* (1934) is a comedy of appearance and reality, a satire on the uses of publicity in the achievement of a literary reputation, which contains little or nothing, other than in its bright and bitter comedy, of what one thinks of as typically Wellsian. Putting it aside, I find that the remaining books all deal with what Wells was perhaps the first to call *the ecological crisis*.

During the twentieth century, Wells said, history has

become ecology, for the human environment has undergone a change so great that the human animal, like any other species faced with such a change, must either adapt or cease to exist. It is a threefold change: first, the abolition of distance effected by radio communication and air travel; second, the tremendous increase in the scale of industrial operations; and third, and great release of human energy resulting from the simultaneous disappearance of widespread illiteracy and of the need for unskilled labor. The first change threatens mankind with destruction by war, and can be met only by the establishment of a worldwide authority to control all use of aircraft. The second change is even more serious than the first, in that the waste and destruction effected by industrial operations is even greater than that caused by war; this change can be met only by the establishment of a worldwide authority for the conservation of resources. The third change threatens the world with anarchy, since social order can no longer be maintained on the basis of master-man relationships, and therefore demands the establishment of an equalitarian social order, for which the first step would be the adoption by all governments of a Declaration of the Rights of Man. Had people read Wells with attention, they would not have been surprised by the sharp increase in crimes of violence, by the riots that have swept cities and campuses, or by the inability of the United States to impose its will on the peoples of Vietnam.[5]

2

If mankind is to survive, Wells adduces from his analysis, three things are needed and needed immediately: a world wide Air Authority, a worldwide Conservation Authority, and a full acceptance of the rights of man. What stands in the way? What prevents man from taking the road to utopia and holds him on the road to destruction? The answer to this question is given most plainly in a book published in 1939, *The Fate of Homo Sapiens*. [6] Here Wells takes up, one by one, the "Existing Forces" that dominate world thought. Let me quote the chapter titles: "The Jewish Influence"; "Christendom"; "What Is Protestantism?"; "The Nazi Religion"; "Totalitarianism"; "The British Oligarchy"; "Shintoism"; "The Chinese Outlook"; "Subject Peoples"; "Communism and Russia"; "American Mentality." Having surveyed the "Existing Forces" and found them all working far more for evil than for good, Wells can only conclude that the possibility of man's survival is very slim indeed:

> The coming barbarism will differ from the former barbarism by its greater powers of terror, urgency, and destruction, and by its greater rapidity of wastage. . . . The average life will be steadily diminishing, health will be deteriorating. The viruses and pestilential germs will resume their experiments in variation and new blotches and infections will give scope for pious resignation and turn men's hearts once again toward a better world beyond the stars. There will be a last crop of saints and devotees. Mankind, which began in a cave and behind a windbreak, will end in the disease-soaked ruins of the slum. What else can happen? What other road can destiny take?
>
> If *Homo sapiens* is such a fool that he cannot realize what is before him now, and set himself urgently to save the situation, while there is still some light, some freedom of thought and speech, some freedom of movement and action left in the world, can there be the slightest hope that in fifty or a hundred years hence, after he has been through two or three generations of accentuated fear, crulty, and relentless individual frustration, with ever-diminishing opportunity of apprehending the real nature of his troubles, he will be collectively any less of a fool? Why should he undergo a magic change when all the forces, within him as without, are plainly set against it? [7]

That was written about the middle of 1939. And then the war came. In several places I have seen it said that the war must have come to Wells as the end of all his hopes. Quite the contrary; for he saw in this war, as he had seen in the war of 1914, the possibility that might set the world free—free, that is, from those forces that blocked the road to survival and utopia.

His first response to the war was the book called *The New World Order* (1939), which was soon followed by other hopeful books and pamphlets—hopeful, at least, in that they called for an effort to save the world. Oddly enough, his having still some hope can be seen from one of his most pessimistic works, *'42 to '44* (1944), his last full-length book—not from its contents, but from the fact that he had it published as an expensive library volume never to be reissued in cheap editions, for he considered it "strong meat for babes," and hence a work that, if widely read, might well do damage to the hope for a new world order (Preface).

3

It has been pointed out by Thomas D. Clareson that much of twentieth-century realism might well be called *scientific fiction* since its peculiar modes derive from the impact of science on the twentieth-century mind.[8] Scientific fantasy and scientific realism are the two sides of the coin of twentieth-century fiction. This concept is especially pertinent to Wells's fiction, including that of his last decade, for there is as much science in the novels as in the romances. *Apropos of Dolores* is the other side of *Star Begotten* (1934). *Babes in the Darkling Wood* is the other side of *The Holy Terror*. And taken together, the six shorter romances are the other side of *You Can't Be Too Careful*.

If one word is needed to name the theme of all these books, that word is *frustration*. The variations on the theme come from the various causes of frustration: sexual repression; class hatred, especially downward class hatred;[9] the addiction of human beings to aggression and cruelty; the fact that very few people can grasp the nature of the world in which they live.

The theme of aggression and cruelty appears in the first book on the list, *The Anatomy of Frustration,* where the story of man is said to be "the story of an excessively pugnacious ape being slowly tamed" (ch. 12)—words that might well remind one of Robert Ardrey and all the other authors who for the past ten years have made instinctive aggression a fashionable topic of conversation. The theme of *The Croquet Player* (1936) is that man's inherent aggression and cruelty are being intensified and released by the changed conditions of the world. The fear of cruelty is the dominant motive in the life of the hero of *The Holy Terror,* who, like Shaw's Caesar, feels that he must either conquer the world or be destroyed by it. In *Babes in the Darkling Wood* the hero is driven mad by the cruelty he sees on the battlefield and—more important—in the wake of battle. Torture and the fear of torture, which began to loom large in his fiction with *Meanwhile* (1927) and *Mr. Blettsworthy on Rampole Island* (1928), run through everything he wrote in his last decade. The subject of the first part of his last full-length book, *'42 to '44,* is the psychology of cruelty, which is the meat that he considered too strong for the babes that read his paperback propaganda.

The most striking science-fictional concept that runs through these last works of fiction is the idea, anticipated earlier in Wells, that mankind consists of two species: one capable and the other incapable of adapting to the new environment. In *Star Begotten* the hero becomes obsessed with the notion that Martians are using cosmic rays to effect mutations in mankind, but after investigating the matter concludes that the new species consists of those people who have evolved to the point that they can see the world for what it actually is, and that he himself belongs to the new species, or at least is a half-breed, rather than what has been called *Homo sapiens* but were better called *Homo superbus*; that is, man foolishly proud (ch. 8, Section 5). In *Apropos of Dolores* the two species are represented by the narrator and his wife, she being *Homo regardant,* "traditional, legal, implacable," and he being *Homo rampant,* "open-minded and futuristic" (ch. 4, Section 16). In *You Can't Be Too Careful,* the old species is renamed *Homo Tewler* in honor of the story's hero, who is as careful as anyone can be. The obdurate blindness to new ideas of *Homo superbus, Homo regardant,* and *Homo Tewler* is basic to the themes of *The Camford Visitation* (1934), *The Brothers* (1938), *All Aboard for Ararat* (1940), and *The Happy Turning* (1945).

4

Both the slight optimism and the almost ovewhelming pessimism of the last full-length books are thus based on the nature of man: the pessimism on the belief that men in general, and especially men of the ruling class, are too prone to aggression, cruelty, and fear to adapt to the new environment; the slight optimism on the hope that there might still be a saving remnant that could, in a world set free by war, lead mankind to utopia rather than destruction. But in that tiny book called *Mind at the End of Its Tether* (1945), the pessimism becomes absolute: "the end of everything we call life is close at hand and cannot be evaded" (ch. 1). Since the book does not support its statements with argument, readers can not be certain why all hope has been lost, but they can perhaps make a pretty good guess on the basis of the book's first sentence:

> The writer finds very considerable reason for believing that within a period to be estimated by weeks and months rather than by aeons, there has been a fundamental change in the conditions under which life . . . has been going on since its beginning.

What is peculiar here is the contrast between months and aeons. What has happened to years and centuries? Up to this time Wells has been saying that a fundamental change had occurred within the last century, in a period to be estimated by years rather than by aeons. Why does he now speak of weeks and months?

Remember that such optimism as Wells had felt had been based on the faint hope that war might sweep away those forces that kept man on the road to destruction. He had never been among those who exaggerate the destructiveness of war. In *The Shape of Things to Come* (1933)—despite whatever memories one may have of the film based on it—it is not war but economic disintegration that brings the old world to ruin. As George Orwell noted in 1941, in a review of *Guide to the New World,* Wells tended to underestimate Hitler's power of destruction.[10] Even so, Wells turned out to be essentially right, and Orwell wrong, as is evident from the recovery of Europe. But with the coming of the atomic bomb, the idea that war might set the world free of its past had to be abandoned. *Mind at the End of Its Tether* was published several months before the existence of the atomic bomb became common knowledge, and I have no facts in my possession to indicate that Wells had somehow penetrated the secrecy that surrounded the development of the bomb. On the other hand, I can think of no other way of making sense out of the strange little book with which he closed a long career of perceptive speculation on the destiny of man.

NOTES

1. The H. G. Wells Society, compilers, *H. G. Wells: A Comprehensive Bibliography,* 2d ed. (Edgeware, Middlesex, England, 1968).

2. Seven or eight brief works that might well be gathered into one volume: *Travels of a Republican Radical in Search of Hot Water* (1939); *The Rights of Man* (1940); *The Common Sense of War and Peace* (1940); *Two*

Hemispheres or One World (1940); *The New Rights of Man* (1942) (not seen by present writer; published only in U.S.; perhaps identical with *The Rights of Man*); *Crux Ansata: An Indictment of the Roman Catholic Church* (1943); *The Mosley Outrage* (1943).

3. *World Brain* (1938) (includes a 1936 and a 1937 pamphlet); *The Outlook for Homo Sapiens* (1942) (an "amalgamation" of *The Fate of Homo Sapiens* of 1939 and *The New World Order* of 1939); *'42 to '44: A Contemporary Memoir on Human Behavior During the Crisis of the World Revolution* (1944) (includes Wells's doctoral thesis at London University, 1942); and four briefer works that might well be gathered into a single volume: *Guide to the New World* (1941); *Phoenix* (1942); *The Conquest of Time* (1942); *Mind at the End of Its Tether* (1945).

4. *The Holy Terror* (1939); and seven shorter stories: *The Croquet Player* (1936); *Man Who Could Work Miracles: A Film Story* (1936); *Star Begotten* (1937); *The Camford Visitation* (1937); *The Brothers* (1938); *All Aboard for Ararat* (1940); *The Happy Turning* (1945).

5. See *The Fate of Homo Sapiens*, ch. 4 (or *The Outlook for Homo Sapiens*, ch. 5); *The New World Order*, chs. 3 and 5 (or *Outlook*, chs. 29 and 31); *The Common Sense of War and Peace*, ch. 4; *Guide to the New World*, Introduction; *Science and the World Mind* (not chaptered; London, 1942), pp. 5–18; *Phoenix*, bk. 1, ch. 2.

6. Published in U.S. as *The Fate of Man* (New York, 1939); *see* also note 3.

7. Ch. 26 in either *The Fate of Homo Sapiens* or *The Outlook for Homo Sapiens*.

8. Thomas D. Clareson, "The Other Side of Realism," in *Sf: The Other Side of Realism*, ed. Thomas D. Clareson (Bowling Green, Ohio, 1971), pp. 5–8.

9. "Downward Class Hatred," ch. 14 of part 1 of *'42 to '44*, is concerned with "the smouldering discontent of the privileged and the advantaged with the development of liberal equalitarianism."

10. George Orwell, *The Collected Essays, Journalism, and Letters of George Orwell*, ed. Sonia Orwell and Ian Angus, 4 vols. (New York, 1968), 2:139–45.

Imagining the Future: Wells and Zamyatin

by PATRICK PARRINDER

> A literature that is alive does not live by yesterday's
> clock, nor by today's but by tomorrow's.
>> Yevgeny Zamyatin, "On Literature,
>> Revolution, Entropy, and Other Matters"[1]

1

In his recent critical biography of Yevgeny Zamyatin, Alex M. Shane wrote that the question of Wells's influence on Zamyatin's *We* "has not yet received extensive, systematic study."[2] I, for one, am glad of this. The connection between Zamyatin and Wells raises problems that can not be solved by the systematic study of influences, or by the purely content-oriented approach that most critics of the anti-utopian novel have adopted. In comparing Zamyatin and Wells critics should at least seek to ask, how should (or how can) science fiction be written?

Zamyatin's reputation in the English-speaking world owes much to George Orwell, who both used *We* as one of the sources of *Nineteen Eighty-Four,* and asserted that Aldous Huxley must have drawn upon it in *Brave New World*[3] (Huxley himself denied this). It has become usual to place *We* in the line that includes these books and other antiutopias such as E. M. Forster's "The Machine Stops" and William Golding's *Lord of the Flies.* Apart from Zamyatin, this is a very English tradition—not merely dystopian, but deliberately and consciously anti-Wellsian—and Mark R. Hillegas has recently argued that their rejection of Wells's values has concealed the basic indebtedness of all these writers to Wells's visions and methods. In Zamyatin's case, Hillegas shows that *We* reproduces the broad topography of the Wellsian future romance: the dehumanized city-state with its huge apartment blocks, its dictatorship, its walls excluding the natural world, and its weird House of Antiquity is built of elements from *When the Sleeper Wakes,* "A Story of Days to Come," and *The Time Machine.*[4] Yet this reveals little about the spirit in which *We* was written. The present essay will emphasize two facts that have been noted and yet have hardly been taken into account by previous critics. The first is that, so far from being a deliberate anti-Wellsian, Zamyatin was the author of a sparkling but little-known essay on *Herbert Wells* (1922), which puts forward its subject as, in some sense, the prototype of the revolutionary-modernist artist. The second is that Zamyatin was himself a notably original modernist writer, and not merely the precursor of Huxley and Orwell. To pass from *The Time Machine* to *We* is to enter a world where the topography may be similar, but the nature of experience is utterly changed, so that readers are faced with two quite different kinds of imagination. In this crucial respect, the "modernist" status, which Zamyatin conferred on Wells in theory, was in practice reserved for himself alone.

A marine architect by profession, and an ex-Bolshevik

who had been imprisoned after the 1905 revolution, Zamyatin was building icebreakers in England when the Tsarist regime was overthrown. He returned to Russia in September 1917 and became a leading figure among the left-wing writers of Petersburg until his outspoken and heretical views came into conflict with the rigid cultural controls of the 1920s. *We*, his major imaginative work, was written in 1920–21, banned in the Soviet Union, and published in English translation in 1924. In ideological terms, it is an expression of his qualms about the technocratic development of Western civilization, with a sardonic relevance to the Bolshevik ideal, notably in the portrayal of the "entropic" stabilization of the once-revolutionary state, and in the restatement of Dostoyevsky's eternal opposition of freedom and happiness. At the same time as writing *We*, Zamyatin, like most of his fellow writers, found himself engaged in educational work and in the organization of new revolutionary publishing houses. One of the first foreign authors to be republished was H. G. Wells. (His works had already been abundantly available under the Tsar.) Zamyatin supervised a series of Wells translations between 1918 and 1926, and *Herbert Wells*, a survey of the whole of his work up to the 1920s, was a by-product of this.

Two factors dominated Zamyatin's enthusiasm for the English writer. There was Wells's standing as a creator of modern myths: Zamyatin saw the "scientific romances," which were his chief interest, as a species of fairy tale reflecting the endless prospect of technological change and the rigorously logical demands of scientific culture. They were the fairy tales of an asphalt-mechanized metropolis in which the only forests were made up of factory chimmeys, and the only scents were those of test tubes and motor exhausts. Thus they expressed a specifically Western experience: for the reader in backward Russia, the urban landscapes that had produced Wells, and not only those that he described, belonged to the future. Zamyatin was enough of a determinist to feel that Wells's expression of the twentieth-century environment alone constituted an essential modernity. He denotes this side of Wells by the symbol of the aeroplane soaring above the given world into a new and unexplored element. Just as terrestrial landscape was transformed by the possibility of aerial photography, war and revolution were transforming human prospects. Zamyatin calls Wells the most contemporary of writers because he has foreseen this, and taught men to see with "airman's eyes."

Zamyatin was forced to admit that Wells himself had "come back to earth," however, in the sense of abandoning science fiction for the realistic-social novel. While suggesting that his social novels were old-fashioned and derivative beside the "scientific romances," Zamyatin used the whole range of Wells's writings to support his second theme, that of Wells as a socialist artist. He quotes passages from Wells's Introduction to a Russian edition of his works (1911) in which he declares himself a non-Marxist, nonviolent revolutionary—in other words, a heretical socialist like Zamyatin himself. The most surprising twist in the argument is the discussion of Wells's most recent phase, his conversion to belief in a "finite God," which was announced in *Mr. Britling Sees It Through* in 1916. Wells's wayward and short-lived attempt to combine rationalism and religion later appeared as an absurdity even to himself; but for Zamyatin it was proof of his independence and of his imaginative daring. In the aftermath of war, Wells's earlier visions had already come true. "The whole of life has been torn away from the anchor of reality and has become fantastic," Zamyatin wrote. Wells's response had been to pursue his method further, until it touched the ultimate meaning of life. The resulting fusion of socialism and religion was a boldly paradoxical feat recalling the joining of science and myth in the early romances:

The dry, compass-drawn circle of socialism, limited by the

earth, and the hyperbola of religion, stretching into infinity—
the two are so different, so incompatible. But Wells managed to
breach the circle, bend it into a hyperbola, one end of which
rests on the earth, in science and positivism, while the other
loses itself in the sky.[5]

Although it made a stir at the time, Wells's spurious religion
hardly merits this engaging metaphor. The figure of the
circle bent into a hyperbola is associated with the spiraling
flight of the aeroplane. Both are found elsewhere in
Zamyatin's writings, serving as cryptic images of his theory
of art.

In his essay "On Synthetism" (1922), he divides all art into
three schools represented by the symbols: +; −; − −
(affirmation, negation, and synthesis).[6] Art develops in
a continual dialectical sequence as one school gives way
to the next. The three schools of art in the present phase
are naturalism(+), symbolism and futurism (−), and
"neorealism" or "synthetism" (− −), a post-Cubist and
post-Einsteinian art that embraces the paradox of modern
experience in being both "realistic" and "fantastic." Characterized by incongruous juxtaposition and the splintering of
planes, Synthetism is identified in the work of Picasso,
Annenkov, Bely, Blok, and, of course, Zamyatin himself.
But this is only a temporary phase, for each dialectical triad
is subject to an ongoing process of replacement and
succession that observes an eternal oscillation between the
extremes of revolution and entropy. Development is a
succession of explosions and consolidations, and "the
equation of art is the equation of an infinite spiral."

These ideas are the formula of Zamyatin's commitments
to permanent revolution and to the heretical nature of the
artist. They are related to his view of Wells in various ways.
In the section of *Herbert Wells* entitled "Wells's Genealogy,"
one reads that the traditional utopian romance from More
to Morris bears a positive sign—the affirmation of a vision

of earthly paradise. Wells invents a new form of "sociofantastic novel" with a negative sign; its purpose is not the portrayal of a future paradise, but social criticism by extrapolation. There is some ambiguity about these categories, and Zamyatin does not elaborate upon them, but it seems evident that there must also be an antiutopian form marked (– –). As the reader follows the struggle of D-503 to achieve mental orthodoxy in *We*, and more fleetingly as he contemplates the brainwashed Winston at the end of *Nineteen Eighty-Four*, the impossibility of the reader's imagining such a future at all—in any full sense—is what the author confronts him with. Is this perhaps the negation of the negation?

Such reasoning would limit Wells to an intermediate place in the dialectic of antiupopia. Zamyatin usually sees him in a more general way as epitomizing the dynamic quality of the contemporary imagination. For Zamyatin— for example, in his "On Literature, Revolution, Entropy, and Other Matters"—the aeroplane spiraling upward from the Earth is not just Wells but a symbol of contemporary writing as a whole. Moreover, Wells's success in terms of actual prophecy confirmed his position as a vanguard artist, and indeed as a "neorealist." Destroying the stable picture of Victorian society with his strange, forward-looking logic, he had foreseen the revolutionary age when reality would itself become fantastic. Zamyatin credited him with the invention of a type of fable reflecting the demands of modern experience—speed, logic, unpredictability. Yet for all this there was one area in which he lagged behind: "language, style, the word—all those things that we have come to appreciate in the most recent Russian writers." One of Zamyatin's metaphors for art is "a winding staircase in the Tower of Babel" ("On Synthetism"). He heralded the verbal and syntactical revolution generating language that was "supercharged, high-voltage," and he tried to create such a language in the writing of *We*.

2

We is written in the form of a diary. It is true that D-503 the diarist, makes some conscientious attempts to explain his society to alien readers, but the social picture that emerges (the sole concern of ideologically—minded critics from Orwell onward) is essentially revealed through the medium of the future consciousness, and even the future language, which are Zamyatin's most radical conceptions. The reflection that a new society entails new conceptions. The reflection that a new society entails new consciousness and language, and that these can only be adequately suggested by a "futuristic" fictional technique, seems obvious once stated. Yet it is Zamyatin's imagination of these conditions—his revelation of the future through its writing—that establishes *We* as a uniquely modernist work of science fiction.

In *The Form of Victorian Fiction*, Hillis Miller has written that "the transformation which makes a man a novelist is his decision to adopt the role of the narrator who tells the story."[7] It is from this point of view that the contrast between the influential Wellsian model of the science-fiction fable, and the form that Zamyatin created, is most clearly seen.

Wells's concern is with *facing* the unknown; Zamyatin's, with *being* the unknown. Wells's narratives always have a fixed and familiar point of reference.[8] Like Swift and Voltaire, he exploits the Enlightenment forms of the travelogue and the scientific report. In his early romances there is always a narrator who brings weird and disturbing news and yet wins the reader's confidence at once by his observance of anecdotal conventions. His audience is either today's audience or that of the very near future, and his assumptions are those of contemporary scientific culture. In *The Time Machine*, the Time Traveller sets out armed with expectant curiosity, quick wits, and cheerful acceptance of danger—the very type of the disinterested explorer. He is also equipped to formulate Social-Darwinist hypotheses, and he arrives by trial and error at unanticipated but presumably correct conclusions. At the end, however, readers are casually told that the Traveller "thought but cheerlessly of the Advancement of Mankind" (ch. 15) even before he set out. The information is held back so that nothing shall interfere with his confidence in the value of exploration—the "risks a man has got to take" (ch. 6). Similarly, in *The Island of Dr. Moreau*, Prendick is a rational, eyewitness observer who only emerges as insanely misanthropic in the final pages. By such concealments the displacement of the whole narrative is avoided.

The reversal in each of these stories shatters the confidence with which Wells's observers set out, but there is no substitute for rationalism as a method. In *The War of the Worlds*, readers are told at the outset that the humanist conception of the universe has been destroyed, but the narrator addresses them in the established terms of rational discourse, and then reassures them of his own essential normality: "For my own part, I was much occupied in learning to ride the bicycle, and busy upon a series of papers discussing the probable developments of moral ideas as civilization progressed" (Book I, ch. 1). In each case, what is portrayed is a biological and anthropological endeavor; the book is an exposition both of an alien society and of the attempts of a representative bourgeois observer to know it empirically (hence the importance of the observation of the Martians from the ruined house, a literal "camera obscura"). The narrator in *The War of the Worlds* is drawn to the Martians, although he does not reject human norms as completely as Gulliver does. Both Swift and Wells recognized the inherent destructiveness of rationalism. Wells's attempt to play down the perception appears more deliberate than Swift's insofar as he was obliged to make a more conscious choice of "eighteenth-century" narrative forms.

In later romances Wells dropped the rational observer in

favor of characters who directly participate in the alien world. Since his imaginative interests were more genuinely anthropological than political, however, the result is the cruder and less exacting form of adventure narrative typified by *When the Sleeper Wakes*. There are some interesting half-experiments that reveal something different: *The First Men in the Moon*, with its split between the earthbound Bedford and the disinterested-rationalist Cavor; and *In the Days of the Comet*, a regrettably slipshod attempt to view the present from the perspective of the future. But *Tono-Bungay* represents Wells's only major advance in technique, with its use of the autobiographical form to combine social analysis and the pragmatic impressions of an uncertain and somewhat manic narrator. Not only is science eventually symbolized as a destroyer, but the whole novel embodies a displacement of sociological discourse to express the drama of radical individualism in the hero's consciousness. This marks an interesting development in the social novel, but in science fiction the Wellsian model remained that of the adaptation of Enlightenment-narrative forms based on the rational, objective observer.

The effect of moving from Wells's romances to *We*[9] might be compared to the experience of Zamyatin's narrator as he passes beyond the Green Wall of the city:

> It was then I opened my eyes—and was face to face, in reality, with that very sort of thing which up to then none of those living had seen other than diminished a thousand times, weakened, smudged over by the turbid glass of the Wall.

> The sun—it was no longer that sun of ours, proportionately distributed over the mirrorlike surface of the pavements; this sun consisted of some sort of living splinters of incessantly bobbing spots which blinded one's eyes, made one's head go round. And the trees—like candles thrusting into the very sky, like spiders squatting flat against the earth on their gnarled paws, like mute fountains jetting green. . . .
>
> (192–93)

This is a new reality, neither seen through a glass (a recurrent mode of vision in Wells), nor in the even light of scientific reason. Experience is splintered and blinding; the head whirls and the self loses its center of gravity. The writer is at the mercy of disparate impressions, and merely records his conflicting impulses as they mount to a nauseous intensity. Although he tries to control his unruly consciousness by a "rational" method, it is the method of an alien society.

We begins with a directive inviting all numbers to compose poems or treatises celebrating the One State, to be carried on the first flight of the space-rocket Integral as an aid to subjugating the people of other planets. To the narrator, D–503 (the builder of the Integral), this is a divine command, but to the reader the forcing of a "mathematically infallible happiness" upon unknown peoples is brutally imperialistic. The value of space travel itself is thus called into question (a very un-Wellsian touch) by means of the ironical device of a narrator who worships mathematical exactitude and straight lines. Yet as soon as the alienness of D–503's values has been established, it becomes clear that he himself is internally torn. He undertakes literary composition as a duty to the state, but chooses to write, not a poem in accordance with the approved, public literary genres (the poetry of the One State is about as rich and varied as that of the Houyhnhnms), but a simple record of his day-to-day impressions. The conflict of group and private consciousness signified by the novel's title is thus outlined by his initial choice of mode of writing; he thinks to express what "We" experience, but his record becomes irretrievably subjective. Already as he begins the diary his "cheeks are flaming" and he feels as though a child stirred inside him—dangerous signs, for the irrationality of sensation and of the philoprogenitive emotion are motifs of rebellion throughout the novel (0–90's longing for a child parallels D–503's creative instinct, and during the brief revolutionary outbreak in the One State, couples are seen shamelessly copulating in the public view). As he writes his diary, D–503 becomes increasingly conscious of the lack of continuity in his thoughts and the disruption of logical processes; finally he goes to the doctors, who diagnose the diseased growth known as a *soul*. A healthy consciousness, he is told, is simply a reflecting medium like a mirror; but he has developed an absorptive capacity, an inner dimension that retains and memorizes. The disease is epidemic in the State, and universal fantasiectomy is ordained to wipe it out. Superficially D–503 develops a soul as a result of falling in love with the fascinating I–330; but really it is constituted by the act of writing. It is his identity as a man who wishes to write down his sensations that throws D–503 into mental crisis.

Fittingly, it is the diary that betrays him, together with his rebellious accomplices, to the secret police. It may seem that the one error of the "mathematically perfect State" was to encourage its members to engage in literary expression at all—as in Ray Bradbury's *Fahrenheit 451*, things might run more smoothly if all the books were burned. But can one be sure of this? At the end, the rebellion is crushed, D–503 undergoes fantasiectomy and watches the torturing of I–330, sensible only of the aesthetic beauty of the spectacle. Notwithstanding the readers' reactions, this appears to be an exemplary tale from the viewpoint of the One State— and might even have been what its propaganda chiefs wanted. Certainly an undue concentration on the political message of *We* should not obscure Zamyatin's attempts to suggest the ultimate inexpressibility of his future society; its experience and its culture are structured in ways that can never be fully understood. The narrator tries to explain things for the benefit of alien peoples stuck at a twentieth-century level of development, but he also feels himself to be in the position of a geometrical square charged to explain its existence to human beings: "The last thing that would enter this quadrangle's mind, you understand, would be to say that all its four angles are equal" (46). A similar argument may apply to the status of the book itself.

The classic, satirical utopia establishes a social picture through incongruous comparisons, and *We* does this, too; the work of ancient literature most treasured in its future society is the book of railway timetables. But Zamyatin suggests a more disturbing and bewildering alienness than this method can convey. A new experience is rendered in an unprecedented language, or perhaps languages, for D–503's diary is a theater of linguistic conflict. His orthodox selfhood is expressed through a logical discourse, syllogistic in form, and drawing repeatedly on mathematics, geometry, and engineering for its stock of metaphors. (There are obvious resemblances to the aggressively "technocratic" style of Zamyatin's essays.) This is the language in which citizens of the One State are trained to reconstruct the infallible reasoning behind the state's bald directives. Even women's faces can be analyzed in terms of geometrical figures—circles and triangles—providing some striking instances of literary Cubism. However, this orthodox, mathematic language is unable to subdue the whole of D–503's experience. He may see his brain as a machine, but it is an overheated machine that vaporizes the coolant of logic. He becomes uncomfortably self-conscious, and his mental operations are no longer smooth and automatic. His analysis of I–330's face reveals two acute triangles forming an "X"—the algebraic symbol of the unknown. More unknowns supervene, and his memory is forced back to the symbol of unreason in the very foundations of the mathematics that he was taught at school—$\sqrt{-1}$, the square root of minus one. So he confronts the existence of a whole "universe of irrationals," of $\sqrt{-1}$ solids lurking in the non-Euclidean space of subjective experience. To his diseased mind, mathematics, the basis of society, seems divided against itself.

The "X" or unknown element in *We* always arises within personal experience. It is identified first in the meeting with I–330, and one senses it in the quality of dialogue— probing, spontaneous, and electric—that clashes sharply with the formulaic responses of the narrator's orthodox discourse. He has been taught to reduce everything to a mathematicized environment, but as soon as he describes impressions and people, his account takes on an acutely nervous vitality. As the diary proceeds, the hegemony of orthodox discourse diminishes, and the "splintered" style of *We* is established—the shifting, expressionistic style that is the basic experience of Zamyatin's reader. The narrator's mood and attention are constantly changing, sensations are momentary, and thoughts, whether "correct" or heretical, are only provisional; utterances are characteristically left unfinished. D–503 is encouraged to bear with the confusion of his kaleidoscopic language by the vaguely pragmatic expectation that self-expression must somehow lead to eventual order and clarification. Yet in fact it leads to the consciousness of a schizoid identity from which only fantasiectomy can rescue him.

We does describe a revolution in the streets, but the narrator's involvement is only accidental, for the real battleground is within his head.[10] The languages involved are futuristic languages and (with some lapses) the fixed points to which D–503 can refer are different from the reader's; thus once his experience has transcended the limitations for which he has been pogrammed, he is unable to make elementary distinctions between dream and reality. It is Zamyatin's resolute attempt to enter the unknowns of consciousness as well as of politics and technology that makes *We* one of the most remarkable works of science fiction in existence.

Not the artistic techniques of *We*, but its topography and social arrangements (down to the Sexual Days and pink tickets) have passed into the subsequent tradition. Verbal innovation and weird experience are part of the stock-in-trade of science-fiction writers, but where the basic assumptions of story and characterization remain unchanged, this is no more than a kind of mannerism. Ivan Yefremov, author of the popular Soviet science-fiction novel *Andromeda,* outlines a typical attitude:

> The mass of scientific information and intricate terminology used in the story are the result of a deliberate plan. It seemed to me that this is the only way to show our distant descendants and give the necessary local (or temporal) colour to their dialogue since they are living in a period when science will have penetrated into all human conceptions and into language itself.[11]

What is conferred is "local colour," and this is done by the insertion of scientific jargon into the emotive narrative of sentimental fiction. My impression is that, despite the variety of available styles and the consciously manneristic way in which a more sophisticated writer like Bradbury uses them, science fiction has preserved a rigid combination of futuristic environment and conventional form. No doubt there are exceptions. Golding's *The Inheritors* involves a highly imaginative projection of "alien consciousness" as I have defined it here. An interesting and perhaps more representative case, however, is that of the one English novel that transmits Zamyatin's direct influence—Orwell's *Nineteen Eighty-Four.*

"Newspeak," perhaps Orwell's most original conception, is based upon developments in the science of propaganda that Zamyatin hardly foresaw. Its penetrating critique of the political uses of language extends what Orwell had done in some of his essays. Yet "Newspeak" is only the public rhetoric of Oceania, it is relegated to an Appendix in the novel, and it is not scheduled for final adoption until 2050. Winston Smith still speaks standard English, and the famous opening sentence in which the clocks are stiking

thirteen is an effective example of "local colour." Winston,
like D–503, is a diarist, but the narrative does not consist of
his diary—which is an economical record of things understood and concluded, and not a day-by-day journal of
uncertainties and confusions. Winston's diary is an outlet for
his rebellious thoughts, but D–503's rebellion is inseparable
from his writing. *Nineteen Eighty-Four* is thus partly a
domestication of the rootless, modernist technique of *We*. It
is a novel grounded in the tradition of English realism and
in the wartime London landscape, with an appended vision
of linguistic change.

3

Zamyatin does not seem to have doubted that science
fiction could be a major literary genre; Wells wrote his
masterpieces in the conviction that it could not. In this essay
I have tried to suggest some considerations that might
apply to science fiction as a mode of imagination, and to
outline two models of major expression within it. The first is
the Wellsian model—the humanist-narrative fable in which
a man whom one accepts as representative of human
culture confronts the biologically and anthropologically
unknown. The second, realized by Zamyatin, aims to create
the experience and language of an alien culture directly.
Each model thus extends social criticism into a more
tentative probing of rational and epistemological assumptions. The books I have considered are essentially future
fantasies in the sense that the century in which they are set
does not greatly matter. But there is a third kind of novel,
concerned with the very near future, of which *Nineteen
Eighty-Four* and Kurt Vonnegut, Jr.'s *Player Piano* are
examples. These novels are science fiction in the sense of
including new gadgetry as well as new social institutions,
and they may be of great political importance. What I

would say of them is that their "feel" now seems very close to that of the contemporary, realistic novel. Perhaps reality has indeed become fantastic as Zamyatin predicted, and critics may apply the label of *realism* to novels of the "recent future" as well as of the recent past.

Wells's own career illustrates the distinction between science fiction and realism that I am proposing, for *When the Sleeper Wakes* (1899) was the first of a series of novels in which he abandoned the science-fiction model he had created and became, instead, a short-term prophet and futurologist. The name that he gave to these realistic-forecast novels (including *The War in the Air* and *The World Set Free*) was "fantasies of possibility." From the context— the 1921 Preface to *The Sleeper Awakes*—it is clear that he was using the word *fantasy* in a very narrow sense. "At the time when I wrote *The Sleeper*," he recalled, "I had a considerable belief in its possiblity."[12] The forecast novel, in fact, is characteristically based on a prediction that the author himself will come to revise. In 1898 Wells expected mankind to desert the countryside for hypertrophied cities; but by 1900 he foresaw population dispersal and creeping suburbanization. At the same time, he began to hope for a regime of benevolent technocrats rather than class polarization. Similarly, Orwell's forebodings must inevitably have changed as his *annus fatalis* approached, while the nightmare of *Nineteen Eighty-Four* shares certain key features with his prewar realistic novels and even with his memoir of his schooldays. Insofar as novels of this kind achieve more than a vigorous adventure narrative or a lucky prophetic guess (as with Wells's forecast of the atom bomb), their crucial quality would seem to be that of continuity—the author's grasp of the real configuration of the present. Many of the best forecast novels have been written by "mainstream" novelists: the Realistic novelist can now naturally take in the near future, toward which his hero would merely have been pointed in the novels of sixty years ago. Doris Lessing's *Children of Violence* sequence, for example, is a Bildungsroman with an epilogue looking forward to A.D. 2000—a modern counterpart to those Victorian novels that end with a detailed résumé of their characters' happily-ever-afters.

Wells and Zamyatin provide models of science fiction because their best works can not be connected to ordinary realism in this way. They look far beyond the author's own probable lifespan and the catastrophe that he might reasonably "expect." Their social criticism is cast in a speculative and imaginative frame, and at its center is a disturbing question that might be formulated in its most general terms like this: what is truly alien to man, and what is not?

NOTES

1. This essay is included in *A Soviet Heretic: Essays by Yevgeny Zamyatin*, transl. and ed. Mirra Ginsburg (Chicago and London, 1970); the sentence quoted is from p. 109.

2. Alex M. Shane, *The Life and Works of Evgeni j Zamjatin* (Berkeley and Los Angeles, 1968), p. 140.

3. George Orwell, review of *We* (London *Tribune*, 4 January 1946), in *Collected Essays, Journalism, and Letters of George Orwell*, ed. Sonia Orwell and Ian Angus, 4 vols. (London, 1968), 4: 72–75.

4. *Hillegas, pp. 99–109.

5. Though *A Soviet Heretic* (*see* note 1) includes a translation of the revised version of Zamyatin's *Herbert Wells*, published as an Introduction to Wells's *Collected Works* in Russian (Leningrad, 1924), I have here followed Lesley Milne's translation of the first edition (published in pamphlet form by Epoka, Petrograd, in 1922). This translation is included in *Parrinder, ed., pp. 258–74; and the quote is from p. 273.

6. "On Synthetism," is included in *A Soviet Heretic* (*see* note 1).

7. J. Hillis Miller, *The Form of Victorian Fiction* (Notre Dame, Indiana, and London, 1968), p. 62.

8. The reading of Wells's romances presented here is a development of that outlined in *Parrinder, p. 16.

9. There are several English translations of *We*. The text followed here is that of the translation by Bernard Guilbert Guerney (London, 1970),

except that Zamyatin's heroine is referred to as "I–330," as Zamyatin intended, and not as Guerney's "E–330"; it is cited by page number in parenthesis.

10. Tony Tanner points out in *City of Words* (New York, 1971), p. 71, that the heroes of many recent American novels are trying to get away from all political commitment, whether pro or anti. Similarly, D–503 is unwillingly led into conspiracy, and tricked by both sides.

11. Quoted on the dust jacket to Ivan Yefremov's novel *Andromeda* (Moscow, 1959).

12. Preface, dated "Easton Glebe, Dunmow, 1921," to *The Sleeper Awakes and Men Like Gods* (London, n.d.).

The Shadow of *Men Like Gods*: Orwell's *Coming Up for Air* as Parody

by **HOWARD FINK**

It was as if I was looking at two worlds at once, a kind of thin bubble of the thing that used to be, with the thing that actually existed shining through it.

Coming Up for Air

It is difficult to know what the lesser prophets of the twentieth century would have done without H. G. Wells. True, a number of antiutopians have a satanic or apostate relationship to Wells's sacred books, but their debt is no less for that—he taught them what to fear, and he also showed them what to desire. Perhaps the clearest evidence for this ambiguous influence is George Orwell's pacifist novel *Coming Up for Air*.[1] Discussing this book in a letter to Julian Symons, Orwell admits, "Of course the book was bound to suggest Wells watered down. I have a great admiration for

144

Wells, i.e. as a writer, and he was a very early influence on me."[2] Orwell's hero's description of his childhood in turn-of-the-century England is in many respects a re-creation of the benign model extracted by Orwell from Wells's earlier novels; as Orwell notes in a review, Wells's "greatest gift . . . was his power to convey the atmosphere of the golden years between 1890 and 1914."[3] George Bowling, the hero-narrator of *Coming Up for Air,* is about ten years older than Orwell, and Bowling's memories date from the decade before Orwell himself was born. On the other hand, a major purpose of *Coming Up for Air* is an attack on Wells—at least, on what Orwell considered dangerous in Wells's later optimistic works. The main narrative and didactic movement of this novel is Bowling's vain search for the utopia of the past. The failure of that search is aimed by Orwell as a rebuttal of what he considers to be the Wellsian vision. Orwell's major technique in communicating his argument with Wells is the parody, especially in the last section, of one of Wells's utopian fictions, *Men Like Gods.*[4]

It is not difficult to see why Orwell chose Wells and his fictions as materials for parody. In a number of places Orwell reveals the strong influence of Wells's writings on the shape of his own ideals; and, even more important, he argues that this influence extended to English society as a whole. In the 1941 essay, "Wells, Hitler, and the World State" (*Collected* 2:139–45), Orwell says: "Thinking people who were born about the beginning of this century are in some sense Wells's own creation. . . . I doubt whether anyone who was writing books between 1900 and 1920, at any rate in the English language, influenced the young so much. The minds of all of us, and therefore the physical world, would be perceptibly different if Wells had never existed." The way in which Orwell defines this influence reveals that he sees Wells's work simply as a guide to technological utopianism (though to be fair, Orwell is not alone in this simplification); and the argument between them grows from the fact that Orwell—like so many Europeans under the cloud of fascist technological prowess in the late 1930s—had come to fear what he had learned from Wells to desire, without quite giving Wells credit for the prophet's own dark side. Wells has become, for this apostate, "the arch-priest of progress." In the London *Tribune* review already mentioned, Orwell is specific: "If, up to the year 1930, any mere novelist could look about him and say, 'This is my work. I did this,' that writer was H. G. Wells. The whole concept of 'progress' (meaning aeroplanes and steel-and-concrete buildings), the vision of a Utopia in which machines do all the work for you, which is definitely a part of the modern mind, owes an immense amount to him."

Orwell judges Wells to be the creator of the modern ethos, and therefore the appropriate scapegoat for an attack on the evils of technological civilization. In *The Road to Wigan Pier*,[5] describing a book by John Beevers extolling modern mechanized society, Orwell comments:

> You can make a fairly good guess at what he would like civilization to be; a sort of Lyons Corner House lasting *in saecula saeculorum* and getting bigger and bigger all the time. And in any book by anyone who feels at home in the machine-world— in any book by H. G. Wells, for instance—you will find passages of the same kind. How often have we not heard it, that glutinously uplifting stuff about 'the machines, our new race of slaves, which will set humanity free'. . . . Barring wars and unforseen disasters, the future is envisaged as an ever more rapid march of mechanical progress . . . until finally you land up in the by now familiar Wellsian Utopia. . . . (*Wigan*:192)

It is clear in the text of *Coming Up for Air* that Orwell is working with his dual attitude toward Wells. The hero Bowling himself has (like the author) come under Wells's influence; the first book Bowling mentions reading at Twelve Mile Dump is an early Wells novel:

"Now and again it so happens that you strike a book which is exactly at the mental level you've reached at the moment; so much so that it seems to have been written especially for you. One of them was H. G. Wells's *The History of Mr. Polly*. . . . I wonder if you can imagine the effect it had on me, to be brought up as I'd been brought up, the son of a shopkeeper in a country town, and then to come across a book like that? . . . Wells was the author who made the biggest impression on me (123, 124).

The other pole of Orwell's ambiguous attitude to Wells, his suspicion of what he reads as the utopian and mechanical quality of Wells's vision, is also obviously present in the novel. Part one of *Coming Up for Air*, dealing with Bowling's revulsion against the modern streamlined world, is an echo of Orwell's attacks on the Wellsian ideal, in its "Lyons Corner House" costume. Bowling's specific experiences— for example, the comedy with the fish-filled frankfurter— are realistic fictionalizations of Orwell's argument in *The Road to Wigan Pier* that the Wells vision has destroyed the rich human texture of life:

You have only to look about you at this moment to realize with what sinister speed the machine is getting us into its power. To begin with, there is the frightful debauchery of taste that has already been affected by a century of mechanisation. . . . As a single instance, take taste in its narrowest sense—the taste for decent food. . . . And what applies to food applies also to furniture, house, clothes, books, amusements, and everything else that makes up our environment. *(Wigan* 202–3)

The main object of Orwell's polemic in the first section of *Coming Up for Air* is the "familiar" Wellsian vision of a machine civilization; the repeated and ominous image of the bombing plane has an important function in relating this theme to the novel as a whole. In his "Wells, Hitler" essay, Orwell uses this same image to make his point:

Unfortunately the equation of science with common sense does not really hold good. The aeroplane, which was looked forward to as a civilizing influence, but in practice has hardly been used except for dropping bombs, is a symbol of that face. . . . Much of what Wells has imagined and worked for is physically there in Nazi Germany. The order, the planning, the state encouragement of science, the steel, the concrete, the aeroplanes are all there, but all in the service of ideas appropriate to the Stone Age. Science is fighting on the side of superstition.[6]

Orwell reveals the symbolic meaning of the bombing-plane image here, a meaning that he applied in *Coming Up for Air:* the aeroplane is the ultimate product of the Wellsian vision; ironically, its effect is the opposite of utopian—the instrument of apocalyptic destruction of society, of which the actual bombing near the end of the novel is a prophetic prefiguration. Orwell's attempt to communicate this criticism in the novel includes Bowling's ironic description of the Left Book Club, which "represents Progress," without ever accomplishing it; in *Wigan* Orwell calls Wells the "arch-priest of progress who cannot write with any conviction *against* progress" *(Wigan* 201).

It can be seen how the general tenor of *Coming Up for Air* is a reaction against the utopian ideas of H. G. Wells. Orwell makes this more specific by including in *Coming Up for Air* a detailed parody of an archetypal Wellsian utopia, *Men Like Gods*. Orwell had created parodies in his earlier works (in *Burmese Days* and *A Clergyman's Daughter*, for example); but in *Coming Up for Air* for the first time he deserts the parody of traditional biblical or classical myth for the parody of a contemporary work. Orwell hints in several places at his model for this new departure, Aldous Huxley's *Brave New World*.[7] In "The Rediscovery of Europe," (1942) *(Collected,* 2: 205), Orwell contrasts Huxley's antiutopia with Wells's utopias, especially *Men Like Gods*. Again, in the passage quoted above from *The Road to Wigan Pier* about the growth of machine civilization, Orwell concludes that "finally you land up in the by now familiar Wellsian utopia, aptly caricatured by Huxley in *Brave New World*, the paradise of little fat men. Of course in their daydreams of the future the little fat men are neither fat nor little; they are Men Like Gods" *(Wigan*: 192). And later in the same section Orwell adds:

> The thought he dare not face is that the machine itself may be the enemy. So in his more characteristic utopias *(The Dream; Men Like Gods)*, he returns to optimism and to a vision of humanity "liberated" by the machine. . . . *Brave New World* belongs to a later time and to a generation that has seen through the swindle of "progress". . . . Allowing for the exaggerations of caricature, it probably expresses what a majority of thinking people feel about machine-civilization *(Wigan*: 201–202).

Frequently in both passages Orwell describes *Brave New World* as a "caricature" of the typical Wells utopia. In another London *Tribune* review (12 July 1940; *Collected 2:* 30–31), Orwell more specifically defines the technique of *Brave New World* as: "a sort of post-war parody of the Wellsian Utopia [in which] the hedonistic principle is pushed to its utmost, the whole world has turned into a Riviera Hotel." Huxley's *Brave New World* provides the precedent and the model for a *parody* on Wells. There are hilarious, if meaningful, parodies in Huxley's novel, ironic exaggerations pointing up the flaws in a pure Wellsian utopianism; for example, the idyllic bath at the disposal of Wells's hero in utopia, complete with buttons for soapy water, pine scent, and chlorine, *(Men*, bk I, ch. 8) is parodied by the crowded dormitory baths in *Brave New World*, with taps for talcum and no less than "eight different scents and eau-de Cologne." *(B.N.W.*:41). But the major Wellsian symbol that Huxley parodies is more somber— the "eugenic beginnings" that Wells describes in his utopia: "an increasing certainty in the science of heredity; and as Mr. Barnstaple contrasted the firm clear beauty of face and limb that every Utopian displayed with the carelessly assembled features and bodily disproportions of his earthly associates, he realized that . . . these Utopians were passing beyond man towards a nobler humanity" (*Men*, bk. I, ch. 6). In Huxley's parody, this epitome of Wellsian utopianism is monstrously transformed into the products of the Central London Hatchery and Conditioning Centre, the Bokanovsky groups of eighty bottle-born mirror-twins who inhabit his brave new world, bred, mind and body, only for their function in the state.

Orwell's numerous references to *Men Like Gods* in all his above critiques of Wells indicate that he considers this book as Wells's most "characteristic" utopia. Not surprising, then, given Orwell's general attack on Wells in *Coming Up for Air*, and the example of Huxley's parody, that Orwell should choose *Men Like Gods* as the source for a structural parody of his own in this novel. To come to specifics, the situation of George Bowling and his trip to Binfield reflect in parody fashion the life and the utopian journey of Mr. Barnstaple, the protagonist of *Men Like Gods*. The first impetus for the voyages of both heroes is a feeling of exhaustion and despair resulting from a negative vision of the future. In the first chapter Wells says of Barnstaple: "The very streets were becoming a torment to him, he wanted never to see a newspaper or a newspaper placard again. He was obsessed by apprehensions of some sort of financial and economic smash that would make the great war seem a mere incidental catastrophe" (*Men*, bk. I, ch. 1). This apocalyptic vision is confirmed in the same passage by Mr. Barnstaple's employer: "Mr. Peeve held very strongly that a belief in progress was at least six years out of date, and that the brightest hope that remained to liberalism was for a good Day of Judgment soon" (*Men*, Bk. I, ch. 1). Wells set up this despair as a straw man; through Mr. Barnstaple's trip to the utopian future, he dispels this negative vision in *Men Like Gods*. In *Coming Up for Air*, however, this progress is reversed, and, at the end, the despairing, apocalyptic vision is triumphant.

The echo of this apocalyptic theme and imagery is

obvious in Orwell's novel. George Bowling, an insurance salesman, fat and forty-five, intermittently poses as the Eastern prophet of an apocalyptic future: "My mind went back to the thoughts of war I'd been having earlier that morning, when the bomber flew over the train. I felt in a kind of prophetic mood, the mood in which you foresee the end of the world, and get a certain kick out of it"; and he explains, "I felt as if I was the only person awake in a city of sleepwalkers because of . . . this prophetic feeling that keeps coming over me nowadays, the feeling that war's just round the corner. . . . I looked at the dumb-bell faces streaming past. Like turkeys in November, I thought. Not a notion of what's coming to them. It was as if I'd got x-ray eyes and could see the skeletons walking" (29). Bowling is a prophet of doom, especially the prophet of *Revelations,* of apocalypse, complete (like the early Barnstaple) with the traditional vision of the Last Judgment when the skeletons rise, but also with more modern images of Doomsday—that of Waste-Land London, and that of the bombing plane, mentioned above. The apocalyptic imagery of bombing and destruction runs through the whole book, becoming an actuality near the end; Orwell appropriately describes the bombing as "a noise like the Day of Judgment, and then a noise like a ton of coal falling on to a sheet of tin" (233). The purpose of this actual bombing is to reinforce the reality of the apocalyptic vision, and to symbolically destroy once, and for all Bowling's illusory vision of the ideal past. By the time Bowling goes home, his vision of the past is exhausted, and he again becomes the prophet of doom: "I felt in much the same mood as I'd felt that day I got my new false teeth. It was as though the power of prophesy had been given me. It seemed to me that I could see the whole of England, and all the people in it, and all the things that'll happen to all of them" (228).

There are other obvious parodistic parallels and reversals of Wells's book in *Coming Up for Air*. Each book opens with the hero's desire for an escape from the present. Both heroes plan a solitary trip in secrecy, without the disturbance of their famiilies. They both resort to furtive scheming to carry out their plans, including melodramatic arrangements for letters to be sent to their wives to put them off the track, with instructions not to try to contact their husbands. An old car figures largely in the escape of both heroes, and their adventures both begin in central London, in the bright summer sunshine of utopian hope. They both avoid the usual route west, the Uxbridge road . . . and at this point the books diverge. It is a fortuitous accident that puts Mr. Barnstaple on the road to Utopia:

> He resumed his seat in his car with such a sense of freedom as he had never felt since his first holidays from his first school. He made for the Great North Road, but at the traffic jam at Hyde Park Corner he allowed the policeman to turn him down towards Knightsbridge, and afterwards at the corner where the Bath Road forks away from the Oxford Road an obstructive van put him into the former. But it did not matter very much. Any way led to Elsewhere. (*Men,* bk. I, ch. 1).

Orwell in *Coming Up for Air*, having left clear evidence of the parody, reacts against the vagueness of Wells's road to utopia; George Bowling consciously chooses his direction. When *he* gets to the "sign-post where the road forks right for Pudley and left for Oxford," he resolutely turns "westward, onto the Oxford Road" (476). This symbolic divergence marks the place where the optimistic utopia of Wells separates from Orwell's antiutopia. Whereas Wells's hero finds himself several hundreds of years in the utopian future, George Bowling, having rejected the Wellsian steel-and-glass future, is attempting to flee to the paradise of his childhood past: "There's a chap who says he won't be streamlined! He's going back to Lower Binfield!" (177).

The dislocation and shock of Barnstaple's translation to the utopia of another dimension is echoed by Bowling's first

shock at the experience of finding himself in sight of
Binfield: "It was as if I was looking at two worlds at once, a
kind of thin bubble of the thing that used to be, with the
thing that actually existed shining through it" (181–82).
This is a typical Wellsian science-fiction image, as Orwell
reveals: "Did you ever read a story of H. G. Wells's about a
chap who was in two places at once—that's to say, he was
really in his own home, but he had a kind of hallucination
that he was at the bottom of the sea? . . . Well, it was just like
that" (201). The ironic-parodistic-quality of Orwell's novel
is again revealed in his echo of Wells's description of the
change in the road at the moment of transition to utopia;
Wells writes: "The road itself, instead of being packed
together pebbles and dirt smeared with tar . . . was apparently made of glass" (*Men,* bk I, ch. 2). Orwell ironically
reverses this in *Coming Up for Air:* "The road was tarmac,
whereas in the old days it used to be macadam" (178).
Bowling's shock when he first arrives at Lower Binfield is
real enough; for, whereas he believes he is escaping to the
past, he discovers that he has been translated to the Binfield
of the future—the future, of course, relative to his childhood memories of the town. In this parody-utopia, Bowling
is continuously making *negative* comparisons between the
raw, ugly, commercial, overgrown "future" Binfield he
discovers, and the ideal Binfield of his childhood past. The
whole situation is a parodic reversal of the awe-inspiring
utopia that Wells's hero compares so favorably to his own
times. Orwell is doing his best to explode Wells's myth of
inevitable progress by this parody: the Binfield of the past is
far more comely and human than modern Binfield. Contrary to Wells's own illusory utopian ideal of progress, the
England before 1914 (which Wells himself had celebrated!)
is preferable to the present or the future; and this is
Orwell's main point.

    The utopian quests in these two novels conclude, once
more, in a contrasting manner. As Wells intended all along,

Mr. Barnstaple leaves utopia cured of his fears of apocalypse. His Day of Judgment has come and gone, and left him—in the optimistic tradition of such things— refreshed and fiilled with an insight into the ideal future. George Bowling, on the other hand, leaves Binfield in the utmost despair of the present and the future, hurried on his way by the symbolic bombing that only confirms the dark apocalyptic vision that he has come there to escape. When Wells's refurbished hero returns home, his admiring wife, incurious about his adventure, welcomes him with the discovery that he has literally (and symbolically) grown two or three inches. He soon sets his life and that of his family in proper order, and the book ends with the happy couple looking forward to the Wellsian future. The end of *Coming Up for Air* is a hilarious, and ominous, parodistic reversal of this optimistic ending. His quest a failure, George Bowling returns home exhausted and depressed, to discover that his nagging wife has exploded the carefully constructed alibi for his absence. His only prophecy for the future consists, ironically, of several weeks of nagging quarrels: "The old life in Lower Binfield, the war and after-war, Hitler, Stalin, bombs, machineguns, food-queues, rubber truncheons—it was fading out, all fading out. Nothing remained except a vulgar low-down row in a smell of old mackintoshes" (236). This, says Orwell, is the *real* world; the way in which this ending parodies that of *Men Like Gods* shows Orwell's view of the great gap between the rosy vision of the Wellsian future and the real ethos of England between the World Wars. Under the level of mundane, comic realism in *Coming Up for Air* there is, then, a controlling level of parody— generally of Wellsian social and political idealism, and specifically a parody of the details and the vision of Wells's most characteristic utopia, *Men Like Gods.*

The parody of utopia is antiutopia. The usual expecta- tions about an antiutopia are of a negative, opposing extrapolation into another time or place—that is, of a negative world that is as much a fantasy as the positive utopia it contradicts. In the case of *Men Like Gods,* such a parody-utopia is *Brave New World,* and indeed Orwell's own *Nineteen Eighty-Four* (which in many ways is a parody of Wells's *The Shape of Things to Come*). Yet it can be seen in Orwell's *Coming Up for Air* (his last fiction before the utopian satires, *Animal Farm* and *Nineteen Eighty-Four*) how antiutopianism can use—for the vehicle of its attack on a specific utopia—a realistic rather than a fantasy construction. This should be interesting evidence for the theory that satiric fiction, including science fiction—no matter how grotesque its fantasy—has for its didactic purpose a reflection back onto the *real* world inhabited by the author. As Northrop Frye would say, Orwell's satire in *Coming Up for Air* undercuts Wells's fantasy-romance or science fiction by "the application of romantic mythical forms to a more realistic context"[8]—not a utopia 3,000 years in the future, but London and suburbs, circa 1938.

Despite the undercutting effect of Orwell's parody, an ambiguity remains in the real relations between these two fictions: as dark as the conclusion of *Coming Up for Air* may be, one of its strongest effects on the reader, and indeed a consciously achieved effect, is to revive the reader's *vision* of utopia. Orwell replaces the modern scientific vision with another ideal, admittedly in and of the past, but lovingly described, and, make no mistake, meant to stand as a model for the future. This is confirmed in *Nineteen Eighty-Four,* in which the simple, hedonistic good life of the past reachieved by Winston and Julia in the country and the upstairs room of Charrington's antique shop is sublimated into the postapocalyptic vision of the future, based on the idealized proles, which dominates the final "washerwoman" scene of part two, and which is confirmed in the "Newspeak" Appendix. The ultimate ambiguity in Orwell's attitude toward Wells is revealed in the source of this vision of Orwell's: as has been seen above, it is the vision of benign

English life that Orwell himself acknowledges to have discovered in the pages of Wells's own early novels. And upon investigation, the quality of life in Wells's utopias is often itself a pure version of this very same turn-of-the-century scene and atmosphere in his early novels. Though Orwell in *Coming Up for Air* and *Nineteen Eighty-Four* rejects Wells's identification of science as the instrument of achieving utopia, he does reinforce Wells's vision of the hedonistic *achieved* utopia in its natural and symbolic terms. In all justice to Wells, he not only taught Orwell the didactic value of projecting an ideal fantasy over the ugliness of the real world, but he even provided Orwell with the materials for such a vision; and even perhaps (in the same washerwoman scene of *Nineteen Eighty-Four*) with the image expressing most powerfully the faith in its realization: the sunset sky overarching the pained and divided world. Winston Smith's "mystical reverence" for the washerwoman is

> somehow mixed up with the aspect of the pale, cloudless sky, stretching away behind the chimney pots into interminable distance. It was curious to think that . . . the people under the sky were very much the same—everywhere, all over the world, hundreds of thousands of millions of people like this . . . people who had never learned to think but who were storing up in their hearts and bellies and muscles the power that would one day overturn the world. . . . The future belonged to the proles.[9]

I suggest that Orwell in the above paragraph is echoing the very imagery of the dream of hope for a human utopia that Wells offered, beyond the scientific revolution, in *Men Like Gods:*

> And yet even in the hate and turmoil and distresses of the Days of Confusion there must have been earnest enough of the ~~exquisite and glorious possibilities of life. Over the foulest~~ slums the sunset called to the imaginations of men, and from the mountain ridges, across great valleys, from cliffs and

hillsides and by the uncertain and terrible splendours of the
sea, men must have had glimpses of the conceivable and
attainable magnificence of being. Every flower petal, every
sunlit leaf. . . . (*Men*, bk. I, ch. 7).

It would be unfair to Orwell to ignore his attack on
Wellsian "Progress" (no matter how limited Orwell's view of
this may be), or to blur the distinction he makes both in
Wigan and in *Coming Up for Air* between the hedonism of the
past and the "little fat men's" hedonism of the future. In
Nineteen Eighty-Four, written in the economically deprived
wartime and immediate postwar period, the hedonistic
vision of the future temporarily failed—but in *Coming Up
for Air* the issue had been a live one for Orwell. Nevertheless, Orwell's own ambiguous identification of these two
Wellsian ideals is clear; and this pushes the didactic
emphasis in *Coming Up for Air* on to Orwell's ironic
skepticism about the *means* Wells had envisioned to achieve
utopia. It is perhaps for this reason that the most detailed
parody in *Coming Up for Air* echoes (as has been argued) Mr.
Barnstaple's *journey* to utopia in *Men Like Gods*, rather
than—what is the main object of the parody in *Brave New
World*—the Wellsian utopian scene.

NOTES

1. George Orwell, *Coming Up for Air* (1939) (London, 1948). Quoted
further by page number in the text.
2. George Orwell, *Collected Essays, Journalism, and Letters,* ed. Sonia
Orwell and Ian Angus, 4 vols. (London, 1968), 4: 422. Quoted further
in the text as *Collected,* by volume: page number.
3. George Orwell, "The Male Byronic," London *Tribune* (21 June
1940), pp. 20–21. This is a review of (among other things) *Two Film Stories*
of H. G. Wells (London, 1940), which was not included in the *Collected
Essays.*
4. H. G. Wells, *Men Like Gods* (London, 1923). Quoted further in the
text as *Men*, by chapter number.
5. George Orwell, *The Road to Wigan Pier* (1937) (London, 1959).
Quoted further in the text as *Wigan*, by page number.

6. *Collected*, 2: 143. Wells uses the symbol of airmen and airplanes in this way especially in *The Shape of Things to Come*.

7. Aldous Huxley, *Brave New World* (1932) (London, 1952). Quoted further in the text as *B.N.W.* by page number. Huxley's acid caricature of Wells's *Outline of History* (the two sketches by Rampion) in *Point Counter Point* clearly reveals Huxley's contemptuous attitude toward the Wellsian "Utopian infinity." See *Point Counter Point* (New York, 1928), pp. 248–49.

8. Northrop Frye, *Anatomy of Criticism* (Princeton, New Jersey, 1957), p. 223.

9. George Orwell, *Nineteen Eighty-Four* (1949) (London, 1950), p. 226.

Borges and Wells and the Labyrinths of Time

by ROBERT M. PHILMUS

> . . . and so on to the end, to the invisible end, through
> the tenuous labyrinths of time.
> Borges, "Avatars of the Tortoise"

1

"For years I believed I had grown up in a suburb of Buenos
Aires, a suburb of random streets and visible sunsets. What
is certain is that I grew up in a garden, behind a forbidding
gate, and in a library of limitless English books." [1] These
words, which begin the Prologue to the second edition of
Evaristo Carriego (1955), evoke, with characteristic conci-
sion, the universe of metaphors their author, Jorge Luis
Borges, still inhabits. The geography is deliberately, symbolically, vague: Borges locates the garden and the library
that created him indefinitely in a labyrinthine suburb of the
Buenos Aires of visible sunsets whose relation to him he is
perhaps no longer certain of, or at least does not choose to

159

define. Where he is definite, circumstantial, the details
reveal one of those secret plots he delights in puzzling out
and perpetrating: the enclosed garden and the library of
(ambiguously) infinite books appear in his parables as
metaphors of the world. "The universe (which others call
the Library) is composed of an indefinite and perhaps
infinite number of hexagonal galleries"[2] wherein men seek,
among a possibly infinite number of volumes, the one book
that may contain their "Vindication." This model of man's
perplexity, and of his extravagant futility, Borges offers in
"The Library of Babel." In "The Wall and the Books" he
suggests elaborate, tentative, and contradictory explanations of the metaphoric significance of "the two vast
undertakings" of the emperor Shih Huang Ti, "the building of the almost infinite Chinese Wall" and "the burning of
all the books that had been written before his time."[3] The
emperor may have begun these monstrous projects at the
same time: the walling in of space and the incinerating of
the past might have been "magic barriers to halt death," or
to delimit the world so that all things might have "the names
that befitted them" (O.I.:2)[4]. Perhaps the two acts "were not
simultaneous," in which case possibly (since the one is
destructive and the other conservative) "the burning of the
libraries and the building of the wall are operations that
secretly nullify each other."[5] Another of Borges's versions
of this crepuscular analogy between the wall and the books,
the garden and the library—a mysterious correspondence
that is "trying to tell us something," or has "told us
something we should not have missed," or is "about to tell us
something" (O.I.:4)[6]—had appeared earlier, in "The Garden of the Forking Paths." There Borges postulates an
identity the basis of which is a tautology: the infinite book
and the labyrinthine garden nominally come together as
The Garden of the Forking Paths, an imaginary novel by the
hypothetical Ts'ui Pên, predicated on the idea of time as a
labyrinth.

Ts'ui Pên [says the sinologist Stephen Albert] must have said once: *I am withdrawing to write a book.* And another time: *I am withdrawing to construct a labyrinth.* Every one imagined two works; to no one did it occur that the book and the maze were one and the same thing. The Pavilion of the Limpid Solitude stood in the center of a garden that was perhaps intricate; that circumstance could have suggested to the heirs a physical labyrinth. Ts'ui Pên died; no one in the vast territories that were his came upon the labyrinth; the confusion of . . . [his] . . . novel suggested to me that *it* was the maze.(*L.*:25; Borges's emphasis)

Ts'ui Pên conceived of a book whose labyrinthine structure depends on the notion of bifurcations in time. Stephen Albert gives an account of that book's mystery to Yu Tsun, a descendant of Ts'ui Pên and a man who, pursued as a spy for the Germans (the story is set during the First World War), has, to elude capture temporarily and to communicate a military secret, conceived of a labyrinthine plan of evasion based on the bifurcations of space.[7] At the center of that labyrinth, which is also a garden of forking paths,[8] Yu Tsun's pursuer will discover the labyrinth-maker and his atrocious mystery, the murdered Stephen Albert, victim of Yu Tsun's monstrous and efficacious attempt to outwit the confines of space. The various labyrinths in the story— Ts'ui Pên's, Yu Tsun's, Borges's—fit each inside the next like a series of Chinese boxes; each is a garden of forking paths and a *Garden of Forking Paths.* The coincidence supposes a clandestine analogy, perhaps an identity; both the garden and the library Borges has, as it were, created as models of the labyrinths of space and time. Thus in saying, "I grew up in a garden . . . and in a library," he is esoterically confessing himself to be the creature of his own creation. (The parable "Borges and I" sets out to distinguish between the two—"I live, let myself go on living, so that Borges may contrive his literature, and this literature justifies me"—but concludes in mock despair, "I do not know which of us has written this page" (*L.*: 246–47).

The self-consciousness involved in portraying oneself as the creature of one's creation is baroque, the sort of self-consciousness Velasquez graphically epitomizes in his masterpiece *Las Meninas* (1656). The scene is the artist's studio. In the foreground the maids of honor assume various attitudes. On the rear wall hangs what at first looks like, but is too luminous to be, another of the many paintings adorning the room: it is a mirror reflecting two figures who do not otherwise appear in the "fictive" space of *Las Meninas*; they belong to the "reality" outside the spatial limits of the canvas. All the same, the presence of their mirror images has the intellectual effect of confounding any nice discrimination of art from life, a confusion Velasquez deliberately intensifies by placing the mirror symmetrically in balance with a door opening on interior space also outside the confines of the space depicted (the symmetry calls attention to this baroque analogy between mirror and door). Initially, the maids of honor detract from the viewer's perception of the artist who stands self-deprecatingly to one side, in partial obscurity, poised with brush and palette before a canvas whose dimensions, it can be inferred, are similar to those of *Las Meninas* itself. This artist, of course, is Velasquez, who has portrayed himself in the act of painting *Las Meninas* from a different angle.[9]

Las Meninas is a compendium of baroque predilections and conceits: the fondness for paradox (which the mirror of art and life typifies); the metaphysical tricks of perspective and point of view (illustrated by the divergent angle of vision of the Velasquez who depicts himself vis-à-vis the self-portrait within *Las Meninas*); the tendency toward infinite regress (consciousness of being self-conscious tends toward consciousness of being self-conscious of being self-conscious . . . ad infinitum—perhaps in the *Meninas*-within-*Las Meninas* there is another self-portrait of Velasquez delineating the maids of honor from yet another angle).

Borges shares this baroque fascination with paradoxes,

metaphysical games, and infinite progressions and regres-
ses. He titles one essay "A History of Eternity," another "A
New Refutation of Time." He defends Berkeleian idealism
and also quotes with relish, twice, Hume's dictum that
"Berkeley's arguments do not admit of the slightest refutation nor do they produce the slightest conviction."[10] He
returns again and again to the paradoxes of Zeno the
Eleatic and cognate *regressus in infinitum.*[11] And in his
formulation of some thoughts provoked by the Quixote,
paradox, metaphysical speculation, and the idea of an
infinite series converge:

> Why does it make us uneasy to know that the map is within
> the map [a reference to Josiah Royce's *The World and the
> Individual*] and the thousand and one nights are within the
> book of *A Thousand and One Nights*? Why does it disquiet us to
> know that Don Quixote is a reader of the *Quixote*, and Hamlet is
> a spectator of *Hamlet*? I believe I have found the answer: those
> inversions suggest that if the characters in a story can be
> readers or spectators, then we, their readers or spectators, can
> be fictitious. In 1833 Carlyle observed that universal history is
> an infinite, sacred book that all men write and read and try to
> understand, and in which they too are written. ("Partial
> Enchantments of the *Quixote*," *O.I.*:48)

The dreamer who is himself dreamed (in "The Circular
Ruins") and the chess player who is a pawn in the hands of
gods who are pawns in the hands of higher gods (in the
poem "Chess") afford Borges other metaphoric disguises
for similar metaphysical paradoxes.

His ultimate theme—perhaps the logical consequence of
the tendency of baroque self-consciousness toward self-
irony—is self-betrayal. Nils Runeberg finally concludes that
God "was Judas" ("Three Versions of Judas"). Of Donne's
Biathanatos Borges writes:

> Christ died a voluntary death, Donne suggests, implying that
> the elements and the world and the generations of men and
> Egypt and Rome and Babylon and Judah were drawn from
> nothingness to destroy Him. Perhaps iron was created for the

nails, thorns for the crown of mockery, and blood and water for the wound. That baroque idea is perceived beneath the *Biathanatos*—the idea of a god who fabricates the universe in order to fabricate his scaffold. ("The *Biathanatos*," *O.I.*:96)

The detective Erik Lönnrot infers from what he believes to have been three murders the existence of a cabalistic pattern analogous to the tetragrammaton, the hidden name of God; he arrives at the point of the compass where he calculates the fourth and last murder will occur and finds that he is the victim of the homocidal labyrinth he has imagined; the name of the murderer (which, redundantly enough, is Red Sharlach) secretly corresponds to his own[12] ("Death and the Compass"). And Borges himself, having attempted to demonstrate the factitiousness, or at least ideality, of space, time, and the self, eventually must admit—

And yet, and yet—To deny temporal succession, to deny the ego, to deny the astronomical universe, are apparent desperations and secret assuagements. Our destiny (unlike the hell of Swedenborg and the hell of Tibetan mythology) is not horrible because of its unreality; it is horrible because it is irreversible and iron-bound. Time is the substance I am made of. Time is a river that carries me away, but I am the river; it is a tiger that mangles me, but I am the tiger; it is a fire that consumes me, but I am the fire. The world, alas, is real; I, alas, am Borges. ("A New Refutation of Time," *O.I.*:197)

For Borges, "universal history," the history of all men and of one man, is the history of the human mind, lost in the labyrinths of time, conceiving labyrinths of vast simplicity wherein to betray itself.[13]

2

"Every writer *creates* his precursors," Borges says in an essay on Kafka; by way of explaining this paradox, he adds:

If I am not mistaken, the heterogenous selections I have mentioned [Zeno, Kierkegaard, and so forth] resemble Kafka's work: if I am not mistaken, not all of them resemble each other, and this fact is the significant one. Kafka's idiosyncrasy, in greater or lesser degree, is present in each of these writings, but if Kafka had not written we would not perceive it; that is to say, it would not exist. ("Kafka and his Precursors," *O.I.*:113)

Some of the authors Borges has talked about (most of whom he read in his paternal grandmother's library of "limitless English books"[14]) are his precursors *in this sense:* among them, the Hawthorne of "Earth's Holocaust" and perhaps "Wakefield" (but not the Hawthorne who imagined a utopian "celestial railroad" that goes to hell);[15] Stevenson in *Dr. Jekyll and Mr. Hyde*; Kipling, the writer of short stories;[16] Oscar Wilde[17]; and G. K. Chesterton.[18] In that sense Poe is perhaps not a precursor (though he was more interested in the mere effect of a bizarre idea than is Borges); H. G. Wells certainly is not.[19] His repeated praise of Wells notwithstanding, Borges has not "created" him as he has, for example, "created" the Chesterton he describes as "a *monstrorum artifex*":

In my opinion, Chesterton would not have tolerated the imputation of being a contriver of nightmares . . . , but he tends inevitably to revert to atrocious observations. He asks if perchance a man has three eyes, or a bird three wings; in opposition to the pantheists, he speaks of a man who dies and discovers in paradise that the spirits of the angelic choirs have, every one of them, the same face he has; he speaks of a jail of mirrors; of a labyrinth without a center; of a man devoured by metal automatons; of a tree that devours birds and then grows feathers instead of leaves; he imagines (*The Man Who Was Thursday*, 6) 'that if a man went westward to the end of the world he would find something—say a tree—that was more or less than a tree, a tree possessed by a spirit; and that if he went east to the end of the world he would find something else that was not wholly itself—a tower, perhaps, of which the very shape was wicked.' (*O.I.*:87)

Here Borges, by enlarging details out of all proportion to

their original context, has perceived an image of Chesterton that, as he admits, Chesterton himself would not have recognized. On the contrary, the Wells of the "scientific romances" is recognizable even in the slightest circumstance Borges singles out. His remark, "the conventicle of seated monsters who mouth a servile creed in their night is the Vatican and is Lhasa," accords with Wells's own summation of *The Island of Dr. Moreau* as a "theological grotesque"[20]; Wells's parable of a man who, as a consequence of the most banal oversight, must dissipate his godlike power of invisibility in futilely trying to satisfy the most basic animal demands encompasses the significance Borges discovers in a minute detail: "the harassed invisible man who has to sleep as though his eyes were wide open because his eyelids do not exclude light is our solitude and our terror" ("The First Wells," *O.I.*:91).

Borges has recorded his admiration for:

> *The Time Machine, The Island of Dr. Moreau, The Plattner Story, The First Men in the Moon.* They are the first books I read; perhaps they will be the last. I think they will be incorporated, like the fables of Theseus or Ahasuerus, into the general memory of the species and even transcend the fame of their creator or the extinction of the language in which they were written. (*O.I.*:92)

He has acknowledged his specific debt to Wells's short story "The Crystal Egg" as the inspiration for "The Aleph" and "The Zahir."[21] Other "inventions" of Wells's (Wells's term), most of which Borges never mentions, further evidence their mutual attraction for "atrocious miracles"[22]: the vampiric plant in "The Strange Orchid"; an imperishable Apple of Knowledge, obtained accidentally, that can not be located again after it has been carelessly thrown away ("The Apple"); the fanatic barbarian who sacrifices another, and then himself, to the dynamo he worships ("The Lord of the Dynamos"); a country whose topography its congenitally blind inhabitants know so well they can move through their world as if they could see ("The Country of the Blind"); eyes whose field of vision is geographically antipodal to the body they belong to ("The Story of Davidson's Eyes"); a man who returns from somewhere that is nowhere or hell "inverted, just as a reflection returns from a mirror" ("The Plattner Story").[23] Although Wells as a writer of science fiction is far more neogothic than baroque, Borges does not have to "create" him as his precursor: the disposition they share to pursue rigorously the "opposite idea,"[24] the conception they both have of fantasy as a mode of subversion, establishes the basis of their affinity.

Only in what he says about *The Time Machine* does Borges come close to refashioning Wells. The Time Traveller, he asserts, "returns tired, dusty, and shaken from a remote humanity that has divided into species who hate each other. . . . He returns with his hair grown gray and brings with him a wilted flower from the future. . . . More incredible than a celestial flower or the flower of a dream is the flower of the future, the unlikely flower whose atoms now occupy other spaces and have not yet been assembled" "The Flower of Coleridge," *O.I.*:10). Wells's is a parable of guarded hope (in an early published draft the Time Traveller confronts the "Coming Beast"[25] in the one hundred and twenty-first century; in the final version that encounter is postponed still further): the future is real, possibly catastrophic, but not beyond redemption; this is the testimony the flower of the future mutely offers. Borges, on the contrary, seems to regard that flower as a hieroglyphic of despair: the future is already inexorably configured in the particulate structure of present time, what will happen is already destiny.[26] What for Wells is an obvious application of the theory underlying time travel—a man who can journey into the future can also come back, into the past as it were, with a flower from that future age[27]—Borges transforms into the metaphysical paradox of a future coexisting with the present.

Borges inverts the significance of the flower of the future by not assuming, as Wells does, that time is a function of space. That assumption is of course the ground of the Traveller's demonstration at the beginning of *The Time Machine*. Time, he argues, constitutes a Fourth Dimension; that is to say, "Time is only a kind of Space" (ch. 1).[28] To define time as a variable and space as the constant obviates any philosophical paradox: the flower then occupies the same space at two different times; space in that view is continuous, and in that sense retains its identity through time—a proposition that, while it is vulnerable to theoretical objections of the sort Borges raises in citing Heraclitus' "You will not go down twice to the same river,"[29] is hardly startling to common sense. However, by reversing the subordination, by supposing, as Borges does, that space is "an episode of time" (*O.C.* 6:43), a paradox, symbolized by the flower, does emerge: the basis of the flower's self-identity then becomes the identity of time, the contemporaneousness, so to speak, of present and future.

3

The essay wherein Borges advances his notion of space as an episode of time, an essay entitled, "The Penultimate Version of Reality" (1928), clarifies the central, but usually implicit, postulate of his fictions. In that discussion, Borges avers an "Opposition between the two incontrastable concepts of space and time" to be delusory—notwithstanding the illustriousness of some of its proponents, such as "Spinoza, who gave his undifferentiated diety—*Deus sive Natura*—the attributes of thought, that is, consciousness of time, and extension, that is, consciousness of space." "According to a thoroughgoing idealism, space is nothing but one of the constitutive patterns in the replete flux of time"; it is "situated in time and not vice-versa." Moreover, space is an accident in time and not, as Kant posited, a universal modality of intuition. There are whole provinces of Being that do not require it: those of olfaction and hearing. Spencer, in his critical examination of the arguments of metaphysicians (*Principles of Psychology*, VII, iv) has elucidated that [notion of] independence and also reinforces it with this reduction to absurdity: "whoever thinks that smell and sound implicate space as intuitive concept can easily convince himself of his error simply by [attempting to] seize the right or left side of a sound or by trying to imagine a color in reverse." (*O.C.* 6:42–43)

The consequence Borges deduces from this reasoning is that a belief in the reality of space can be dispensed with: without spatial referents, without an awareness of corporeality, humanity would still continue "to weave its history" (*O.C.* 6:44). Time alone is the universal substratum of perception.

Borges's conception of space accounts for, and perhaps also reflects, his mature concern for geography only as the geometry of space.[30] "Death and the Compass" (1942) is an instance where this is clearly the case. Less obviously in a story like "The Immortal" (1947), the cartographical details conform to a geometrical pattern. The antiquary Joseph Cartophilius, whose life history is found in a manuscript in his copy of Pope's translation of the *Iliad,* begins his quest for immortality in Berenice, a seaport in Eritrea, as the Roman tribune Marcus Flaminius Rufus, and recovers the mortality he longs for "in a port on the Eritrean coast," the name of which Borges ostentatiously withholds.[31] The circularity of the geography is thus an objective correlative of the circularity of the immortal's search.[32]

That image of eternal recurrence, in "The Immortal" as in "A New Refutation" (1944, 1946), represents a negation of time. Such a repudiation may afford the *ultimate* version of reality; at least Borges sees it as the final, perhaps logically inevitable, extension of idealist philosophy.[33] Its paradoxical consequences he adumbrates in "Tlön, Uqbar, Orbis Tertius," an encyclopedic account of a world that mirrors—that is, inverts—the model of the universe that philosophic materialism proposes (the story opens, "I owe the discovery of Uqbar to the conjunction of a mirror and an encyclopedia" [*L.*: 3].

The inhabitants of Tlön are "congenitally idealist":

> The men of this planet conceive the universe as a series of mental processes which do not develop in space but successively in time. Spinoza ascribes to his inexhaustible divinity the attributes of extension and thought; no one in Tlön would understand the juxtaposition of the first (which is typical only of certain states) and the second—which is a perfect synonym of the cosmos. In other words, they do not conceive that the spatial persists in time. The perception of a cloud of smoke on the horizon and then of the burning field and then of the half-extinguished cigarette that produced the blaze is considered an example of the association of ideas. (*L.*:9)

Here the equivalent of the Eleatic paradoxes, which call into question the (orthodox) spatial continuum by assuming the infinitesimal divisibility of infinite time as a series of discrete moments, is "the sophism of the nine copper coins," which insinuates the (in Tlön, paradoxical) existence of spatial continuity as the ideational adjunct of temporal continuity. To obviate the need for supposing what would subvert idealism—that it is possible for Y and Z to find certain coins that X lost as a previous time because space does persist in time independent of its being perceived—one of the philosophers of Tlön formulates "a very daring hypothesis":

> This happy conjecture affirmed that there is only one subject, that this indivisible subject is every being in the universe and that these beings are the organs and masks of the divinity. X is Y and is Z. Z discovers three coins because he remembers that X has lost them; X finds two in the corridor because he remembers that the others have been found. . . . The Eleventh Volume [of *A First Encyclopedia* of Tlön] suggests that three prime reasons determined the complete victory of this idealist pantheism. The first, its repudiation of solipsism; the second, the possibility of preserving the psychological basis

of the sciences; the third, the possibility of preserving the cult of the gods. *(L.*: 12)

In other words, the solution to the paradox of the coins postulates the unitary nature of mind. Gradually it becomes apparent that Tlön is a world in the flux of time, an amorphous world in the process of conforming to the full implications of its idealist premises. Gradually it becomes apparent that the incidental details of Borges's fiction reflect that process (the words *descubrimiento* and *descubrir,* meaning *discovery* and *to discover,* recur frequently in the story; the conversation at the outset that leads to the "discovery" of Tlön concerns "a novel in the first person, whose narrator would omit or disfigure the facts and indulge in various contradictions which would permit a few readers—very few readers—to [divine] an atrocious or banal reality" *(L.*: 3). The intellectual *voyage imaginaire* in search of Tlön begins with Bioy Casares's putative discovery of certain pages in volume 16 of the 1917 edition of what is "fallaciously called" the *Anglo-American Cyclopædia,* pages that appear in some copies of that book (at least in one) but not in others. (Later, following the demise of one Herbert Ashe, a volume 11 of the *First Encyclopedia of Tlön* adventitiously comes into Borges's possession. Its contradictions, when one considers the "lucid and exact . . . order observed in it" *(L.*: 8), constitute a proof that companion volumes must exist. In a postscript it is revealed that forty volumes of the encyclopedia were subsequently located "in a Memphis library" *(L.*: 17). The postscript also confirms the existence of a vast and labyrinthine conspiracy to disintegrate this world by perpetuating and spreading the habits of thought of an "imaginary planet": "The world," Borges asseverates, "will be Tlön" *(L.*: 17–18).

The facts admit, indeed demand, something more than this credulous and literal rehearsal of them. A careful examination of other details of Borges's account discloses their true and clandestine meaning. The discovery of Tlön

begins as the revelation that certain pages occur in some
copies of a particular book but not in all; later it is learned
that the encyclopedia of Tlön has, as it were, disappeared at
times. Those details call to mind Ts'ui Pên's delphic clue to
his labyrinth—"*I leave to various futures (not to all) my garden of
forking paths*" (*L.*: 25, 26; Borges's emphasis)—and with it
his idealist conception of the multiplicity of time. The
article purportedly contained in volume 16 of the *Anglo-
American Cyclopædia* deals with Uqbar and supplies "fourteen names" as its geographical coordinates; a note to "The
House of Asterion" alleges that "as used by Asterion" this
number stands for infinity (*L.:*4–5, 138). The language of
Tlön, in accord with idealist thought, excludes all substan-
tives; " 'The moon rose above the river' is *hlör u fang
axaxaxas mlö*, or literally: 'upward behind the onstreaming it
mooned' " (*L.:*8); *Axaxaxas mlö* is the title of a book in one "of
the many hexagons under my administration" (*L.:*57) in
"The Library of Babel." A Princess Faucigny Lucinge
figures in the postscript to "Tlön" in connection with a
compass; in "The Immortal" Joseph Cartophilius offers
"the Princess of Lucinge the six volumes . . . of Pope's *Iliad*"
(*L.:*105). The elusive pages of the *Anglo-American Cyclopædia*
inform its readers "that the literature of Uqbar was one of
fantasy and that its epics and legends never referred to
reality, but to the two imaginary regions of Mlejnas and
Tlön" (*L.:*5). The allusive pages of "Tlön, Uqbar, Orbis
Tertius" insinuate that Borges's fictions comprise the
definitive encyclopedia of Tlön.

The world of Borges's fictions generally, like the world of
Tlön, is a predicate of idealist philosophy, which premises
that nothing exists independently of perception. But if
space does not exist outside the human mind, then the
perceptions the mind has when waking and the visions
arising in a dream become indistinguishable from one
another. It becomes as impossible to differentiate the
imaginary Uqbar from the real world as it is to differentiate

Uqbar from Tlön, the fantasy from the fantasy-within-a-fantasy. (Borges illustrates this point elsewhere with the parabolic anecdote about a certain Chuang Tzu who "dreamed that he was a butterfly and when he awakened . . . did not know if he was a man who had dreamed he was a butterfly, or a butterfly dreaming it was a man" ("A New Refutation of Time," *O.I.:* 194). The confusion of real with imaginary names that proliferates in "Tlön, Uqbar, Orbis Tertius" and everywhere else in Borges's fantasies is another deliberate example of this consequence.

To suppose that time as well as space is not absolute means to relinquish the temporal coordinates of individual identity. In a world where space is merely a perception, during Chuang Tzu's dream "he was a butterfly" *(O.I.:* 195). In a world where time is merely a sense of time, whoever dreams he is Chuang Tzu dreaming he is a butterfly—at that moment, which is identical with the moment of Chuang Tzu's dream—is Chuang Tzu. Any chronological determination to the contrary, inasmuch as it belongs to the realm of absolute time, is inadmissible. For similar reasons, the man who imagines he is immortal is immortal; if he chooses as well to think of himself as Homer, whom he conceives of as an almost speechless Troglodyte, then he is Homer; and Pierre Menard, the symbolist poet who undertakes to write *Don Quixote* without becoming Cervantes, has as good a claim to its authorship as Cervantes. These consequences inhere in the "idealist pantheism" of Tlön.[34]

"Tlön, Uqbar, Orbis Tertius" to some extent imitates an idealist universe: the unstated premise of the fiction posits the narrative order as the order of discovery; its narrative sequence, manifestly at variance with absolute chronology, supposedly follows exactly the sequence of the author's perception of events. The story abounds in accidents because causality requires that space persist in time, in apparent irrelevancies because the sequence of human perceptions is not logical but random.

The idealist universe wherein a sense of time derives from a web of perceptions that contradict or coincide with or complement one another is a vertiginous universe of "divergent, convergent, and parallel times," a labyrinthine universe analogized as the Lottery of Babylon, which consigns identity to chance, or Library of Babel, with its indefinite, perhaps infinite, number of books composed of all the possible combinations of orthographic symbols. These labyrinths the mind constructs are mirrors that reflect itself and also maps of the world.

"Work that endures . . .," Borges asserts, "is a mirror that reflects the reader's own traits and . . . is also a map of the world." He speaks of Wells's enduring legacy as a "vast and diversified library": "he chronicled the past, chronicled the future, recorded real and imaginary lives" ("The First Wells," *O.I.:* 91, 92). These words secretly acknowledge the profound debt Borges, the contriver of fictional labyrinths that are also maps of the mental cosmos, feels toward the Wells who has outlined the past and future history of the mind as much as toward the Wells who plausibly traces the absurd consequences of a more or less improbable idea. In the philosophically idealist sense, the "vast and diversified library" of Wells's opus *is* the "library of limitless English books" of which Borges confesses himself to be a creature and in which he has sought a model of the universe.

NOTES

1. *Evaristo Carriego,* in Jorge Luis Borges, *Obras Completas,* 10 vols. (Buenos Aires, 1953–1967), 4: 9. All subsequent citations from this source, in my own translations from the original Spanish, will be abbreviated as *O.C.* volume: page (for example, *O.C.* 4:9). This edition, incidentally, despite its title, by his own choice does *not* include all of Borges's works up to 1967.

2. "The Library of Babel," in Jorge Luis Borges, *Labyrinths,* ed. and trans. Donald A. Yates and James E. Irby (New York, 1962), pp. 51 and further. References to this volume are hereafter cited parenthetically in the text as *L.:* page (for example, *L.:* 51 and further).

3. "The Wall and the Books," in Jorge Luis Borges, *Other Inquisitions,* trans. Ruth L. C. Simms (New York, 1966), p. 1. References to this translation are hereafter cited parenthetically in the text as *O.I.*: page.

4. For clarification of this idea about the names of things, *see* R. M. Philmus, "Swift, Gulliver, and 'The Thing Which Was Not,' " *ELH* 38(1971): 62–79.

5. Alexander Pope, whom Borges quotes in the epigraph of his essay, takes "Chi Ho-amti" (Pope's spelling) to have been simply one more enemy of learning (the Queen of Dulness praises him in *The Dunciad,* bk. 3, ll. 75–78).

6. Compare "Forms of a Legend," *Other Inquisitions,* pp. 157–62.

7. In "The Wall and the Books" another of Borges's speculations is that Shih Huang Ti undertook the building of the wall so that a future emperor would "destroy the wall, as I have destroyed the books, and he will erase my memory and will be my shadow and my mirror and will not know it" (*O.I.*:3); Shih Huang Ti himself, in burning the books, would, according to this baroque notion, be just such a shadow and a mirror of "that legendary Huang Ti, the emperor who invented writing" (*O.I.*:2). Similarly, Yu Tsun is the negation (shadow) and inversion (mirror) of his ancestor Ts'ui Pên, of whom Yu Tsun says, "the hand of a stranger murdered him" ("The Garden of Forking Paths," *L.*: 23).

8. The labyrinthine nature of Yu Tsun's journey to Stephen Albert's becomes explicit as Yu Tsun reflects on the unsolicited directions given him at the Ashgrove railroad station: "The instructions to turn always to the left reminded me that such was the common procedure for discovering the central point of certain labyrinths" (*L.*:22). A road that "forked among the now confused meadows" takes him to the "rusty gate" that opens on Stephen Albert's garden: "Between the iron bars I made out a poplar grove and a pavilion" (*L.*:23)—suggesting Ts'ui Pên's "Pavilion of the Limpid Solitude." Thus, Borges insinuates, *The Garden of Forking Paths* and the Garden of Forking Paths converge at the center of Yu Tsun's labyrinth—a spatial correlative to Ts'ui Pên's idea of "an infinite series of times . . . divergent, convergent, and parallel" (*L.*:28).

9. In *The Structure of Spanish History,* trans. Edmund L. King (Princeton, New Jersey, 1954), pp. 236, 662, Américo Castro connects some of these features of *Las Meninas* with those observable in Spanish literature of the Golden Age, especially in the *Quixote. See also* Wylie Sypher, *Four Stages of Renaissance Style* (Garden City, N.Y., 1955), pp. 171–72.

10. Borges quotes this comment of Hume's in an essay in *Discusión,* "La Postulacion de la Realidad" (*O.C.* 6: 67) and in "Tlön, Uqbar, Orbis Tertius" (*L.*:8).

11. In "La perpetua carrera de Aquiles y la tortuga" and "Avataras de la tortuga" from *Discusión* (the second essay appears again in *O.I.*); "Kafka and his Precursors" (*O.I.*); and "Tlön, Uqbar, Orbis Tertius"

(*Ficciones*). There is also an allusion to Zeno in "The Lottery of Babylon" (*L.*:34).

12. I notice that Borges himself makes this point in his notes to *The Aleph and Other Stories, 1933–1969,* ed. and trans. Norman Thomas di Giovanni "in collaboration with the author" (New York, 1970):

> The killer and the slain, whose minds work the same way, may be the same man. Lönnrot is not an unbelievable fool walking into his own death trap but, in a symbolic way, a man committing suicide. This is hinted at by the similarity of their [*sic*] names. The end syllable of Lönnrot means red in German, and Red Scharlach is also translatable, in [*sic*] German, as Red Scarlet. ("Commentaries," p. 269)

13. The Borgesian notion of universal history as the history of all men and of one man is implicit in many of his writings, particularly in "The God's Script," "The Immortal," and "Pascal's Sphere." The latter begins: "Perhaps universal history is the history of a few metaphors" (*O.I.*:5); a corollary of this notion can be found in "The Wall and the Books," where Borges defines "sacred books" as those "that teach what the whole universe or each man's conscience teaches" (*O.I.*:3). Here and in the discussion above of Borges's baroque qualities, I have made no attempt to exhaust the possible examples.

14. Along with his grandmother's books, Borges seems to have inherited her idosyncratic taste in literature. In "An Autobiographical Essay" (*The Aleph and Other Stories,* p. 206) he recalls: "when she was over eighty, people used to say, in order to be nice to her, that nowadays there were no writers who could vie with Dickens and Thackeray. My grandmother would answer, 'On the whole, I rather prefer Arnold Bennett, Galsworthy, and Wells.'"

15. See Borges's "Nathaniel Hawthorne" in *O.I.,* especially pp. 56–62.

16. Among the works of Kipling, Borges singles out *The Finest Story in the World* and *Many Inventions* ("La Postulacion de la Realidad," *O.C.* 6: 73n.).

17. See "About Oscar Wilde," *O.I.*: 83–85. Borges's first published work was a translation of *The Happy Prince.*

18. See "On Chesterton," *O.I.*: 86–89. Also below.

19. Ronald J. Christ, in *The Narrow Act: Borges' Art of Allusion* (New York, 1969), maintains that the "authors who really influence [Borges's] work, the reflection of whose writing can be seen in his fiction, are Chesterton, Wells, and Kipling" (p. 43). Of the three, Christ focuses mainly on Wells (for example), on pp. 144–45, 164–65); he also presents a convincing case for an affinity between Borges and De Quincey (pp. 148–210).

20. Preface to *The Island of Dr. Moreau,* in *Works* (London, 1924–27), 28 vols. [The Atlantic Edition], 2: ix.

21. Epilogue to *El Aleph* (Buenos Aires, 1968), p. 198.

22. This phrase, quoted from "The First Wells" (*O.I.:* 92), originally occurs in a review Borges reprints in *Discusión,* where he speaks of Wells as the "ancient [in the sense of ageless] narrator of atrocious miracles: that of the voyager who brings back from the future a wilted flower; of the Beast Men who gabble a servile creed in the night; of a traitor who flees from the moon" (*O.C.* 6: 164–65).

23. The same story contains this hellish speculation: "It may be . . . that, when our life has closed, when evil or good is no longer a choice for us, we may still have to witness the working out of the train of consequences we have laid."

24. Wells uses this term in his essay on "Zoological Retrogression," *The Gentleman's Magazine* 271 (7 September 1891): 246.

25. "Zoological Retrogression," p. 253.

26. Compare Yu Tsun's precept: *"The executer of an atrocious undertaking ought to imagine that he has already accomplished it, ought to impose upon himself a future as irrevocable as the past"* (*L.:*22; original emphasis).

27. "The Flower of Coleridge" goes on to give a brief account of Henry James's *Sense of the Past,* where, "The cause follows the effect, the reason for his [Pendrel's] journey is one of the consequences of the journey." Borges finds this "an incomparable *regressus in infinitum*" (*O.I.:*11)—that is, the future determines the past that determines the future, and so on. Could he be hinting, by his juxtaposition, that he perceives this regress in embryo in *The Time Machine,* where, as it were, the present identity of the Traveller is dependent on the future?

28. For a further analysis of how the Fourth Dimension functions in *The Time Machine,* see R. M. Philmus, "*The Time Machine*; or, The Fourth Dimension as Prophecy," *PMLA* 84 (1969): 530–35.

29. "A New Refutation. . . ," *O.I.:*187: "I admire his [Heraclitus'] dialectic skill, because the facility with which we accept the first meaning ('the river is different') clandestinely imposes the second one ('I am different')."

30. Compare this sentence from "The Man on the Threshold": "The exact geography of the facts I am going to report is of very little importance" (*O.C.* 7: 143).

The abstractness of space in Borges's fictions undoubtedly has something to do with his congenitally bad eyesight. Compare T. S. Eliot's discussion of Milton's "auditory imagination" in his first essay on the poet, in *On Poetry and Poets* (New York, 1961), pp. 157ff.

I speak of Borges's *mature* concern for the geometry of space because in his early work, "in books now happily forgotten, I tried to copy down the flavor, the essence of the outlying suburbs of Buenos Aires" ("The

Argentine Writer and Tradition," *L.*:181).

31. Borges's footnote at this point in the text says, "There is an erasure in the manuscript; perhaps the name of the port has been removed" (*L.*:116n).

32. Compare L. A. Murillo, *The Cyclical Night: Irony in James Joyce and Jorge Luis Borges* (Cambridge, Mass., 1968), pp. 237–38.

33. *See* "A New Refutation. . . ," in *O.C.*, especially pp. 186–87.

34. "Today, one of the churches of Tlön Platonically maintains that . . . all men, in a vertiginous moment of coitus, are the same man. All men who repeat a line from Shakespeare *are* William Shakespeare" (*L.*:12n.).

H. G. Wells and Japanese Science Fiction

by SAKYO KOMATSU*

The appearance of a Japanese equivalent to the kind of science fiction H. G. Wells was writing back before the turn of the century is a relatively recent phenomenon, barely more than twenty-years old. Equally recent is any real understanding in Japan of what H. G. Wells is about. The parallel between the fortunes—and misfortunes—of the two is not accidental. The reasons for the retarded development of science fiction in Japan are precisely the ones that stood in the way of any recognition of the real significance of Wells's ideas, and of the aims and methods of his works. My discussion of those reasons, I would venture to claim, has more than limited interest, for I think they reveal not only certain historical and cultural predilections and prejudices that persisted in Japan much longer than their analogues did in Europe and North America, but also

*Translated from the Japanese by the author with the help of Judith Merril and Tetsu Yano, and revised by R. M. Philmus.

some of the basic assumptions that Wells was working from and that in a society long used to science and technology often go unrecognized.

Among the cultural and historical factors inimical not only to Wells but also to all science fiction is the presumption that literary genres can be classed hierarchically in order of importance. The notion that certain kinds of literature are more respectable and are to be taken more seriously than others was not totally alien to Europe, especially (as far as modern history is concerned) during the period when this view gained official sanction in Japan, the Edo Period (1615–1866). But in Japan the evaluation of genres on a scale ranging through degrees of "high" and "low" became institutionalized as a matter of dogma. It was an intrinsic part of Confucianism, which permeated Japanese society under the auspices of the Tokugawas, the *shogun* family that dominated the Edo Period. According to the Confucianism that the Tokugawas imported from China, the "highest" literature is the classic teachings of the ancient sages Confucius and Mencius. These sacred books are nonpareil; and the most significant and serious contribution of any thinker is to arrive at exegeses or new applications of them, to write commentaries interpreting the ancient wisdom and relating it to contemporary situations. Next in prestige and respectability, after the sacred books and the explanations thereof, is poetry: in poetic forms the adept presents a human orientation toward time and eternity, the individual's position and opposition to history and politics. Below the sacred books and poetry is history, and below that again are writings temporally narrower in scope, commentary and criticism, especially regarding politics. All these kinds of "Great Writings" are deserving of serious attention: they deal with what is eternally important or socially and politically of weight. No such consideration was thought to apply to prose fiction and drama—the "lowest" genres—which, having as their subject the quotidian or the fantastic, merited no intelligent regard. They were fit amusements for the minds of women, children, and socially inferior beings, but hardly for a gentleman of substance and intellectual purpose. This, as I say, was the traditional approach to literature on the part of the Chinese intelligentsia, and it became firmly rooted in Japan in the Edo Period. The Tokugawa regime adopted an educational policy whose intent was to implant Confucianism in the basic culture of all Japanese. The attempt was not entirely successful in respect to literature: the tradition of what Confucianism categorized as "low" genres did not die out. The taste of many Japanese for myth, legend, romance, and fantasy—a taste that before the Edo Period had produced the *genji monogatari* (*Tales of the Genji*, a classic of Japanese fiction completed at the beginning of the eleventh century) and the *heike monogatari taiheiki* (a medieval compilation that included legends and myths from ancient times)—continued to find expression in a popular literature in and after the Edo Age in fiction, drama, and illustrated stories.

This popular literature prepared the way for the reception of Jules Verne, whose works began to appear in Japan in the late 1870s and who was the beneficiary of a publishing "boom" in the 1880s. Verne's *Voyages extraordinaires* found an audience already familiar with Chikamatsu's *kabuki* drama based on an old legend of a journey underground; with *furyu shidohken*, a Swiftian satire by the talented and versatile scientist-writer Gennai Hirage that describes many strange lands—one is inhabited solely by women, in another the people have large holes in their bodies—and with Bakin Takizawa's *chinzei yumiharizuki*, tales of heroic adventure across the seas, reminiscent in some ways of the *Odyssey*. These and other popular works provided the common people—confined as they were to a small island-country geographically and culturally cut off from all communication with other countries and cultures—their only chance to be in touch at least with imaginary worlds beyond their own. These popular "low" forms were the only ones available, within the framework of Tokugawa restrictions, for the expression of imaginative and intellectual energy in a free play of thought. In the restrictive world of Tokugawa Japan, which excluded interchange with the rest of the planet and confined itself to Confucian traditions of scholarship, the intellectually adventurous writers often found themselves perforce borrowing the style and techniques of such "low entertainments" as the satires, fantasies, and romances supposedly suitable only for "tradesmen and commoners."

Verne's works began appearing in Japanese translation within a decade or so after the Meiji Restoration of 1868. The Jules Verne boom was an indirect consequence of Meiji policies designed to reverse the trends of two hundred and fifty years of Tokugawa isolation by opening Japan to the world and reorganizing it as a modern nation. Many of the customs and much of the social structure of the Tokugawa Period underwent drastic changes. The samurai class lost its special privileges: samurais at this point had no more rights than farmers or tradesmen, who in turn were entitled to study the culture of the samurai and scholars, to participate in political organizations, and in general to take a position in society equal to that of the samurai. But these changes in the social caste system began affecting the cultural caste system only very much later: the intellectual and psychological hierarchy of the Tokugawas remained long after its politicoeconomic counterpart had declined. The first performance of kabuki theater before the emperor, for example did not take place until many years after the Meiji Restoration. Until then, kabuki was still considered to be "low-grade" entertainment and was scorned as an art form by the nobility.

Prose fiction was likewise dismissed as "vulgar," regardless of the content or quality of the work. Verne, and later

Wells, were classed in the "lowest" order of literature; and the more popular they became, the more they were despised by intellectuals. Furthermore, the "cultural-caste" prejudice against science fiction lasted beyond that against most other "low" genres. Science fiction has become recognized as reading matter suitable for serious adults only in the 1960s (the first Japanese science-fiction magazine began appearing in 1959; there is still only one such magazine and a dozen writers of science fiction). Up to that time, it was considered either as a species of juvenile literature or a subspecies of the mystery story. Even now there is a tendency among critics and publishers to think in these terms. I myself, when I began to get a reputation as a writer of science fiction, was advised by several editors not to write science fiction forever: "You must write 'genuine' literature sometime."

I understand that this sort of attitude toward science fiction is not entirely unknown elsewhere. But the Japanese perhaps have a clearer perception of the basis of that attitude in a "cultural-caste" system. Among Japanese science-fiction writers there is a joke extrapolating from the Tokugawa order of classes: *shi noh koh sho science fiction sakka*, which means, "The order of caste is Military, Agricultural, Industrial, Mercantile, and Science-Fiction-Writer Classes"—that is, science-fiction writers realize the traditional view places them at the bottom of the social and cultural hierarchy. Still, taking their example from Wells, they look upon science fiction as a genre for expressing serious ideas, however others may regard it.

The point I have made may seem relevant to explaining the predicament of science fiction in Japan, but of little importance with respect to Wells, who, after all, must have been undaunted by any "cultural" prejudices against the "scientific romance" as a serious form. But however that may be, the animosity between science fiction and a literary "caste" system that I have talked about both prepares for

and has certain resemblances to other sociocultural conditions that make Wellsian science fiction possible—or impossible.

As I have already hinted, Verne was available (in more
than one sense) to the Japanese reader long before Wells.
In the 1880s, at a time when Japan was importing and
assimilating American and European technology, Verne's
Voyage extraordinaires, adapted and rearranged, were published in Japanese. The adventures of Captain Nemo as he
takes on all the world over—and under—the seven seas; the
global travelogue of *Around the World in Eighty Days;* the
trials and success of the international fraternity of youth
reinventing the technological world in *The Mysterious
Island*—all these stories of Verne's now had meaning in a
country that was being "westernized" and opened to the
world. A new sense of spaciousness and of technological
possibilities prepared the way for them, and they in turn
further stimulated that sense. For young people especially,
reading Verne then was like unlocking a door to the future
and to the big "international" world outside, after all the
years of claustrophobic existence on the four small islands
of Japan.

The Jules Verne boom soon produced many native
imitations, with the result that the original Verne books—
which in any case had been badly translated and arranged
(thanks to the academic prejudice against fiction and
romance)—vanished in a wave of trash. However, Verne
did not disappear for long. Some thirty years later, better
translations started appearing. In the meantime, the first
Japanese science-fiction writer of note had come on the
scene. Shunroh Oshikawa, who wrote military science
fiction, began publishing during the Russo-Japanese War,
and had considerable influence, especially on the thinking
of young people.

During this period, when the impact of technology was
generating an interest in Verne's kind of science fiction,

Wells was not entirely neglected. *The Time Machine* appeared as an adaptation entitled *The World After Eight Hundred Thousand Years* about 1905. Over the next twenty-odd years, *The War in the Air, The War of the Worlds, The Invisible Man,* and *The Island of Dr. Moreau* were all published in Japanese versions. Significantly, all of them appeared first in adventure-story magazines for boys; but gradually they were reprinted in magazines for adults and eventually even in book form.

Wells's ideas did not begin to attract serious attention until the 1930s. In 1931 *Tono-Bungay* was published for the first time, in the second series of a "collection of world novels," by the Heibonsha publishing company. Once complete translations of *The Outline of History* and *The Science of Life* could be had—which was not until the late 1930s—a few young scholars began to study Wells as a thinker. Unfortunately, this was also the time when the Sino-Japanese War was rapidly militarizing Japanese society: the authorities began suppressing left-wing or radical thought, deteriorating relations between Japan and England, and Japan and America, led to a fanatic "Anti-Anglo-American Ideas" movement that utilized a mystical emperor-worship to monger war and justify imperialist rule over Asia, and the promulgation of Wells's works became difficult. Just when Wells's ideas were starting to circulate, he was branded, along with other English and American authors, as an "enemy" writer.

Yet even in these difficult times Wells's science fiction continued to be published. In 1941 a series of his scientific romances came out from a publisher called "Diamond"; and as late as 1943 *The War in the Air* was printed again in magazine form. Apparently, Japanese wartime leaders and administrators permitted this because they thought that such fiction was harmless entertainment.

After the war, Wells was not published at all for a while. The World Declaration of Human Rights got a certain amount of attention from Japanese thinkers, but no one seemed to recognize any connection between it and Wells's efforts concerning the Sankey Committee Declaration of 1940. Marxism was a strong influence on the Japanese intelligentsia at this time, perhaps as a reaction against the severe repression of leftist thought both before and during the war. There was a tendency to regard Wells as a "trivial low-grade popular thinker," perhaps because of his confrontation with Lenin after the Russian Revolution. And the fact that Wells had once been a leading member of the Fabian Society made radical thinkers consider him a "half-hearted reformist." But actually Wells's thought was less criticized and attacked than it was ignored. For ten years after the war, most Japanese intellectuals passionately focused on bitter and fanatical arguments about world revolution, internal revolution, and the decline and fall of capitalist society.

I do not mean to imply that no attention was paid at all to science fiction. Aldous Huxley's *Ape and Essence* aroused interest because it concerned the atom bomb. Orwell's *Animal Farm* and *Nineteen Eighty–Four* irritated the leftist press because these books dealt with the corruption of the revolution and the terrors of totalitarianism. But Wells's science fiction was by and large passed over; and a reevaluation of his thinking did not begin until quite recently.

In 1966, the last volume of his important trilogy, *The Work, Wealth, and Happiness of Mankind*, was finally brought out under the title *gendai sekaibunmei no tenbo (Perspectives on the Civilization of the Modern World)* by Mr. Teru Hemano, who also founded the H. G. Wells Society of Japan. Both literary scholars who had been studying Wells and some of the new futurologists joined the Society, and now a systematic movement is under way to introduce and popularize all of Wells's works.

Why did it take so long for Wells's thought to be recognized in Japan for what it really is? From what I have said, there emerge four sociocultural obstacles that prevented clear-sighted perception of what Wells is getting at in his opus. The first was the deeply rooted "cultural-caste" system already discussed. In addition, the absence of a truly scientific world view, then the predominance of a militaristic nationalism, and finally the preoccupation with narrow-minded ideological squabbles—each of these in turn thwarted an understanding of Wells. Wells's vision comes from a global-mindedness that in Japan is now taken for granted.

Wells's vision has, at least partially, become reality. Beginning in the latter half of the nineteenth century, the development of scientific civilization under the leadership of Western countries has produced significant changes in the flow of human history. First of all, there is the impact of new technologies on life-style and environment: the systematization of human life; the explosive increase in productivity resulting from mass production and other technological advances; the bringing together of peoples from all parts of the planet through electronic communication; and the accelerating of transportation to enable movements of men and materials over the surface of the Earth on a scale completely unimaginable in an earlier age. Subtler but perhaps more important has been the impact not of technology but of scientific thinking. Science offers a new way of looking at the universe, and at humanity within that universe, so as to allow a degree of objectivity concerning the "shape of humanity," both historically and in the present. The world is a single tiny planet called Earth, and this planet is just one of the planets circling the star called the sun; and this sun is only one star among many many billions of stars in the galaxy; and the whole universe contains many many such galaxies, each with its billions of stars billions of light-years from one another. Today, nobody disbelieves all this. Man also accepts that the universe is made up of certain kinds of atoms and elementary particles, and that on Earth certain accidental conditions enabled these atoms to combine in highly complex stages culminating in the strange phenomenon called *life*. And after four billion years there evolved creatures called *humans* who in time became aware of the "universe itself." This is man's "common sense." It was also, largely, Wells's.

Wells was acutely sensitive to mankind's evolution from what might be termed the *alluvial epoch* to a *scientific epoch*. Wells was aware of the new thinking and new world views taking shape in modern science, especially in Darwinian and post-Darwinian biology. He was aware that men could use their new and unprecedented technological powers to hurl themselves precipitously toward unknown dangers. And his works are full of warnings, appeals, and prophecies about the dangers, as well as the possibilities, of the new scientific epoch. Above all, Wells was perhaps the first to use "mankind," in the scientific sense, as the subject of fiction.

I do not expect what I am saying to be regarded as a startling revelation about Wells. But I do think that the fortunes of Wells's opus in Japan provide a kind of empirical verification. Once the Japanese had the "experience" of modern technology, there was an audience to appreciate Jules Verne. Verne was sensitive to some of the tendencies of technology, and his science fiction deals with more than technological gadgetry wondrously regarded for its own sake; but his heroes, after all, in traditional novelistic fashion, are "men," not "mankind." Wells, on the other hand, presupposes more than an acquaintance with mere technology. Only when there is a conception of man as a species and of his place in universal space and time do Wells's speculations about the shape and destiny of mankind become intelligible. For that reason, Wells was not comprehensible in the Japan of the late nineteenth or early twentieth centuries. For that reason also, his ideas were not accessible at a time when thoughtful people in Japan were involved with imperialistic nationalism or labor internationalism. Only now that a scientific view of the universe,

Earth, and mankind has been accepted, are Wells's science fiction and discursive writings—premised as they are on "mankindism" or "Earthism"—coming to be understood.

As for Wells's influence on Japanese science fiction, let me speak somewhat autobiographically. My choice of science fiction as the genre best suited to expressing the ideas I wanted to express was very much influenced by my reading of Wells. When I was in my teens, during the horrible war, I read *The Science of Life* and *The Outline of History* avidly, and they made a permanent impression on my thoughts and feelings. This impact seemed to lessen through certain stages of growing up, through the period of intellectual trial and error and mental agitation; but in retrospect I can see that their influence was guiding me all along. As a university student, I majored in Italian literature, motivated to do so by my acquaintance with Dante, whose *Divine Comedy* I looked upon as a sort of grand space-opera. I wrote my thesis on Pirandello: in his "relativization of recognition" I sensed something in common with the basis of science fiction.

It strikes me that of all the Japanese writers and translators of science fiction, there is not one over fifty years old; only three are in their forties; and the rest are in their twenties and thirties. For them and myself, growing up in the 1930s and 1940s, Wells's science fiction, and his outlook generally, was a marvelous contrast to daily life in the world Verne had described—the world of World War II, with its sometimes awesome, sometimes terrifying technological inventions. This was the world of *Twenty Thousand Leagues Under the Sea* and *The Master of the World* (in Japanese, *Battleship in the Sky*), of missiles and heroism, earnest patriotism and adventure, territorial expansion, and friendships born in battle. World War II could easily be called *the War of Verne*—and the postwar age, with its crisis of humanity first brought on by the use of atomic weapons, *the Wellsian Postwar Age*.

Wells's impact on Japanese science fiction can not easily

be traced in the usual manner of a literary historian in terms of resemblances between this work and that. Rather it is more elusive—and deeper. Wells's thought—also his mode of thinking—has become axiomatic. In the face of the vast and manifold problems confronting humanity, men try to follow his example, to see with the same grand scope and depth of vision. And with every attempt, Wells's greatness becomes clearer.

A Selective Bibliography (with Abstracts) of H. G. Wells's Science Journalism, 1887–1901

by DAVID Y. HUGHES
and ROBERT M. PHILMUS

This survey is a selective record of H. G. Wells's science journalism, from his earliest surviving efforts up to 1901 (with the exception made for "The Scepticism of the Instrument," included as an appendix to *A Modern Utopia* [1905] but also essentially related to these early writings, especially "The Rediscovery of the Unique," and thus an important nexus between Wells's interest in science and his later sociological concerns). Without claiming to be exhaustive, the listing comprises sixty articles derived from a comprehensive sifting of periodical contributions attributed to Wells by Geoffrey Wells or Gordon Ray;[1] augmented by thirty-five previously unnoticed pieces, most of which are assigned to Wells on the basis of evidence found in the Wells Archive at the University of Illinois. Included are all the essays and reviews that were deemed relevant to Wells's science fiction, as well as two uncollected short stories of a somewhat essayistic nature (nos. 86, 93). The arrangement of the material is alphabetical, by title, though a chronological index has been appended.

Of the thirty-five previously unlisted articles, one is a transcript of a lecture by Wells, five are signed, thirteen are identifiable from Amy Catherine Wells's cue-titles on a document in the Wells Archive (these are quoted in the attribution brackets that follow the bibliographic information), and sixteen (of which six allude to, or are alluded to, in essays or reviews known to be by Wells) are included on grounds of style and content (in which case there is a bracketed asterisk after the entry).[2]

The ninety-five items listed here—most of them unsigned and unreprinted[3]—make up an otherwise unavailable record of Wells's overt scientific beliefs and shifts in belief in the period before *Anticipations*—before, that is, he turned his attention decisively toward sociological issues. While his science journalism prepares for that development, it does not reveal Wells as committed to any particular blueprint for society. It does, however, reveal him as committed to science in its literary use as a basis for science fiction.

The reviews and essays fall into three groups, partly overlapping. One group involves science education or science popularization; another expresses a more or less passive delight in the wonders and mysteries of science; and the third deliberately challenges received opinion by proposing novel or paradoxical ideas and backing them up with an appeal to science. Of course, all three types reveal Wells as attempting to widen the reader's range of perceived possibilities and to encourage his power and desire to extend it for himself.

1 SCIENCE EDUCATION AND POPULARIZATION

A. Education

Having dropped science teaching in 1893, Wells as a journalist urged reform. The core of his position is the need for a sequence of studies. Mind and hand should be trained in integrated class and laboratory work leading step by step through the intellectual hierarchy of the sciences. Common sense dictates that studies like metallurgy or physiology should rest on prior study of physics and chemistry. Science consists neither in technical proficiency nor in pure knowledge of fact, but in a method of discovery, and science teaching must impart that method. Wells was Baconian, largely—he stresses inferential reasoning and slights mathematics—but he prizes the inductive method itself, not its material fruits. (*See* nos. 35, 78, 80, 82, 83, 87).

He was consistently Baconian concerning fields of learning as well as ways of teaching. He mistrusts both the a priori state of academic psychology and the nonrepeatable data of psychic research. In a lighter vein, he intimates that "pure" reason may be unhygienic; he shows up the usual "proofs" that the earth is round as false inductions; and he deplores the taxonomic pedantry of the South Kensington Science Library, which catalogues the lives of entomologists under "Insects" and the subject "Meteorology" before 1891 under "Physics" and after 1891 under "Astronomy." Finally, recalling his education as being in many ways a typical one, he discovers all his teachers deficient in the faculty of significant inductive generalization, even at the Royal College of Science, except of course T. H. Huxley. (*See* nos. 9, 31, 39, 64, 67, 72, 77, 79).

B. Popularization

In "Scientific Research as a Parlour Game" (no. 81) and

especially in "Popularising Science" (no. 66), Wells states
the requirements of works of popularized science. Primarily, he urges the imparting of a sense of intellectual
discovery to the reader. The popularizer must shuck off
specialized language as a mark of "intellectual
parochialism" and employ general literary (or at least
literate) English; his delight in technical problems must be
subsumed in the larger scheme that gives them significance;
and he must build up this scheme in an orderly, causal, and
logical sequence in support of an opening generalization, so
as to give the reader an idea of scientific method. The
result, says Wells, is the pleasure of "inductive reading."
Since his model of what the popular exposition of scientific
ideas should be like closely parallels the plan of a number of
his works of science fiction, it is significant that he also
remarks, "the fundamental principles of construction that
underlie such stories as Poe's 'Murders in the Rue Morgue,'
or Conan Doyle's 'Sherlock Holmes' series, are precisely
those that should guide a scientific writer."

At this time, in mid-1894, he had done little science
popularization himself; he alludes instead to his experience
"as a reviewer for one or two publications,"[4] evidently
referring to his *Pall Mall Gazette* science reviews (listed for
the first time in this bibliography). In these reviews, he
develops the critical principles that later work well for him
in his *Saturday Review* popularizations. The *P.M.G.* reviews
employ the technique of evaluation through direct quotation (an analogue of the inductive policy). Among them are
amusing yet slashing reviews attacking jargon, bad construction, false sentimentality, sham induction, and
amateurish theorizing; faint commendations of technical
guides and supernumerary surveys of already familiar
fields; and unreserved recommendations of original research presented lucidly as an imaginative and encompas-
sing vision (for example, no. 85).

Wells's own popularizations, despite their brevity, succeed through causal connection of illustration and generalization. Sometimes they pose the question: What general principle does a given set of phenomena illustrate?—the answer being unknown. This provides "inductive reading": the quality of significance of a phenomenon is revealed or problematically raised as a function of its illustrating a principle of things. For example: no conspicuously colored or scented flower exists without relation to insects (no. 41); or, a recent transit of Mercury, though a minor event, might, under proper conditions of weather and geographical accessibility, have helped determine the presence or absence of an atmosphere on that planet as well as the extent of its curious orbital aberrancies (no. 89). In general, the expository essays on science manifest a reasonable care for accuracy, a strong emphasis on factual up-to-dateness, and a sure eye for salient, problem-focusing detail (the erratic behavior of Mercury that Wells singles out for attention, for instance, not long afterward gave Einstein evidence for his Theory of Relativity). (Other examples of basically neutral expository essays: nos. 1, 14, 23, 30, 46, 62).

2 THE WONDERS AND MYSTERIES OF SCIENCE

The wonders and mysteries of science mean the secrets of nature that science discloses. Essays with such titles as: "An Excursion to the Sun" (no. 28), "Through a Microscope" (no. 88), "From an Observatory" (no. 34), and "A Vision of the Past" (no. 93), are exercises in dissolving the limitations of human perception. Through science, one can imagine having telescopic or microscopic eyesight or conceive of a lifespan enduring through eons. Science thus can aid imagination and enlarge human understanding. True, some deficiencies may not be remediable. If the moon were brighter, man might never suspect the existence of the stars (no. 34); the human brain, not merely the eye, is doubtless a provisional and unreliable instrument (no. 77), a mere "by-product" of the evolutionary process (no. 13); and science itself is a matchflare that "man has just got alight," beyond which is "darkness still" (no. 74). Yet these arguments of human limitation bespeak wonders and mysteries in nature discoverable, if at all, only through the scientific method. Case in point: precise measurement of the weight and density of gases reveals the existence of argon, the otherwise unsuspected element in the air one breathes (nos. 59, 69, 84).

At times Wells appears almost ready to abandon Baconian principles outright and commit himself to a belief in a universe of unpredictables. At other times, he faces what he calls the "Calvinism of science" (nos. 12, 38). That is, when science enables man to take his bearings against the immensities of nature, his sense of wonder and mystery and his fine free sense of enlarged vision may be overshadowed by a feeling of impotence amid inexorable forces (*see* nos. 34, 86). The ability to envision the man of the year million confers no power to alter the cosmic forces that will have shaped him. This awareness on Wells's part permits him to see that the scientific enterprise is apt to be regarded as a "systematised Fetishism," a substitute for religious magic in offering cosmic correspondences among phenomena—correspondences well beyond the pale of cause and effect (no. 60).

On the other hand, always alive to the dialectical possibilities of the "opposite idea" (no. 95), Wells attributes to science "the Rediscovery of the Unique" (no. 74). Man is finally liberating himself from "the trim clockwork thought" of the eighteenth century: because evolutionary biology now teaches that *"all being is unique."* There are no principles, no ontological generalizations, but only individualities—"unique threads flying," in Goethe's figure of the loom of time. Perhaps nothing is impossible in nature and perhaps nothing is repeated. Perhaps, Wells suggested in "The 'Cyclic' Delusion," the only universal principle is change, that is, novelty and death in a cosmos moving "from the things that are past and done with for ever to things that are altogether new" (no. 19). Yet such a view renders science powerless to reveal nature's secrets, because it amounts to dissolving the system of uniformities upon which all science rests. For that reason, Wells was only sporadically tempted by unpredictability.

3 UNORTHODOX SPECULATIONS

Unorthodox speculation was congenial fare to Wells. In part, it was a matter of intellectual play. Civilization was engendered by the flint and could have been engendered by nothing else (no. 33); "mimetic" coloration is not protective but irrelevant, since most predators hunt at night and by smell (no. 15); not only are rigid skeletons not needed for support of musculature, as witness the octopus, but also silica skeltons—if rigidity be desired—would far surpass the lime-salt structures actually possessed by vertebrates (no. 17); on the moon there may be considerable and continuous change, the possibility of which is discounted without reckoning that such change might be invisible to man (no. 91). These are fair samples of sheer speculative play.

The most paradoxical of Wells's notions have to do with man's place in nature, a theme so pervasive in these early essays (as it is in his science fiction) that it is possible here to suggest only the briefest outline of his thought.[5] His starting point is unorthodox from any standpoint but that of mainstream British biology, especially as exemplified by Thomas Huxley. Wells did not really regard evolution as a "theory" at all. Whatever its consequences might be, it was the central fact of biology, geology, and solar physics. The corollary was that *Homo sapiens* is an accident and an episode. Essay after essay—at least until about 1896— hammers away at the anthropocentric fallacy. Life could be built out of compounds other than carbon (no. 8) and might somewhere have reached or surpassed man's present mental level (nos. 42, 48). Animals (nos. 53, 93) and plants (no. 46) possess nervous organizations higher than is commonly recognized, while the human brain is an instrument of dubious precision and accuracy (no. 77). Man, moreover, remains subject both to instinctual drives inherited from apelike ancestors and to the accidents and necessities imposed on him by nature (no. 38); so that from both within himself and without, he faces powerful adversaries to his humanity. Natural law is as unethical and un-"human" as it is universal and absolute (nos. 12, 36, 58).

After Wells came round to accepting—by early March 1895—Weismann's Theory of Germ Plasm[6] (which directly opposed the older Lamarckian theory that acquired characteristics are inheritable), he gradually but decisively turned his attention away from the long-range prospects of evolutionary change through natural selection (as exemplified in *The Time Machine*) and toward the immediate possibilities of what he termed *artificial evolution* (no. 38)—meaning education and behavioral engineering. Having discovered in *The Island of Dr. Moreau* that the mind presents more of an obstacle to "individual plasticity" than does man's physical form, he concluded that man may be redeemed from the bondage of cosmic biological laws only through education (*see* no. 2), which confirms him in his capacity of "artificial man," "the highly plastic creature of tradition, suggestion, and reasoned thought" (no. 38). Here Wells speaks as he would for years to come: in 1897, he already imagines the vanguard of the New Republicans, Samurai, and Open Conspirators, "One may dream," he writes , "of an informed, unselfish, unauthorised body of workers, a real and conscious apparatus of education and moral suggestion . . . shaping the minds and acts and destinies of men" (no. 55).

In the bibliography that follows, these abbreviations are employed: *E.T.—The Educational Times; F.R.—The Fortnightly Review; G.M.—The Gentleman's Magazine; P.M.G.—The Pall Mall Gazette; S.R.—The Saturday Review;* and *S.S.J.—The Science Schools Journal.* For abbreviations of book titles, *see also* the note to the Introduction of this volume.

BIBLIOGRAPHICAL LIST

1. "About Telegraphs." *P.M.G.* 60 (5 January 1895): 4 [A.C.W.: "Telegraphs"]. Wells praises A. L. Ternant's *The Telegraph* (trans. R. Routledge) for its wide-ranging historical exposition of the development of various telegraph systems, ancient and modern.
2. "Acquired Factor, The." *Academy* 51 (9 January 1897): 37 [signed]. Wells approves of the constructive Weismannism of C. Lloyd Morgan's *Habit and Instinct* (so like his own position in no. 38). Morgan infers from analysis of the proportionate shares of instinct and habit (that is, education) in higher animals, including man, that the human body and instincts are no longer evolving. The mental environment alone evolves. Despite his brute ancestry, man can shape his world through science, art, and education, and so "cease to be driven, a dry leaf before the wind."
3. "A.D. 1900." *P.M.G.* 59 (12 October 1894): 3 [GW]. In 1900 the giving of a dinner party or the hanging of a picture may be forbidden by court order if either is deemed unwholesome by Mrs. Hallelujah, Mr. Peahen, or other guardians of public morality.
4. "Advent of the Flying Man, The" *P.M.G.* 57 (8 December 1893): 1–2 [G.W.; but G.W. inadvertently

masks the identity of this unreprinted essay by confusing it with "The Flying Man"; the latter, a short story collected in *The Stolen Bacillus, and and Other Incidents*, appeared in *P.M.G.* 60 (4 January 1895): 1–2]. Wells portrays the flying man, present and future. The nineteenth and twentieth centuries witness his fiascos and hardier triumphs. By A.D. 21,000 (Wells adopts the quasi-visionary tones of no. 52) batlike human swarms darken the evening air, homing to suburban "rookeries" from the dome of Saint Paul's. The flying man holds the future: "Even now the imaginative person may hear the beating of his wings."

5. "Ancient Experiments in Co-operation." *G.M.* 273 (October 1892): 418–22 [signed]. The "element of individual competition" in the struggle for existence is "over-accentuated in current thought," while biological cooperation has been ignored. Wells gives a few examples of the kind of cooperation he is referring to, pointing out that man himself "is an aggregate of [cooperating] amoeboid individuals in a higher unity." The essay closes with speculation on the social significance of this fact.

6. "Angels and Animalculae." *P.M.G.*, 59 (9 October 1894): 4 [A.C.W.: "Angels and Animalculae"]. Wells cheerfully labels J. W. Thomas's *Spiritual Law in the Natural World* "what one may perhaps call the New Theology, theology 'up-to-date,' " scientifically "smartened" up.

7. "Angels, Plain and Coloured." *P.M.G.* 57 (6 December 1893): 3 [G.W.]. Wells catalogues angels: the common white angel of "the oleograph, the Christmas card, the illustrated good book, and the plaster cast"; the art angel of "fiery red and celestial blue," "of brightness rather than sentiment"; and the biblical angel of the Hebrew and of Milton, "a vast winged strength, sombre and virile."

8. "Another Basis for Life." *S.R.* 78 (22 December 1894): 676–77. [G.W., G.R.]. In addition to organic compounds as the basis for life, there may be other elements that "would afford the necessary material basis for a quasi-conscious and even mental superstructure"—such as the silicon-aluminum cycle. This inspires Wells with "visions of silicon-aluminum organisms."

9. "At the Royal College of Science." *E.T.* 46 (1 September 1893): 393–95 [About 893–94, *E.T.* "paid Low 50 a year as editor and another 50 a year for contributors. He and I found it convenient that I should be the contributors—all of them": *Wells, *Exp.*, 291] [*]. Things have changed little, Wells writes, since his student days at South Kensington; and he hopes that through brief "glimpses of the hall, the lift and staircase, a laboratory full of students, methodical teaching, and errant rebels sitting over rare books in the 'Dyce and Forster,' or cultivating art in the picture galleries," he can give the reader a student's view of that institution.

10. "Belated Botanist, A." *P.M.G.* 59 (13 November 1894): 4 [A.C.W.: "Belated Botanist"]. E. Sandford, author of *A Manual of the Exotic Ferns and Selaginella*, is "an extreme expression of the specialist type." Knowing all about the cultivation of ferns, he has not a suspicion of the findings of botany in the last forty years—facts of fertilization, reproduction, and classification, known to "almost any high-school girl."

11. "Biological Problem of To-Day, The." *S.R.* 78 (29 December 1894): 703–4 [G.W., G.R.]. Wells here presents a brief expository critique of August Weismann's Theory of Germ Plasm, against which his main objection is that the immortality of germ cells seems to be another version of mystical theories of the

preformation of all individuals at the beginning of time (compare no. 2).

12. "Bio-optimism." *Nature* 52 (29 August 1895): 410–11 [signed]. In this review of *The Evergreen*, by Patrick Geddes, et al., Wells resists Geddes's arguments against the idea that the struggle for existence is the prime mechanism in evolution: "As a matter of fact, Natural Selection grips us more firmly than it ever did, because the doubts thrown upon the inheritance of acquired characteristics have deprived us of our trust in education as a means of redemption for decadent families." Moreover, "a static species is mechanical, an evolving species suffering." "The phenomena of degeneration rob one of any confidence that the new forms [of life] will be . . . 'higher' . . . than the old."

13. "Bye-products in Evolution." *S.R.* 79 (2 February 1895): 155–56 [G.W., G.R.]. "Modification . . . involved in the change [designated] A," required for successful adaption, brings with it "other consequent changes . . . the directly unserviceable and yet absolutely necessary modifications B, C, and D." Hence, a perfectly useless organ may be just this kind of "bye-product" and does not necessarily pose an objection to the theory of natural selection. Wells then goes on to speculate whether the higher attributes of mind might be such "bye-products" of evolutionary adaptation.

14. "Centre of Terrestrial Life, The." *S.R.* 79 (16 February 1895): 215 [G.W., G.R.]. On the basis of the geological theory that continental land masses have persisted fundamentally unchanged in scope in geological time, Wells reasons that terrestrial life must have begun in the higher northern latitudes and "in the struggle for existence between the older and newer type [that is, species], generally the newer prevailed and drove the older southwards."

15. "Colours of Animals, The." *P.M.G.* 60 (25 January

1895): 3 [A.C.W.: "Mimicry of Animals"]. Whereas the man in the street supposes that "everything is trying its very best to resemble something else," the truth is that "many such resemblances are still unaccountable and apparently quite accidental." Wells cites as his main source F. E. Beddard's *Animal Colouration*.

16. "Concerning Our Pedigree." *G.M.* 274 (June 1893): 575–80 [signed]. Wells muses, with satirical overtones, on the evolutionary ancestry of man, which he follows from the anthropoid apes *backward* in time.

17. "Concerning Skeletons." *S.R.* 81 (27 June 1896): 646–47 [G.W., G.R.]. Wells begins by raising the questions: why a skeleton of phosphate and carbonate of lime rather than silica, which would be sturdier and more durable; and why a skeletal structure at all, which is "not simply explicable as a response to the need for support and armature"? These as yet unanswerable questions suggest "that the line of advance in biology lies now along the path of physiological chemistry" (that is, biochemistry).

18. "Concerning the Nose." *The Ludgate,* n.s. 1 (April 1896): 678–81 [signed]. Light hearted speculation, with satiric undertones, on the future evolution of the inexplicable human nose. "The nose of to-day . . . is in . . . a transitory and developing stage. One may conceive 'advanced' noses, inspired with an evolutionary striving towards something higher, remoter, better—we know not what. We seem to need ideals here."

19. " 'Cyclic' Delusion, The." *S.R.* 78 (10 November 1894): 505–6 [G.W., G.R.]. While the tendency to perceive every process as cyclical is "woven into the texture of our being," many times this perception is delusive—for example, "one day the sun will rise for the last time." On the cosmic level, "the main course is forward, from the things that are past and done with for ever to things that are altogether new."

20. "Darwinian Theory, The." *P.M.G.* 60 (1 January 1895): 4 [A.C.W.: "Darwinian Lectures"]. For the general reader, A. Milnes Marshall's *Lectures on the Darwinian Theory* is "the clearest modern exposition"; and, says Wells, "when such dark speculations as those of Weismannism" are used by the "small fry of science" to belittle Darwin, Marshall's encomium is "a needful tribute to the memory of the greatest biologist" of all time.

21. "Death." *S.R.* 79 (23 March 1895): 376–77 [G.W., G.R.]. Complex organisms are mortal, but "death is not inherent in living matter. Protoplasm may live forever." Nevertheless, "mortal man and the immortal protozoa have the same barren immortality; the individuals perish, living on only in their descendants . . .; the type alone persists."

22. "Decadent Science." *P.M.G.* 58 (5 April 1894): 4 [allusions in nos. 66, 81][*]. Wells demolishes Henry Pratt's *Principia Nova Astronomica* and its "brand-new" solar system, "a very nice affair, with a Central Sun, and a Polar Sun, and an Equatorial Sun, over and above the visible sun of your vulgar astronomers."

23. "Discoveries in Variation." *S.R.* 79 (9 March 1895): 312 [G.W., G.R.]. A discussion of new biometric studies of variation in species, wherein Wells observes: "Variation occurs in every direction [that is, all possibilities are tried], with complete symmetry) it does not occur in a definite direction as if it were following some inherent tendency of the animal to develop in a particular fashion. These minute variations offer a fair field for natural selection to reject or select."

24. "Diseases of Trees, The." *S.R.* 79 (19 January 1895): 102–03 [G.W., G.R.]. A review of R. Hartig's *The Diseases of Trees,* together with a brief discussion of plant pathology.

25. "Dream Bureau, The." *P.M.G.* 57 (25 October 1893): 3

[*]. With increasing knowledge of dream physiology, the time approaches for investigators "to bring the control of dreaming as a fine art into the realm of possibilities." Men may imagine the dream addict someday ordering up a night's supply, of any sort he pleases.

26. "Duration of Life, The." *S.R.* 79 (23 February 1895): 248 [G.W., G.R.]. "The business of the animal seems to be, not to live its own life, but to reproduce its own kind, and the term of life at its disposal is adjusted accurately to the special difficulties of this purpose." The generalization also applies to man under natural conditions.

27. "Electricity." *P.M.G.* 59 (22 December 1894): 4 [*]. Wells reviews J. A. Fleming's *Electric Lamps and Electric Lighting* and R. Mullineux Walmsley's *The Electric Current.* The one is a "readable volume" for nontechnical people, the other a secondhand handbook of batteries, circuitry, and "professorial disregard" of "the real substance of electrical engineering" at the time, the dynamo.

28. "Excursion to the Sun, An." *P.M.G.* 58 (6 January 1894): 4 [*]. Wells admires the plain style and "inhumanity and serene vastness" of subject of Sir Robert Ball's *The Story of the Sun.* The idea of electromagnetic tides brushing by "our little eddy of planets," unsettling compasses, making solar storms, then passing on to "the illimitable beyond," is "so powerful and beautiful as to well-nigh justify that hackneyed phrase, 'the poetry of science.' "

29. "Extinction of Man, The." *P.M.G.* 59 (25 September 1894): 3 [reprinted, with a slight addition, in *Wells, C.P.M.*]. Man is dominant today, but the fossil record never shows "a really dominant species succeeded by its own descendants." Man may be displaced by crustaceans, cephalopods, ants, or even plague bacilli—to

name but four possibilities "out of a host of others."
30. "Fallacies of Heredity." *S.R.* 78 (8 December 1894): 617–18 [G.W., G.R.]. This essay raises, but leaves unanswered, the problem of what causes genetic "idiosyncrasy"—that is, differences among offspring of the same parents, even among twins—that Wells finds one of the fascinating enigmas of heredity.
31. "Flat Earth Again, The." *P.M.G.* 58 (2 April 1894): 3 [A.C.W.: "The Flat Earth Again"]. In dialogue form, a perverse person challenges a schoolmaster to prove the Earth round. "The point is that you teach things at school as proofs the world is round that are no more proofs than they are poetry."
32. "Flint Implements, Old and New. *P.M.G.* 58 (3 April 1894): 4 [*]. Wells recommends Worthington G. Smith's *Man, the Primeval Savage* to the general reader for its accounts both of ancient bones and implements and of modern forgeries of same.
33. "Foundation Stone of Civilization, The." *P.M.G.* 58 (22 May 1894): 3 [G.W.]. A cyclist with a tire ripped up by flints listens perforce to an old man's dissertation showing that flints attended the demise of savagery and were, in fact, "the only thing that could engender civilization."
34. "From an Observatory." *S.R.* 78 (1 December 1894): 594–95. [reprinted in *Wells, *C.P.M.*]. If the moon were brighter, man might never suspect the existence of the stars. "We can imagine men just like ourselves [but] without such an outlook"; in that case, what an enlargement of vision it would be if that bright moon faltered in its luminosity—perhaps perturbed by the passing of a dark star—and the heavens were unveiled. There is a fear of the night "that comes with know-ledge, when we see in its true proportion this little life of ours."
35. "Geology in Relation to Geography." *E.T.* 47 (1 July

1894): 288–89 [signed]. Using England as an example, Wells points out that "all the chief facts in the geography of a country may be obtained in a quasi-inductive fashion from its geological structure." Thus "a few elementary geological considerations . . . bind together what are otherwise disconnected facts in a singularly powerful manner." (The argument here anticipates Wells's position in no. 82; *see also* no. 87).

36. "Good Intentions of Nature Explained, The." *P.M.G.* 58 (9 February 1894): 4 [*]. Wells regrets Edith Carrington's *Workers Without Wage,* a children's nature book that holds up to "vile" man the "lowly goodness" of the "affectionate" spider and the "patient" snail. Hiding nature's cruelty from children is bad practice.

37. "Human Evolution." *Natural Science* 10 (April 1897): 242–44 [signed]. This open letter of Wells's defends the position he had taken in no. 38. "My interest in these theories [about the nature of man]," he writes, "lies chiefly in their application. . . . After Darwin, it has become inevitable that moral conceptions should be systematically restated in terms of our new conception of the material destiny of man."

38. "Human Evolution, An Artificial Process." *F.R.,* n.s. 60 (October 1896): 590–95 [signed]. Because for various reasons man is not as subject to the rigors of natural selection as, say, rabbits, *"man has undergone . . . but an infinitesimal alteration in his intrinsic nature since the age of unpolished stone"* (emphasis in original), especially since civilization impedes the working of natural selection. Civilized man is a composite of "the natural man . . . the culminating ape" and "the artificial man . . . the highly plastic creature of tradition, suggestion, and reasoned thought." Save for the "padding of suggested emotional habits" (Wells's definition of morality), he is no different from the Paleolithic savage. Wells concludes by saying that "in Education lies the possible salvation

of mankind from misery and sin"—that is the "suffering and 'elimination' " entailed by the evolutionary process.

39. "Huxley." *Royal College of Science Magazine* 13 (April 1901): 209–11. [signed]. Wells recalls his student days under T. H. Huxley: "I believed then he was the greatest man I was ever likely to meet, and I believe that all the more firmly today."

40. "Influence of Islands on Variation, The." *S.R.* 80 (17 August 1895): 204–5 [G.W., G.R.]. "Isolation on islands has played a larger part in the evolution of the animals and plants than is usually attributed to it," since this isolation—which, according to modern geological findings, is intermittent—gives rise in its periodicity to "an immense number of new species." Among these natural selection takes place when the island resumes its connection with the mainland again.

41. "Insects and Flowers." *S.R.* 79 (6 April 1895): 440–41 [G.W., G.R.]. A discussion of examples of pollination by various insects.

42. "Intelligence on Mars." *S.R.* 81 (4 April 1896): 345–46 [G.W., G.R.]. Conditions on Mars could have led to the evolution of protoplasmic forms, but "granted that there has been an evolution of protoplasm upon Mars, there is every reason to think that the creatures on Mars would be different from the creatures of Earth, in form and function, in structure and in habit, different beyond the most bizarre imaginings of nightmare." "No phase of anthropomorphism is more naive than the supposition of men on Mars." A report in the *Science Schools Journal,* no. 15 [November 1888], pp. 57–58: "Mr. Wells on the Habitability of the Planets," indicates that at least part of the substance of what Wells advanced in his *S.R.* essay he had already formulated as early as October 1888.

43. "In The New Forest." *S.R.* 79 (27 April 1895): 544–45

[G.W., G.R.]. Wells mentions some animals to be met with in the forest and raises some questions about their behavior.

44. "J.F.N." *Academy* 56 (6 May 1899): 502–4 [signed]. Wells pays tribute to the philosopher J. F. Nisbet and his "quest—that perpetual quest!—of the unassailable truths of being." "It has a touch of the heroic," says Wells, that Nisbet, "feeling, as he certainly did, a strong attraction towards certain aspects of devotion . . . would defile himself with no helpful self-deceptions . . . but remained, as he was meant to remain, outside, amid his riddles." (Compare the conclusion of no. 60, where Wells defines his own, similar position in regard to the "imperative to believe".)

45. "Life in the Abyss." *P.M.G.* 58 (9 February 1894): 4 [*]. In this review of Sidney J. Hickson's *The Fauna of the Deep Sea*, Wells recounts some oddities in a field just opening up. He concludes: "our knowledge is in a very pleasant phase; enough to stimulate the imagination, and not enough to cramp its play."

46. "Life of Plants, The" *S.R.* 82 (8 August 1896): 131–32 [G.W., G.R.]. The differences between animals and plants are not so great as most people imagine. All plants have at least local motion, with the "lower forms of plant life" moving "as actively as animal protoplasm." Also, the process by which plants absorb and assimilate nourishment is not so mechanical as it is usually supposed to be.

47. "Limits of Individual Plasticity, The." *S.R.* 79 (19 January 1895): 89–90 [G. W., G. R.] "It often seems to be tacitly assumed that a living thing is at the utmost nothing more than the complete realization of its birth possibilities. . . . We overlook only too often the fact that a living being may also be regarded as raw material, as something plastic, something that may be shaped and altered . . . and . . . developed far beyond

its apparent possibilities." "There is in science . . . some sanction for the belief that a living thing might be . . . so moulded and modified that at best it would retain scarcely anything of its inherent form and disposition; that the thread of life might be preserved, while the shape and mental superstructure were so extensively recast as even to justify our regarding the result as a new variety of being." Wells argues for this idea by using familiar examples, such as those drawn from surgery. "If we concede the justification of visection, we may imagine as possible in the future, operators, armed with antiseptic surgery and a growing perfection in the knowledge of the laws of growth, taking living organisms and moulding them into the most amazing forms." (*See The Island of Dr. Moreau*, ch. 14.)

48. "Living Things That May Be, The." *P.M.G.* 58 (12 June 1894): 4 [allusion to no. 33] [*]. A review of J. E. Gore's *The Worlds of Space*. Finding Gore unimaginative when it comes to extraterrestrial life, Wells suggests such possibilities as a silicon base for life outside planet Earth (*see* no. 8).

49. "Luminous Plants." *P.M.G.* 59 (25 August 1894): 4 [A.C.W.: "Pr. v. Kerner"]. In the interests of "the general reader," Wells approves Anton Kerner von Marilaun's *The Natural History of Plants* (trans. F. W. Oliver). In particular, the section on luminous lichens and seaweeds inspires Wells to regard the deepest growths (which overhang "the perpetual night of the plant world" and glow red in utilizing their chlorophyll) as emblems of apocalypse—"so to speak, the sunset of marine vegetation."

50. "Making of Mountain Chains, The." *Knowledge* 16 (1 November 1893): 204–06 [signed]. An account of various contemporary hypotheses—which Wells illustrates with homely examples—about how mountains

are formed, concluding with his own synthesis of these ideas.

51. "Mammon." *S.S.J.*, no. 2 (January 1887), pp. 53–54 [G.W.; signed "Walter Glockenhammer"]. Thoughts on two paintings by G. F. Watts, *Mammon* and *Visit to Aesculapius*: together these canvases "signify . . . that this nation is, as it were, two dissevered parts . . . ease, elegance, and pleasure are floated to-day on an ocean of toil and ignorance and want."

52. "Man of the Year Million, The." *P.M.G.* 57 (6 November 1893): 3 [Reprinted in *Wells, *C.P.M.* as, "Of a Book Unwritten"; a lost version, "The Past and Future of the Human Race," went back to 1885 (*see* *West, p. 111) or perhaps 1887 (*Wells,*Exp.*, 549)]. As man evolves, says Professor Holzkopf of Weissnichtwo, the "purely 'animal' about him is being, and must be, beyond all question, suppressed in his ultimate development." He forecasts the hypertrophy of the organs of intellect—head, eyes, hands—and the atrophy of the "animal organs"—nose, external ears, digestive tract. Man's descendants, immersed in nutritive baths deep underground, will survive until the sun itself burns out.

53. "Mind in Animals, The." *S.R.* 78 (22 December 1894): 683–84 [G.W., G.R.]. In this review of Lloyd Morgan's *An Introduction to Comparative Psychology*, Wells intimates that he has a higher opinion of animal intelligence than Morgan. "It may be that Professor Lloyd Morgan's dog, experimenting on Professor Lloyd Morgan with a dead rat or a bone, would arrive at a very low estimate indeed of the powers of the human mind."

54. "Modest Science, The." *P.M.G.* 58 (19 February 1894): 4 [allusion in no. 79] [*]. To the general reader, says Wells, H. N. Dickson's *Meteorology* is exceptionally entertaining," combining "the most modern conclu-

sions" with accurate" folk-knowledge" of the still un-
predictable ways of the weather.
55. "Morals and Civilisation." *F.R.*, n.s. 61 (February
    1897): 263–68 [signed]. "We must needs regard social
    organization and individual morality as determining
    one another." Wells takes sexual morality as an exam-
    ple of man's ethical progress and then asks whether "a
    rational code of morality" can not be formulated at this
    point in man's history. "One may dream of an informed,
    unselfish, unauthorised body of workers, a real and
    conscious apparatus of education and moral sugges-
    tion . . . shaping the minds and acts and destinies of
    men."
56. "More Bacon." *P.M.G.* 58 (22 June 1894): 4 [allusion in
    no. 66] [*]. Wells expounds the "scientific method" of
    Orville W. Owen's *Sir Francis Bacon's Cipher Story*. Owen
    pasted up pages of all "Bacon's" works—*The Faerie
    Queene, The Anatomy of Melancholy*, Shakespeare's plays,
    and the rest—rolled them back and forth on a
    thousand feet of canvas until every line mated with a
    physically distant one to produce a secret history of
    Elizabethan profligacy. Two earlier Bacon articles—
    "Mysteries of the Modern Press," *P.M.G.* 58 (23 April
    1894): 3 and "A Remarkable Literary Discovery,"
    P.M.G. 58 (3 May 1894): 3—may also be Wells's.
57. "Mountains out of Molecules." *P.M.G.* 59 (29
    November 1894): 4 [allusion in no. 81] [*]. Wells
    debunks both the thesis that "heat is a current of ether
    running in and out of molecules" and the overblown
    style of its presentation in Frederick Hovenden's *What
    is Heat? A Peep into Nature's Most Hidden Secrets*.
58. "New Optimism, The." *P.M.G.* 58 (21 May 1894): 4
    [Wells mentions Kidd in no. 38] [*]. In reviewing
    Benjamin Kidd's *Social Evolution*, not only does Wells
    doubt Kidd's belief that nations survive in the struggle
    for existence by subordinating intellectual develop-

ment to "virtue, altruism, and the habit of self-sacrifice" but he also questions the name *optimism* for a creed that gives the future to the Anglo-Saxons because they are "so stupid, so pious, so sentimental."

59. "Newly Discovered Element, The." *S.R.* 79 (9 February 1895): 183–84 [G.W., G.R.]. A popularized account of Lord Rayleigh's discovery of argon. "All their lives [people] had, without knowing it, been breathing argon."

60. "On Comparative Theology" *S.R.* 85 (12 February 1898): 212–13 [signed]. A review of Grant Allen's *The Evolution of the Idea of God* (together with an anonymous work called *The [Cabalistic] Canon*), wherein Wells, while admitting that Allen's "certainly . . . is a book to be read," disagrees with Allen's notion that man could have come to the worship of God in only one way: "it is certain," writes Wells, "there are at least a dozen different ways . . . by which a man may arrive at worshipping a stone." "The modern method of inquiry, as Bacon described it, was of course systematised Fetishism, the natural human method in all ages. . . . The essential idea of Fetish is that cause follows effect . . . the fault of the system is that each savage who practices it has to discover for himself for the most part what is adequate fetish for the effect he desires and what is not. He dies before his system is clarified." But even scientists feel the need of superstition and fetishistic cosmic correspondences among phenomena. Another, far less interesting, review of Allen's book by Wells is "Grant Allen's 'Idea of God,' " *Daily Mail*, 27 November 1897, p. 4 [signed].

61. "On Extinction" *Chambers's Journal* 10 (30 September 1893): 623–24 [G.W.]. Extinction—the "saddest chapter of biological science"—is a tragedy true as any by a Shakespeare, a Sophocles, or an Ibsen. Perhaps, moreover, the victims feel: perhaps the bison senses

that those "seas of grass were the home of myriads of his race, and now are his no longer." The loneliest of pinnacles is man's present triumph. Visions of the future must include the doom hit upon in Thomas Hood's "The Last Man": "the earth [a] desert through a pestilence, and two men, and then one man, looking extinction in the face."

62. "Origin of the Senses, The." *S.R.* 81 (9 May 1896): 471–72 [G.W., G.R.]. Wells talks about the evolution of three organs of sense: the nose, from primitive chemotropic mechanisms; the eye, from primitive phototropic ones; and the ear, as "an organ for translating vibrations into touches."

63. "Pains of an Imagination, The." *P.M.G.* 59 (20 September 1894): 3 [G.W.]. The author used to be cursed with a restless, florid imagination that led him about as if tied by a string. But he cured himself of it. He proposed that it earn him a living by writing a book, and it has never troubled him since.

64. "Peculiarities of Psychical Research." *Nature* 51 (6 December 1894): 121–22 [signed]. Wells in this review of Frank Podmore's *Apparitions and Thought Transference* attacks "psychical research" into occult phenomena as unscientific because its results are unverifiable by repeated experiment.

65. "Polyphloisballsanskittlograph,' The." *P.M.G.* 58 (8 May 1894): 3 [*see* no. 22] [*]. Wells spoofs apparatuses of unknown function exhibited by unintelligible foreigners at Royal Society soirées.

66. "Popularising Science." *Nature* 50 (26 July 1894): 300–301 [signed]. Wells begins by pointing out the need for popularizing science, then criticizes how scientists usually go about it (in language that is too technical and jargonized or absurdly and condescendingly simplistic). "Intelligent common people come to scientific books . . . for problems to exercise their

minds upon . . . there is a keen pleasure in seeing a previously unexpected generalisation skilfully developed."

67. "Position of Psychology, The." *S.R.* 78 (29 December 1894): 715 [G.W., G.R.]. Wells uses George Trumbull Ladd's *Psychology, Descriptive and Explanatory* to launch an attack on the state of contemporary psychology, which he regards as being weighed down by a priori, hence unscientific, assumptions.

68. "Possible Individuality of Atoms, The." *S.R.* 82 (5 September 1896): 256–57 [G.W., G.R.]. The fact that oxygen, for example, responds in more than one way to spectroscopic analysis means "that there are two kinds of oxygen, one with an atom a little heavier than the other. And this opens one's eyes to an amazing possibility . . . that, after all, atoms might not be all exactly alike, that they might have individuality, just as animals have."

69. "Protean Gas, The." *S.R.* 79 (4 May 1895): 576–77 [G.W., G.R.]. A quizzical discussion of the controversy surrounding the discovery of argon.

70. "Province of Pain, The." *Science and Art* 8 (February 1894): 58–59 [signed]. After tracing gradations of animal and human pain, Wells concludes that "the province of pain" may be no more than "a phase through which life must pass on its evolution from the automatic to the spiritual."

71. "Pure and Natural Man, The." *P.M.G.* 57 (16 October 1893): 3 [G.W.]. Wells's hero, a rigid logician, recognizing that "the essence of all civilized ills" is man's "entirely artificial life," retires from society, goes nudist, and abstains altogether from the use of soap.

72. "Pygmy Philosophy." *P.M.G.* 60 (11 April 1895): 4 [A.C.W.: "Pigmies"; G. R. links this cue-title to *S.R.* (13 July 1895), but A.C.W. enters it under "Sat. Review" and "P.M.G." in title-groups published no later than

April, and only "P.M.G." crossed off (indicating publication); also, the *S.R.* (but not the *P.M.G.*) review is uncommonly colorless for Wells]. Wells rejects the efforts of J. L. A. de Quatrefages, in *The Pygmies* (trans. Frederick Starr), "to establish the high moral standards of these primitive people, and to imply the primordial elevation of humanity."

73. "Rate of Change in Species, The." *S.R.* 78 (15 December 1894): 655–56 [G.W., G.R.]. One thing that biologists have not emphasized about evolution is that the rate of change in species, and hence their "plasticity," varies in direct proportion to their fecundity and the time span between generations. Thus the "true heirs of the future are the small, fecund, and precocious creatures. . . . No doubt man is lord of the whole earth to-day, but the lordship of the future is another matter."

74. "Rediscovery of the Unique, The." *F.R.*, n.s. 50 (July 1891): 106–11 [signed]. Wells maintains that science, by insisting on the importance of minute differences among phenomena, substantiates the contention that *"All being is unique*, or, nothing is strictly like anything else" (emphasis in original; see also no. 77).

75. "Reminiscences of a Planet." *P.M.G.* 58 (15 January 1894): 4 [allusion in no. 66] [*j**]. Wells commends an "able and popular exposition of modern geology," Thomas Bonney's *The Story of Our Planet*. The earth's age and life span are the main topics of this review.

76. "Rudis Indigestaque Moles." *P.M.G.* 60 (13 March 1895): 4 [A.C.W.: "Rudis Indigestaque Moles"]. Wells reviews Sir Archibald Geikie's *Memoir of Sir A. C. Ramsay*, in which one eminent geologist shuffles the life of another into a detritus "shaken up together and thrown down before the reader."

77. "Scepticism of the Instrument, The." *Mind*, n.s. 13 (July 1904): 379–93 [signed; given first as a paper to the

Oxford Philosophical Society, 8 November 1903; reprinted, altered, and abridged by about 15%, in *A Modern Utopia*]. This essay develops ideas first bruited in nos. 68 and 74. Wells mistrusts the uniformity of formal logic because: (1) it classifies "uniques as identically similar objects" under some term that automatically accumulates a specious significance thereby; (2) "it can only deal freely with negative terms by treating them as though they were positive"; and (3) it projects onto one plane at a time, and thus places in mutual opposition, ideas that in fact are stratified at various levels of meaning, and thus really complementary. In Wells's universe of "uniques," "ethical, social and religious teaching [come] into the province of poetry." Since philosophy, too, is self-expression, this essay contains much autobiographical material.

78. "Science, in School and after School." *Nature* 50 (27 September 1894): 525–26 [signed]. Mainly in school; a critique of the predominant pedagogical approach to science, which inculcates fact but not the method of discovery (compare nos. 80, 82, 87).

79. "Science Library, South Kensington, The." *P.M.G.* 58 (3 May 1894): 2 [G.W.]. Wells slashes the cataloguing system of the Science Library of the Royal College of Science, which classifies the lives of entomologists under "Insects" and the subject "Meteorology" before 1891 under "Physics" and after 1891 under "Astronomy" (among other examples).

80. "Science Teaching—An Ideal and Some Realities." *E.T.* 48 (1 January 1895): 23–29 (identified in *E.T.* as a transcript of Wells's lecture before the Royal College of Preceptors, 12 December 1894]. Wells contrasts the "idealistic standpoint" toward the curriculum with "things as they are." Ideally, education should be primarily and fundamentally scientific: there should be an overall sequence of studies, emphasizing the

interrelatedness of various disciplines. Structurally also, within any given area of study, "generalizations" should be arrived at "inductively" on the basis of "object lessons and physical measurements" that enable the student to "see certain visible facts as connected with certain other visible facts. In practice, on the other hand, school curricula are unorganized and chaotic. Rather than providing "an ample background of inductive study"—the prerequisite for "exact thinking" and consequently for exactness of expression—schools instead offer a bewildering array of courses in which facts—purveyed as dogma—are presented in isolation from one another and without regard for any experiential or experimental basis. (This lecture is the fullest expression of notions Wells brings up in nos. 78, 82, and 87).

81. "Scientific Research as a Parlour Game." *S.R.* 79 (20 April 1895): 516 [G.W., G.R.]. A review of I. W. Heysinger's *The Source and Mode of Solar Energy Throughout the Universe*, in which Wells, pointing out Heysinger's ignorance in equating solar energy with electricity, attacks this kind of dilettantism generally.

82. "Sequence of Studies, The." *Nature* 51 (27 December 1894): 195–96 [signed]. Wells here reviews three scientific textbooks and criticizes them all for the absence "of that progessive reasoning process which is the very essence of genuine scientific study"—that is, the process of establishing evidence for why something is so.

83. "Sins of the Secondary Schoolmaster, The." *P.M.G.* 59 (15 December 1894): 1–2 [A.C.W.: "Sins of the Schoolmaster"; this, the last of three parts, deals with science teaching; two earlier parts appeared on November 28, pp. 1–2, and December 8, pp. 1–2]. Generally ignorant of the present state of science, schoolmasters must needs teach it anyway. They do so

mechanically, without sequential progression and without realizing that "not knowledge, but a critical and inquiring mental habit, is the aim of science teaching" (*see* no 80).

84. "Strangeness of Argon, The." *P.M.G.* 60 (15 March 1895): 3 [A.C.W.: "Argonn"]. Many are the curious properties of argon, not least the lateness of its recognition: "Surely there are still wonders left in the world, and the healthy discoverer may keep a good heart yet, though Africa be explored." (*See also* nos. 59 and 69.)

85. "Sun God and the Holy Stars, The." *P.M.G.* 58 (24 February 1894): 3 [*]. In this review of Norman Lockyer's *The Dawn of Astronomy,* Wells focuses upon man's early atunement to the cycles of the sun and the stars. Now, he adds, churches look onto gaslit streets where "the Great Democracy circulates forever" and "the silent and eternal stars are forgotten."

86. "Talk with Gryllotalpa, A." *S.S.J.,* no. 3 (February 1887), pp. 87–88 [G.W.; signed "Septimus Browne"]. A dialogue wherein the anthropocentric view of the universe confronts the cosmic perspective of the "infinitesimal littleness of man."

87. "Teaching of Geography, The." *E.T.* 46 (1 October 1893): 435–36 [signed]. Ranged in ascending order of complexity, the pedagogical approaches to geography proceed from "where is A?" through "what kind of a place is A?" to why is A what it is? They proceed, that is, toward a "descriptive"—"inductive" or scientific—view of the subject. Ideally, with a proper sequence of studies (*see* nos. 80 and 82), the study of geography can become "something altogether wider, a great and orderly body of knowledge centering about man in his relations to space." (*See also* no. 35.)

88. "Through a Microscope." *P.M.G.* 59 (31 December 1894): 3 [reprinted, slightly modified, in *Wells,

C.P.M.]. "All the time these creatures are living their vigorous fussy little lives in this drop of water, they are being watched by a creature of whose presence they do not dream." "Even so, it may be, the [observer] himself is being curiously observed."

89. "Transit of Mercury, The." *S.R.* 78 (24 November 1894): 555 [G.W., G.R.]. There are many things about the planet Mercury worth noting as it crosses the sun's disc—its erratic behavior, for example.

90. "Very Fine Art of Microtomy, The." *P.M.G.* 58 (24 January 1894): 3 [G.W.] Wells describes the preparation of a variety of substances for observation under the microscope and whimsically envisions a time when the slides prepared in his day will become collector's items.

91. "Visibility of Change in the Moon, The." *Knowledge* 18 (October 1895): 230–31 [signed]. While it is popularly believed that the lunar surface has not changed, there is every reason to suppose that it has, and that this change has escaped observation not only because the process of lunar transformation would be less noticeable than its terrestrial counterpart, but also because "the eye that watched" expected to find no changes in the Moon.

92. "Visibility of Colour, The. *P.M.G.* 60 (7 March 1895): 4 [A.C.W.: "Colour Vision"; G.R. linked this cue-title to *S.R.* (14 September 1895), but A.C.W. entered it under *P.M.G.* only and in a group all published by mid-April; again, the *S.R.* (but not the *P.M.G.*) review is uncommonly bland for Wells]. Wells welcomes W. de W. Abney's *Colour Vision,* a "fairly exhaustive account of the sensations of colour from the scientific side" and a work particularly stimulating to "the artist and art critic among those who find pleasure in untechnical scientific books addressed to the general reader."

93. "Vision of the Past, A." *S.S.J.,* no. 7 (June 1887), pp.

206–9 [G.W.; signed "Sosthenes Smith"]. A vision of reptilians in the distant past: they have three eyes and believe the world was made for them, "the noblest of all beings who have ever existed or ever will exist." When the time traveler points out to them that this can not be so, for they will soon become extinct, they attempt to refute him with an *argumentum ad stomachum;* but he saves himself from being eaten by waking up.

94. "Yards Sacred and Profane." *P.M.G.* 60 (4 March 1895): 4 [A.C.W.: "Measures"]. With a perfunctory nod to reform, Wells turns with relish from the rationalized standards of measurement urged in Wordsworth Donisthorpe's *A System of Measures* to Donisthorpe's account of such "natural" standards as the hand's length or the ox's "furrow-long" ("growing," says Wells, "visibly out of the soil"). (Compare no. 85.)

95. "Zoological Retrogression." *G.M.* 271 (September 1891): 246–53 [signed]. Contrary to popular belief, evolution is a process of twists and backslidings. Degeneration is common and not always a dead end but sometimes "a plastic process in nature." The degenerate upper-Silurian "mud-fish" is the ancestor of the land animals; and who knows the future of the "last of the mud-fish family, man"? His varied existence and variable structure probably assure him "a long future of profound modification." Yet nature may even now be equipping some "humble" successor. "The Coming Beast must certainly be reckoned in any anticipatory calculations regarding the Coming Man."

CHRONOLOGICAL LIST

1893: 4, 7, 9, 16, 25, 50, 52, 61, 71, 87
1894: 3, 6, 8, 10, 11, 19, 22, 27–36, 45, 48, 49, 53, 54,
56–58, 63–67, 70, 73, 75, 78, 79, 82, 83, 85, 88–90
1895: 1, 12–15, 20, 21, 23, 24, 26, 40, 41, 43, 47, 59, 69,
72, 76, 80, 81, 84, 91, 92, 94
1896: 17, 18, 38, 42, 46, 62, 68
1897: 2, 37, 55
1898: 60
1899: 44
1901: 39
1904: 77

NOTES

1. *G. H. Wells; and Gordon N. Ray, "H. G. Wells's Contributions to the *Saturday Review,*" *The Library,* 5th series, 16 (1961): 29–36.

2. Arguments for some attributions are implicit in the introduction. Where there is not the authority of Geoffrey Wells (G.W.), Amy Wells (A.C.W.), or Gordon Ray (G.R.), an asterisk (*) has been placed after the bibliographical information. It was decided to record these asterisked items after a study of all the issues of the *Pall Mall Gazette* from August 1893 to May 1895, the inclusive dates for Wells's contributions to that paper. For comparison, there were twelve reviews in the *P.M.G.* that were known to be Wells's, plus his work for the *Saturday Review* (S.R.) and, more generally, the body of his other science essays and his science fiction. In addition to the aid of published bibliographical sources, the authors would like to acknowledge the kind assistance of Professor Harris Wilson, University of Illinois Wells Archive, and Professor J. P. Vernier, Université de Rouen.

3. Up to now (*see* n. 5), the few reprinted include nos. 31, 34, 52, 88, in *Wells, *C.P.M.;* and no. 77, in a *Modern Utopia* (London, 1905; rptd. Lincoln, Neb.: 1967). Nos. 88 and 77 are also included in the Atlantic Edition.

4. No. 65; also, *Wells, *Exp.* states that Harry Cust, editor of the *P.M.G.,* permitted Wells to do some reviewing: "Books for review came to hand" (p. 310).

5. This aspect of Wells's thought is explored in some detail in introductory material for an anthology of Wells's hitherto unreprinted writings, *H. G. Wells: Early Writings in Science and Science Fiction* (Berkeley and Los Angeles, 1975).

6. For the dating of Wells's "conversion" to Weismannism, compare no. 11; *see also,* "Incidental Thoughts on a Bald Head," in *Wells, *C.P.M.,* p. 158 (first printed in *P.M.G.,* 60 [1 March 1895]: 10).

An Annotated Survey of Books and Pamphlets by H. G. Wells

by R. D. MULLEN

The major portion of this essay deals with books and pamphlets as abstract units rather than as physical objects. The place of publication is noted only when necessary for other purposes and then only as U.K. or U.S. The dates given are for first book or pamphlet publication, except that in item no. 71 the dates for first serial publication are also given if the intervening period was of any appreciable length. For each book or pamphlet the length is given in the pages of the Atlantic Edition (*See* part 2 of this survey) or, in the case of Wells's uncollected works, in the estimated number of pages the book would take up if it were reset in the format of that edition (hereafter referred to as "abstract pages"—abbreviated abs.pp.). All references are to chapter or section: for example, no. 102:4:1:2, means item no. 102 (*Babes in the Darkling Wood*), book 4, chapter 1, section 2; for a second example, no. 102:0, indicates the Introduction to the same work. The volumes of the Atlantic Edition are cited as A1, A2, and so forth. For detailed information on the various first editions, the reader is respectfully referred to the two major bibliographies.[1]

Wells began his book-publishing career in 1893 with *Text-Book of Biology* and *Honours Physiography.* Although I have glanced at copies of these books, I have not read them and so do not presume to include them in the Chronological Survey. Besides, it seems eminently fitting to begin the survey with *The Time Machine,* whose first U.S. edition is now known to have preceded by several weeks, even though its first U.K. edition followed by one day, the first edition of *Select Conversations.*[2]

Except for any work appearing in the Atlantic Edition, I have also *excluded* publications of certain types listed in the major bibliographies: first of all, in order to avoid duplication, stories or essays first published separately but later made part of a collection, as well as regrouped collections and omnibus collections other than the comprehensive *Short Stories* of 1927; second, books to which Wells was merely a contributor; third, pamphlets printed for private circulation, issued as advertising brochures, or of less than thirty-two pages.[3]

With one exception (no. 20), the annotations in the survey are intended to be not evaluative as to literary quality, but factually descriptive as to content and reputation; that is, terms like *classic* or *notable* are used to indicate not just opinions that I happen to share, but also opinions that seem to be widespread. The length of each annotation is determined not by the supposed importance of the work, but by the amount of detail necessary to indicate the interrelations between Wells's various books and to suggest both the continuities and the changes in his thought. Considerations of space have in general precluded the noting of conflicting interpretations of the various works, but in one case (no. 21) I have ventured to correct interpretations that seem to me both grossly mistaken and too often repeated.

In classifying the various works of fiction, I have counted as *fantasy* (supernatural fantasy, if the distinction between nature and supernature can be allowed for this one purpose) those stories that deal with the prehistoric past as traditionally envisioned in theology or mythology; with future time as leading to judgment day: with outer space as envisioned in theological astrology; or with the traditional personae of demonology and mythology: angels, devils, and the demons of the air, ghosts and human souls waiting to be born, magicians and witches, mermaids, and fairies, and the like. Counted as *delusional fantasy* are stories that center on a dream or daydream, or a sleeping or waking nightmare, of the protagonist.

On the other hand, I have counted as *science fiction* stories that deal with imagined developments in applied science, including social science and the psychic; with imagined biological species, imagined survivals in presumably extinct species, or imagined mutations in existing species; with natural catastropes of a nature or scope unparalleled in history, though perhaps not in myth; with the prehistoric past as reconstructed in paleontology; with the fourth dimension as a short-cut through time or space or as a link between parallel worlds; or with outer space as an extension of the material world perhaps inhabited by beings with humanlike or even godlike powers but not exclusively or primarily by traditional beings behaving in the traditional ways. Also counted as science fiction are those stories in which apparently supernatural phenomena are made subject to natural law, as in no. 7:6.

In both fantasy and science fiction there are stories of the *unresolved* type: those in which narrator and reader are left in doubt as to whether the ghost was real or merely a delusion, or the claimed invention or discovery merely a fraud.

For stories counted neither as fantasy nor as science

fiction, I have used four terms: the noun *novel* or the adjective *mundane* for stories predominantly concerned with the world of the here and now as empirically verified in daily life; *colonial romance* for the adventures of Europeans or Americans ("white men") among the natives of the far places of the world; and *ruritanian romance* for stories laid in imaginary small kingdoms of the white man's world.

Finally, I have used *mundane* in two paradoxical ways: in *mundane fantasy* for stories that contain nothing of the supernatural or science fictional but are too dreamlike to be called *realistic* and too reasonable to be called *surrealistic;* and in such phrases as *mundane farce on the wonders of science* for stories centering on astonished, marveling, or worshipful reactions to the actual achievements of modern science.[4]

1 CHRONOLOGICAL SURVEY

1. *The Time Machine: An Invention.* U.S. 1895. U.K. 1895, rev. A1 (116 pp.; rechaptered). Science Fiction. Evolution to the end of time: social, biologic, geologic, solar. Forms with nos. 5, 8, 10, and 14 the group of five scientific romances that have won virtually universal acclaim.

2. *Select Conversations with an Uncle (Now Extinct) and Two Other Reminiscences.* 1895. (74 abs. pp.). Fourteen familiar essays in which provincial common sense is pitted against the artistic and social fashions of the metropolis.

3. *The Wonderful Visit.* 1895. A1 (155 pp.). Science Fiction. The first book-length story in which Wells uses the method that predominates in his short stories, "the method of bringing some fantastically possible or impossible thing into a commonplace group of people, and working out their reactions with the completest gravity and reasonableness" (A1:0).

An angel falls from his world (man's land of dreams) through the fourth dimension to this world (his land of dreams), where he is immediately shot down by a bird-hunting vicar, who then takes him home to nurse back to health. The townspeople refuse to believe that he is anything other than some queer kind of hunchback. He gradually deteriorates as he breathes Earth's "poisonous air" (ch. 48), so that when his wounds heal, he finds himself not only unable to fly again but also suffering from all the human passions; cf. no 23. Science fiction, if barely so: although the protagonist is called an *angel*, he is not from the traditional heaven; moreover, the concept of parallel worlds with each being the other's land of dreams would seem to belong to psychic science fiction rather than to traditional fantasy.

4. *The Stolen Bacillus and Other Incidents.* 1895 (168 abs. pp.).
    1. "The Stolen Bacillus." Mundane farce on the wonders of science. A jesting bacteriologist tells a visitor that the bottle in his hand contains enough bacteria to poison London's entire water supply. Since modern science can do anything, the credulous visitor, who happens to be an anarchist, takes him at his word and runs away with the bottle to do just what the bacteriologist has suggested.
    2. "The Flowering of the Strange Orchid." A1. Biological science fiction.
    3. "In the Avu Observatory." Biological science fiction.
    4. "The Triumphs of a Taxidermist." Mundane satire on the passion to make a name for onself by the discovery of new species.
    5. "A Deal in Ostriches." Mundane farce.
    6. "Through a Window." Ironic mundane melodrama.

7. "The Temptation of Harringay." Fantasy: the infernal pact and artistic integrity.

8. "The Flying Man." Colonial romance with the wonders of technology: the natives astounded by the use of a parachute.

9. "The Diamond Maker." Science fiction of the unresolved type; cf. no. 7:5.

10. "Aepyornis Island." A1. Biological science fiction.

11. "The Remarkable Case of Davidson's Eyes." A1. Science fiction: the fourth dimension.

12. "The Lord of the Dynamos." A1. Mundane tragedy, involving the wonders of science: a white man's brutal jest and a black man's religious response; cf. no. 4:1.

13. "The Hammerpond Park Burglary." Mundane farce.

14. "The Moth." A1. Delusional fantasy satirizing the rivalry of biologists in the discovery of new species.

15. "The Treasure in the Forest." Colonial romance.

5. *The Island of Dr. Moreau.* 1896. A2 (170 pp.). Described by Wells as a "theological grotesque" (A2:0), this science-fiction story of animals turned into men by surgery has been given various parabolic interpretations.

6. *The Wheels of Chance: A Holiday Adventure.* 1896. A7 (231 pp.). Novel. This story of the misadventures of a draper's assistant on a bicycling holiday is the first of the five comedies of lower-middle-class life: "close studies" of "personalities thwarted and crippled by the defects of our contemporary civilization" (A7:0). Cf. nos. 13, 22, 32, 44.

7. *The Plattner Story and Others.* 1897 (296 abs. pp.).

1. "The Plattner Story." A1. Science fiction. The Fourth dimension.

2. "The Argonauts of the Air." Science fiction. The building and launching of the first successful aeroplane; compare no. 19:1.

3. "The Story of the Late Mr. Elvesham." A1. Somatopsychic science fiction. A drug-induced exchange of bodies.

4. "In the Abyss." Biological science fiction. A manlike species on the ocean floor.

5. "The Apple." Unresolved fantasy. A schoolboy dreading examinations is given, by a mysterious stranger, an apple said to be from the Tree of Knowledge, but he loses it before he can nerve himself up to trying it out.

6. "Under the Knife." A1. Science fiction in a delusional-fantasy frame. When soul and body separate at the moment of death, the soul, being immaterial and hence unaffected by either inertia or external force, remains fixed in space while body, earth, and solar system speed away.

7. "The Sea Raiders." Science fiction: man's predominance challenged by a hitherto unknown species from the depths of the sea.

8. "Pollock and the Porroh Man." Colonial romance: the white man's arrogance and the black man's magic.

9. "The Red Room." A10. Psychic science fiction: fear as an externalized force.

10. "The Cone." A1. Mundane melodrama involving the wonders of technology.

11. "The Purple Pileus." A1. A mixture of mundane comedy and delusional fantasy resulting from the eating of a mushroom.

12. "The Jilting of Jane." A1. Mundane comedy.

13. "In the Modern Vein: An Unsympathetic Love Story." Mundane comedy.

14. "A Catastrophe." A10. Mundane comedy.

15. "The Lost Inheritance." Mundane comedy.

16. "The Sad Story of a Dramatic Critic." Mundane comedy.

17. "A Slip Under the Microscope." A6. Mundane comedy (bitter comedy in the closing pages) of student life at the Normal School of Science; compare no. 13.

8. *The Invisible Man: A Grotesque Romance.* 1897. A3 (203 pp.). Science fiction. Remains the model of stories using the method specified for no. 3 and one of the chief models of the (failed) superman story.

9. *Certain Personal Matters: A Collection of Material, Mainly Autobiographical.* 1897 (240 abs. pp.). Thirty-nine familiar essays, "the stuff of which novels are made" (A6:0), of which twenty-two appear as *The Euphemia Papers* in A6 (115 pp.). Among those not in A6 are the two of most direct science-fiction interest: "The Extinction of Man" and "From an Observatory," the stuff of no. 7:7 and no. 12:2.

10. *The War of the Worlds.* 1898. A3 (241 pp.). Science fiction. Martians invade England with a technological superiority as overwhelming and a ruthlessness as complete as that with which Europeans have invaded Africa and Australia. Remains the standard of comparison for all stories on the world-catastrophe theme.

11. *When the Sleeper Wakes.* 1899 (326 abs. pp.). 1910 (rev. as *The Sleeper Awakes*). A2 (text of 1910; 304 pp.). Science fiction. The revolt of the proletariat in the megalopolis of 2100—a future extrapolated on the basis of Marxist theory and the assumption of continued technological advance under laissez-faire government; thus a dystopia in that free enterprise is shown as leading to monopoly, political oligarchy, and a disaster for the human spirit. Although Wells regarded this work as artistically and intellectually unsatisfactory (A2:0; no. 24:1), it has probably been the most influential of his scientific romances. The

revisions of 1910 consist in the elimination from Ch. 14 of an eleven-page account of the history of the period 1899–2100, from ch. 16 of a four-page account of flying inconsistent with the actual flying of 1910, and from ch. 23 and elsewhere of about seven pages that suggest a love affair between the Sleeper and the heroine. (*see* no. 30).

12. *Tales of Space and Time.* 1899 (269 abs. pp.).

   1. "The Crystal Egg." A10. Science fiction. Interplanetary television.

   2. "The Star." A10. Science fiction. A sixteen-page epitome of the colliding worlds theme.

   3. "A Story of the Stone Age." 79 abs. pp. Science fiction. The invention of the axe, the taming of the horse, and so forth.

   4. "A Story of the Days to Come." 124 abs. pp. Science fiction. Pastoral dream and megalopolitan reality in the laissez-faire dystopia of 2100; cf. no. 11.

   5. "The Man Who Could Work Miracles." A10. Science fiction: like no. 7:6 in bringing supernatural phenomena into conflict with the Newtonian laws of motion. For the film, *see* no. 90.

13. *Love and Mr. Lewisham.* 1900. A7 (278 pp.). Novel. The ambitions of youth abandoned under the pressures of sexuality for the comforts of marriage. This second of the five comic novels (*see* no. 6) was Wells's first laborious attempt at realistic fiction and his bid for reputation as a serious novelist. Although it failed in its immediate purpose, its depiction of student life at the Normal School of Science and its portrait of Chaffery the Medium have since made it one of his most popular novels.

14. *The First Men in the Moon.* 1901. A6 (265 pp.). Science fiction. Regarded by Wells as the best of his scientific romances and by many readers as the unrivaled masterpiece of the cosmic voyage.

15. *Anticipations of the Reaction of Mechanical and Scientific*

Progress upon Human Life and Thought. 1901. A4 (273
pp.). In this book, which was more responsible than
any other for the development of futurology, Wells
turned from the Marxist thinking of no. 11 to the
development of his own vision of the future. The
improvements in locomotion already well under way
will cause cities to grow, not in the immense vertical
concentrations described in no. 11, but horizontally
along great roadways (chs. 1–2). The old social classes
will dissolve into a new mixture of four main elements: first, the Efficients, "more or less capable
people engaged more or less consciously in applying
the growing body of scientific knowledge to the
general needs"; second, and perhaps as numerous as
the Efficients, the Speculators, "nonproductive per-
sons living in and by the social confusion"; third, the
unemployables, or People of the Abyss, those unable
for one reason or another to develop the skills
required by mechanized industry; fourth, the Irresponsible Rich—rich because of their ownership of
shares in corporations, irresponsible because the
control of those corporations will be in other hands
(ch. 3). In the earlier years of the century there will be
not one but many moralities, not one but many
reading publics, and so forth, but as the years pass the
Efficients will develop a common body of ideas and
gradually segregate themselves from the functionless
elements (ch. 4). Since popularly elected governments
inevitably drift into war, but can not fight a war
effectively, they will give way to governments that can
(ch. 5). The nations that survive the pressures of war
and preparation for war will be those that achieve the
largest proportional development of Efficients; that
is, those that are most successful in eliminating, in one
way or another, the Speculators, the People of the
Abyss, and the Irresponsible Rich (ch. 6). The grow-

ing unity of the world will result in the spread of those languages that offer the largest bodies of imaginative and scientific literature, and also in the aggregation of smaller states into larger ones; by the end of the century the world will probably be dominated by three great powers: an English-speaking union, a federated Western Europe, and an East Asian union, with Russia absorbed into the second or third or divided between them (chs. 7–8). In the English-speaking union, at least, the Efficients will become a New Republic, with a religion stripped of superstition and with a morality and public policy shaped to favor the procreation of the "fine and efficient and beautiful" and to prevent that of "the mean and ugly and bestial in the souls, bodies, or habits of men" (chs. 8–9).

16. *The Discovery of the Future: A Discourse Delivered to the Royal Institution.* 1902. A4(33 pp.). The classic statement of the difference between the kind of mind that looks to the past and the kind that looks to the future.

17. *The Sea Lady:A Tissue of Moonshine.* 1902. A5 (167 pp.). Fantasy. The method of nos. 3 and 8 with the subject matter of no. 13, except that here the youthful ambitions include an advantageous marriage already arranged and are abandoned for the "better dreams" advocated by the mermaid heroine.

18. *Mankind in the Making.* 1903 (371 abs. pp.). A4 (74 pp.; selections as indicated below). Concerned with education, health care, and social legislation as the means of making ordinary people Efficients rather than unemployables and thus of saving them from the Abyss of no. 15.

    1. "The New Republic." This first of the Wellsian manifestos (*see* nos. 59, 69, and 75) calls upon the reader to dedicate himself to "the service of the future of the race."

    2. "The Problem of the Birth Supply." A4. Argues

against positive eugenics and ridicules the fear of the rapid multiplication of the unfit.

7. "Political and Social Influences." A4 (first half only, as "The Case for Republicanism"). The first of Wells's many attacks on the English monarchy and aristocracy.

8. "Thought in the Modern State." A4 (last paragraph only). On the publishing and distributing of books.

12. "Appendix: A Paper on Administrative Areas Read Before the Fabian Society." A4 (as "Locomotion and Administration"). This argument that the administrative areas planned by the Fabians are far too small for the demands of the modern world is mentioned frequently by Wells in his later work. *See* no. 20.

19. *Twelve Stories and a Dream*. 1903 (274 abs. pp.).

1. "Filmer." Science fiction. The building of the first aeroplane. Cf. no. 7:2.

2. "The Magic Shop." A10. Unresolved fantasy. Magic is in the eye of the beholder. A classic story of the conflict between the child's vision and the adult's mundaneness.

3. "The Valley of Spiders." A10. Biological Science fiction within a parable of the ruler and the ruled.

4. "The Truth about Pyecraft." A10. Science fiction. The difference between fat and weight in a story that brings supernatural phenomena into conflict with natural law; cf. no. 7:6.

5. "Mr. Skelmersdale in Fairyland." Fantasy. An epitome of one side of the theme most pervasive in Wells's mundane fiction: Mr. Skelmersdale declines the invitation of the fairy queen and then regrets having done so for the rest of his life in this dreary world. Cf. no. 17 and 33.

6. "The Inexperienced Ghost." A ghost story.

7. "Jimmy Goggles the God." A10. Colonial romance. The effect of the wonders of technology on the superstitious natives.

8. "The New Accelerator." A10. Science fiction. A drug that accelerates human reactions a thousandfold.

9. "Mr. Ledbetter's Vacation." Mundane farce.

10. "The Stolen Body." Science fiction. Psychic research.

11. "Mr. Brisher's Treasure." Mundane farce.

12. "Miss Winchelsea's Heart." A6. Mundane comedy.

13. "A Dream of Armageddon." A3. Science fiction. Love and honor in the world of 2100; that is, the world of nos. 11 and 12:4.

20. *The Food of the Gods and How It Came to Earth.* 1904. A5 (299 pp.). Said by Wells to be "the idea of the first chapter of 'Anticipations' and of the essay on 'Locomotion and Administrative Areas' transmuted into fantasy" (A5:0; *see no. 12),* this story of children grown so gigantic that they can not "get inside a church, or a meeting-house, or *any social or human institution"* (1:4:2; emphasis added), is his most elaborate application of the method of nos. 3 and 8 and his most extensive venture into allegory. Let me add here some words of a kind that might also be applied to no. 11 and all the later romances. Although it does not have the concentrated impact of Wells's five most widely admired romances (nos. 1, 5, 8, 10, and 14), it is still by the standards commonly applied in science fiction criticism a quite satisfactory superman story, as well as, in chs. 1:3–7, a successful thriller on the theme of growth run wild. (On a number of occasions in his later writings, Wells used the expressions "Food of the Gods" and "Sea Lady" for opposing forces in the human heart; for one example, *see* no. 35.)

21. *A Modern Utopia.* 1905. A9 (350 pp.; including the Appendix, "Scepticism of the Instrument," which is of some importance in the history of semantics). Science fiction. The world as it might have been in 1905 if history had been somewhat different, as shown by a parallel world out beyond Sirius; that is, a world more technologically advanced than Edwardian England only in the ways and to the degrees that would have been possible through the wider application of techniques already available. The Irresponsible Rich of no. 15 have no existence in Utopia, but the Efficients are present as the Poietic and Kinetic; the Speculators as the Base, mostly banished to islands where they may cheat each other to their heart's content (5:2); the People of the Abyss as the Dull, those failing in the educational program, then about 13% but a constantly decreasing proportion of the population (9:4); and the New Republicans of no. 15 and no. 18 as the Order of Samurai, in which Wells anticipates such organizations as Lenin's Communist Party. Since the Order is open to 87% of the population, subject only to one's willingness to abide by the Discipline, it can not be said, several critics to the contrary, to be anything like a managerial elite. Furthermore, since the great cities of Utopia are mere dots on the surface of a world whose great geographic areas are either tended as gardens or held as wilderness preserves into which anyone may, and every Samurai must, make periodic retreats for self-renewal (9:7), it is not an urbanized nightmare like that of no. 11.

22. *Kipps: The Story of a Simple Soul.* 1905. A8 (442 pp.). Novel. With this story of a draper's assistant who inherits a fortune, Wells achieved the success that had eluded him with no. 13. Henceforth for many readers, he was to be the supreme interpreter of the life of

the lower-middle class—the "new Dickens." *Kipps* was originally planned as part of a larger work; Harris Wilson has compiled a continuous narrative from the surviving pages of the discarded manuscript and published it as *The Wealth of Mr. Waddy* (Carbondale, Illinois: Southern Illinois University Press, 1969).

23. *In the Days of the Comet.* 1906. A10 (313 pp.). Science fiction. The world before and after the passage of a comet that purifies the air men breathe and thus awakens "the Spirit of Man that has drowsed and slumbered and dreamt dull and evil things" (2:1:3; cf. no. 3). The first half of this book presents a considerably darker picture of lower-middle-class life than that presented in no. 22 or any of the other early comedies. There seems to be no term in current usage, though *eucatastrophe* might serve, for a nonmillenial world-shaking natural event of beneficial effect, the theme not being common in literature.

24. *The Future in America: A Search After Realities.* 1906. A26 (238 pp.). An examination of various aspects of American life in an effort to determine whether the United States is on the way to becoming the kind of "Great State" that Wells envisioned in such works as nos. 15, 21, 27, or 38:7.

25. *Socialism and the Family.* 1906. A16 (36 pp.). A pamphlet on matters more fully covered in no. 27.

26. *This Misery of Boots.* 1907. A4 (25 pp.). A frequently reprinted essay in which shoddy footwear is made to stand for all the inefficiencies of the capitalist system.

27. *New Worlds for Old.* 1908 (272 abs. pp.). An exposition of "modern Socialism," directed primarily at the middle classes, and said to have been the most widely influential socialist propaganda of its day. Includes the matter of two pamphlets: *Will Socialism Destroy the Home?* (1907) and *A Walk Along the Thames Embankment* (1923).

28. *The War in the Air, and Particularly How Mr. Bert Smallways Fared While It Lasted.* 1908. A20 (377 pp.). Science fiction. Notable for its blending of the science fiction of great events with the comedy of lower-middle-class life. After a series of misadventures, Mr. Smallways finds himself on the flagship of the German Aerial Navy and thus with a grandstand seat for the beginning of the war that destroys civilization. Unlike nos. 39 and 84 in that the destruction of civilization has no utopian aftermath.

29. *First and Last Things: A Confession of Faith and a Rule of Life.* 1908 (212 abs. pp.); 1917 (with addition of 1:12–15); *see* note on no. 109. A11 (182 pp.; 1917 text with deletion of 3:10–19). An introduction to philosophy. Begins with an exposition of the "neo-nominalism" that Wells began to develop as early as 1891 in "The Rediscovery of the Unique" (*Fortnightly Review*, July), which he developed further in "Scepticism of the Instrument" (no. 21, Appendix), which he continued to work at for the rest of his life (see no. 111:4), and which forms the philosophical foundation for his view of what life is in the modern world and what one should do about it. Of the sections omitted in A11, the first seven deal with the possibility of organized brotherhoods along the lines of the Samurai (no. 21), and the last three with an attitude toward war rendered difficult to defend if not untenable by 1914–1918.

30. *Tono-Bungay.* 1909. A12 (520 pp.). Novel. Widely regarded as Wells's masterpiece, this is the autobiography of a scientist involved in the rise and fall of a financial empire that originates in the success of the eponymous patent medicine. In its concluding chapters, with the world collapsing around the protagonists, it becomes somewhat farcical and science-fictional in the search for science-fictional metal and

the use of a science-fictional aircraft. As has been noted by several critics, this book does for turn-of-the-century England, especially with respect to advertising, corporate finance, and class relationships, what no. 11 attempted to do for the future. The most cogent account of the relationship between the two books is given by Wells in a 1921 Preface that appears in the Collins edition of *The Sleeper Awakes* (reprinted as recently as 1964).

31. *Ann-Veronica: A Modern Love Story.* 1909. A13 (390 pp.). Novel. The first of Wells's novels to deal primarily with the upper classes, and the first to include extensive discussions of morality and politics, this story of a young woman from a respectable home who defies her parents, first in going to London to study biology and live on her own, then in demonstrating with the suffragettes and going to jail for the cause, and finally in setting up housekeeping with the man she loves even though he already has a wife, scandalized a vocal segment of the older generation and became an international success among young people.

32. *The History of Mr. Polly.* 1910. A17 (280 pp.). Novel. A return to the comedy of lower-middle-class life, this book had a success comparable to that of no. 22 and continues to be one of Wells's most popular books.

33. *The New Machiavelli.* A14 (553 pp.). Novel. The autobiography of a politician who chooses, at the height of his career, to abandon politics for an illicit love (cf. no. 17). For the scandal that arose from the similarity of two of the characters to Sidney and Beatrice Webb, and from the similarity of the crucial love affair to an affair of Wells's own, *see* Lovat Dickson, *H. G. Wells: His Turbulent Life and Times* (1969), ch. 12. This is the first of the five Prig Novels—stories that "turn on a man asking himself what he shall do with his life" (A19:0), in each of which

the protagonist is frustrated in the attempt to live a nobly constructive life by the pressures of sexuality or by the demands of a wife or husband interested only in mundane success (*see* nos. 35, 37, 40, 45). Together with nos. 13, 17, and 62, they thus present Wellsian variations on the ancient theme of love and honor.

34. *Floor Games*. With marginal drawings by J. R. Sinclair. 1911 (63 abs. pp.). An introduction to the art. (*See* no 36).

35. *Marriage*. 1912. A15 (577 pp.). The second of the prig novels (*see* no. 33): "Trafford has eaten the Food of the Gods, and Marjorie is immune to the stimulant and plays, in holy wedlock, the role of the Sea Lady" (A15:0).

36. *Little Wars: A Game for Boys from Twelve Years of Age to One Hundred and Fifty and for That More Intelligent Sort of Girl Who Likes Boys' Games and Books. With an Appendix on Kriegspiel. By . . . the Author of "Floor Games" and Several Minor and Inferior Works*. With marginal drawings by J. R. Sinclair. 1913 (103 abs. pp.). 1970 (facsimile edition with Foreword by Isaac Asimov and Introduction by Christopher Ellis). Ellis indicates that a considerable literature has grown up in this field, all deriving from this book. If so, it has in its field the same kind of importance that nos. 15, 56, and 80 have in theirs.

37. *The Passionate Friends*. 1913 (376 pp.). Novel. The most romantic of the prig novels (*see* no. 33)—and the book in which the phrase "open conspiracy" first appears (*see* no 75).

38. An Englishman Looks at the World: Being a Series of *Unrestrained Remarks on Contemporary Matters*. 1914 (443 abs. pp.; in U.S. as *Social Forces in England and America*). A9, 18, 20, 27 (217 pp.).

   1–3. "The Coming of Bleriot"; "My First Flight"; "Off the Chain." A20. Of the 1909 channel crossing that demonstrated the practicability of heaver-than-air flight; of Wells's own venture three years later; and of the inevitable effects of the abolition of distance on commerce, politics, and social life.

4–5. "Of the New Reign"; "Will the Empire Live?" A20. Argues against imperial tariffs, imperial military establishments, and so forth; argues for a great effort to make the empire worthy of the loyalty of its various peoples.

6. "The Labour Unrest"; "Social Panaceas"; "Syndicalism or Citizenship." 1912 pamphlet. Argues that modern conditions demand not mere tinkering with wages and hours, which seems to be the sole concern of the labor unions, but fundamental changes in the social structure.

7. "The Great State." A18 (40 pp.). Appeared in a book of the same title by Wells and thirteen others (1912) as, "The Past and the Great State." An epitome of Wells's social thought, with a remarkable diagram that makes Wells's view of past and future immediately clear.

8. "The Common Sense of Warfare."A20. 1913 pamphlet. Argues against conscription, for education.

9. "The Contemporary Novel." A9. The major statement of Wells's literary theory. Cf. no. 85:7:7; also nos. 74:25–26, and 102:0.

10. "The Philosopher's Public Library." A description of what a public library should and very economically could be.

11. "About Chesterton and Belloc." A9. On the most persistent of his friendly enemies, who fought at his side against the capitalist order, but parted from him in advocating distributism rather than socialism and who are the objects of friendly comment or gentle satire in many of his books (not always gentle in the case of Belloc; *see* especially no. 70).

12. "About Sir Thomas More." Originally the

Introduction to an edition of *Utopia* published in 1905, the year no. 21 appeared.

13. "Traffic and Rebuilding." Suggests that it might be more economical to rebuild London on a new site.

14. "This So-Called Science of Sociology." 1907 pamphlet. Against Comte, Spencer; for Plato and the utopian approach.

15. "Divorce." A18. Changing mores.

16. "The Schoolmaster and the Empire." Against regarding Polonius as the ideal schoolmaster.

17. "The Endowment of Motherhood." A18. The most convenient statement of an idea also treated in nos. 21, 27, and 33.

18. "Doctors." For medicine as a "sanely organized public machine."

19. "An Age of Specialization." Argues that this is instead an age of the decline of specialization.

20. "Is There a People?" Argues that there is not.

21. "The Disease of Parliaments." Argues for proportional representation. Compare no. 52:9–11.

22. "The American Population." A9 (as "The American Outlook"). A more pessimistic forecast than that of no. 24.

23. "The Possible Collapse of Civilization." A20. The great dangers are financial panic and modern warfare.

24. "The Ideal Citizen." A9. He is, in sum, a student and philosopher, understanding the society in which he lives.

25. "Some Possible Discoveries." The most sensational discoveries of the century are likely to be in biology.

26. "The Human Adventure." A27. Surely the most eloquent statement of Wells's vision of the future, this essay is an elaboration of the last pages of no. 20.

39. *The World Set Free: A Story of Mankind.* 1914. A21 (247 pp.). Science fiction. An experiment in narrative structure, this romance tells of the development of atomic energy, of the use of atomic bombs in the most destructive of all wars, and with the world thus freed of its past, of the establishment of the world state and building of utopia. From this time on, despite the apparent optimism of many of his books, Wells seems always to have believed that only after some great cleansing, some catastrophe of worldwide scope, would the leaders of mankind leave the road to destruction and set out upon the road to utopia.

40. *The Wife of Sir Isaac Harman.* 1914. A16 (500 pp.). Novel. The fourth of the prig novels (*see* no. 33): large-minded wife, small-minded husband; thus in direct contrast with no. 35.

41. *The War That Will End War.* 1914 (88 abs. pp.). A pamphlet reprinting eleven newspaper articles in which Wells viewed the war less as a great disaster than as a great opportunity. With one exception ("The Liberal Fear of Russia"), they deal with matters more fully covered in no. 46.

42. *The Peace of the World.* 1915. A21 (33 pp.). Discusses the forces that make for war and calls for a world congress to replace the ambassadorial system.

43. *Boon, The Mind of the Race, The Wild Asses of the Devil, and The Last Trump: Being a First Selection from the Literary Remains of George Boon, Appropriate to the Times: Prepared for Publication by Reginald Bliss, with an Ambiguous Introduction by H. G. Wells.* 1915 (198 abs. pp.). A13 (166 pp.; omits chs. 0 and 6–7). Novel: despite the title, this book is not a collection of papers by George Boon, the "remains" having turned out to be merely a few scraps of paper, but instead a narrative by Reginald Bliss in which he talks about Boon and his friends, reports their conversations, and reconstructs from memory never-written papers that Boon had

told him about, including the (in)famous "Of Art, of
Literature, of Mr. Henry James." Of the "selections"
only one is a complete literary work: "The Story of the
Last Trump," a fantasy in which the world continues
on its merry way, the last trump having been heard
but not believed. Chs. 6–7, a lively but rather frivolous
debate on metaphysics and religion, were perhaps
omitted from A13 as being inconsistent with the views
set forth on these matters in A11, for which *see* no. 50.
44. *Bealby: A Holiday.* 1915. A17 (278 pp.). Novel: the last
and most farcical of the five comedies of lower-
middle-class life; *see* no. 6.
45. *The Research Magnificent.* 1915. A19 (436 pp.). The
quintessential prig novel (*see* no. 33) in that it explores
most fully the motivations and difficulties of a man
attempting to lead a completely noble life. Benham is
the first of Wells's heroes to develop religious ideas
along the lines of those more fully propounded by Mr.
Britling (no. 47) and by Wells himself in no. 50.
46. *What is Coming? A Forecast of Things After the War.* 1916
(248 abs. pp.). Looks forward first to a long war (being
here different from nos. 41 and 47) and then to the
bankruptcy of the exhausted nations, which will force
upon them a considerable degree of socialism; to the
liberation of women, made inevitable by their partici-
pation in the war effort; to a reformation of the
universities, made possible by their then being virtually deserted; to a Europe made less quarrelsome by
the rationalization of national boundaries; to the
beginnings of a world state in the Permanent Alliance
made necessary by the fear of a resurgent Germany;
to the end of the various colonial empires, backward
countries being prepared for statehood by the members of the Permanent Alliance; and to the eventual
absorption of a chastened Germany into the new
world order. For the way in which this "very loose-

lipped" book was viewed by Wells eighteen years later, *see* no. 84:9:5.

47. *Mr. Britling Sees It Through.* 1916. A22 (as *Mr. Britling*; 538 pp.). Novel. This story of life during wartime at the home of a famous author was Wells's greatest popular success in fiction, ranking second among American best-sellers in 1916 and first in 1917. Many reviewers, and presumably large sections of the general public, found reassurance in Mr. Britling's religious conversion; on the other hand, many of Wells's most loyal followers felt themselves betrayed.

48. *The Elements of Reconstruction: A Series of Articles Contributed in July and August 1916 to The Times: With an Introduction by Viscount Milner.* [Articles signed "D. P."]. 1916; 1917 (as by Wells). This pamphlet calls for increasing the size of British industrial units so that they can compete with those of Germany and the United States; for an imperial constitution and parliament (not wholly consistent with no. 38:4–5); in general for adapting British institutions to the demands of the new age.

49. *War and the Future: Italy, France, and Britain at War.* 1917 (240 abs. pp.; in U.S. as *Italy, France, and Britain at War*). A26 (106 pp.).

   0. "The Passing of the Effigy." A26 as ch. 1. Discusses the absence of "great and imposing leaders, Napoleons, Caesars."

   1. "The War in Italy: August 1916." A26, abridged, as chs. 2–3.

   2. "The Western War: September 1916." A26, abridged, as chs. 4–7. One chapter tells of Wells as the grandparent of the tank, because of his 1903 story, "The Land Ironclads" (no. 70:1:4), of the old-line opposition to the development of tanks, and of their potential as the decisive weapon of the war.

   3. "How People Think of the War." In comparison

to no. 46, a more restrained but still hopeful forecast
of the world after the war.

50. *God the Invisible King.* 1917. A11 (147 pp.). An
introduction to theology. From first to last (or at least,
from no. 15:9 to no. 113) Wells saw man as struggling
to survive in a hostile universe, and saw religion as the
dedication of the individual to this larger purpose.
This book forms with nos. 51 and 54 what may be
called a Manichaean trilogy, for in them, as less
centrally in nos. 45 and 47, the spirit of man is seen as
embodied in a finite personal god. Although Wells
repudiated this book from 1926 on (nos. 69:1:3,
85:9:4, and 109:10), he was defending it as late as
1925 against both orthodox Christians on the right
and the Rationalist Press Association on the left
(A11:0), and it remains an accurate statement, except
in the concept of a personal god, of his religious views.

51. *The Soul of a Bishop: A Novel (with Just a Little Love in It)
about Conscience and Religion and the Real Troubles of
Life.* 1917. A25 (309 pp.). Novel: the second part of
the Manichaean trilogy. Having unwittingly taken a
mind-expanding drug, the Bishop experiences the
reality of the living God and eventually comes to find
that he can serve Him best by leaving the established
church.

52. *In the Fourth Year: Anticipations of a World Peace.* 1918.
A21 (125 pp.; omits ch. 0, 5 abs. pp.).

0. Preface. Of the various proposals made since
1914 for a league of nations.

1–8. "The League of Free Nations." Argues that the
League can be successful only if all the civilized
peoples of the world are pledged to a common law and
a common world policy. Includes the 1917 pamphlet
A Reasonable Man's Peace.

9–11. "Democracy." Argues for proportional representation.

53. *Joan and Peter: the Story of an Education.* 1918. A23–24 (819 pp.). Novel. The story of how Oswald Syndenham, bruised in body and spirit after serving the Empire in Africa for seventeen years, returns to England to become the guardian of Joan and Peter, of how he undertook their education, and of what he and they learned in the years before and during the Great War. Of all Wells's novels, this one has the broadest sweep, the largest cast of characters, and the greatest variety of matter and manner.

54. *The Undying Fire: A Contemporary Novel.* 1919. All (170 pp.). Fantasy. This last part of the Manichaean trilogy (*see* no. 50) tells of a new wager in Heaven; of how Job Huss, headmaster of a school similar to Oundle (*see* no. 65), suffered through a series of blows to himself, his family, and his school; of how he kept the faith; and of how all things were restored. Although repudiating its theology, Wells continued to regard this dialogue on religion and education as one of his finest artistic achievements (no. 84:7:5). Listed among Wells's works sometimes as a novel, sometimes as a romance; cf. no. 66.

55. *History Is One.* 1919. A27 (14 pp.). Prolegomena to no. 56.

56. *The Outline of History: Being a Plain History of Life and Mankind.* 1920 (1,950 abs. pp.). Numerous editions in various formats; one of the best-selling books of all time. As for the first full-scale history of mankind, and as by far the most widely read, this book was more important than any other in establishing world history as a field of study. The note that dominates Wells's work from this time on is struck in the final chapter, "The Possible Unification of the World into One Community of Knowledge and Will." Although Wells the erstwhile school-teacher had labored extensively along conventional lines for the improvement of

schools, teaching methods, and so forth (in numerous never-reprinted articles in the educational press and in no. 18), he had come to believe that such efforts would be largely futile until there had been broad changes in the attitudes of the members of the educated classes, especially with respect to religion and patriotism. In devoting its first fourteen chapters to scientific concepts of the origin and prehistorical development of earth, life, man, language, and in devoting many of its other chapters to religions, cultures, and empires outside the Ancient-Medieval-Modern scheme that conventionally culminated first in Christian Europe and then in modern England (or modern Anycountry) as the crown of civilization, the *Outline* was consciously intended to reshape the outlook of its readers. It aroused intense opposition in many quarters; *see* nos. 60 and 70.

57. *Russia in the Shadows.* 1919. A26 (75 pp.; omits six-page Envoy). Tells of a visit made in October 1920 to Petersburg and Moscow, including an interview with Lenin, and argues that the Allies should seek not to overthrow but instead to aid the Bolshevik government, it being the only conceivable government that can save the country from complete collapse.

58. "A Memorandum on Peace Propaganda." In Campbell Stuart, ed., *Secrets of Crewe House* (London, 1920). A21 (13 pp.). Written in 1918 while Wells was officially engaged in the propaganda campaign directed at the German people; published as evidence of the failure of the government to keep its wartime promises; cf. no. 73:3.

59. *The Salvaging of Civilization.* 1921 (186 abs. pp.). Ch. 1, the second of the Wellsian manifestoes (*see* no. 18), anticipates the Three-fold Imperative of no. 108 by declaring that "unless the ever more violent and disastrous incidence of war can be averted, unless

some common controls can be imposed on the headlong waste of man's limited inheritance of coal, oil, and moral energy that is now going on, the history of humanity must presently culminate in some sort of disaster, going on thereafter in a degenerative process towards extinction" (1:2) and then calls for "propagandist cults to which men and women must give themselves and their energies regardless of the consequences to themselves" (1:4). Chs. 2–3 distinguish between a true world state and such organizations as the League of Nations. Chs. 4–7 discuss a possible "Bible of Civilization" and the schooling of the world. In sum, the salvaging of civilization, to use the famous phrase from no. 56:41:4, is a race between education and catastrophe.

60. *The New Teaching of History: With a Reply to Some Recent Criticisms of "The Outline of History."* 1921 (42 abs. pp.). Defends the concept of world history; expresses a willingness to accept corrections in matters of detail; complains that many critics attack the work for errors that appeared only in the serial version; and so forth.

61. *Washington and the Hope for Peace.* 1922 (189 abs. pp. in U.S. and in A26 as *Washington and the Riddle of Peace*). A26 (155 pp.; omits seven chapters). Twenty-nine newspaper articles on the Washington Disarmament Conference. The victorious Allies having imposed a punitive peace, the League having emerged as a mere paper organization, and this conference having actually achieved some success, Wells turned from the idea of an immediate world parliament to the hope that from this and similar conferences may come the establishment of worldwide limited-purpose organizations that can gradually become numerous enough and strong enough to create the conditions necessary for world peace, order, and development. Compare no. 77.

62. *The Secret Places of the Heart.* 1922. A25 (250 pp.).

Novel. Like nos. 13, 17, and 33, this is a love-and-honor story, but in this case the lovers choose honor rather than love, separating so that they can devote themselves more effectively to the creation of the new world order.

63. *A Short History of the World.* 1922, A27 (457 pp.). Numerous editions, including paperback editions and updated revisions.

64. *Men Like Gods.* 1923. A28 (321 pp.). Science fiction. A group of Englishmen pass through the F dimension to a utopian world such as Earth might become in a thousand years if it manages to survive the present Age of Confusion.

65. *The Story of a Great Schoolmaster: Being a Plain Account of the Life and Ideas of Sanderson of Oundle*, 1924. A24 (130 pp.). Wells's theory of what a school should be was closely approximated by Oundle School, to which he sent his own sons, and on which he modeled the school attended by Peter in no. 53 and the one presided over by Job Huss in no. 54.

66. *The Dream: A Novel.* 1924. A28 (318 pp.). An inhabitant of the utopian world of the fortieth century dreams of life in the twentieth century. The result is essentially a realistic story of working-class life. Although it can hardly be called *science fiction*, the story is given a distancing and coloring by the narrative device that might justify calling it a *romance*. Students of science fiction as popular literature might well be interested in the account of Thuderstone House, an English equivalent of the American publisher of pulp magazines.

67. *A Year of Prophesying.* 1924 (302 abs. pp.). A26 pp.; fourteen selections as *Articles Written in 1923–1924*). Fifty-five newspaper articles on a wide variety of subjects. A 1924 pamphlet, *The P. R. Parliament* [proportional representation], appears here and in A26 as "The Extinction of Party Government."

68. *Christina Alberta's Father*. 1925 (466 abs. pp.). Novel. Partly the story of the growth to maturity of the heroine, and partly that of the belief of her putative father that he is a reincarnation of Sargon, King of Kings, and has only to proclaim his kingdom in order to bring it into being. This is the first of five stories making extensive use of formal psychology and centering on a protagonist who suffers from some form of psychosis. (*See* nos. 75, 82, 97, and 102).

69. *The World of William Clissold: A Novel at a New Angle*. 1926 (860 abs. pp.; three volumes in U.K.; two volumes in U.S.). A survey of the world of 1926, and of its history, purportedly written by a scientist of such vision and directive capability as to have been important in the development of a worldwide industrial organization similar to Brunner Mond and Co. Not more than a third of the book can be described as narrative, and even this tends to be synoptic rather than detailed. Ch. 5 presents the first extensive exposition of the Open Conspiracy for a world state, an idea that Wells thought should be especially attractive to men engaged in commerce or industry on a worldwide scale, hampered and restricted as they presumably are by the division of the world into numerous small states. (*See* no. 75).

70. *Mr. Belloc Objects to "The Outline of History."* 1926 (76 abs. pp.). Wells's part in the no-holds-barred contest that Belloc began with a series of articles in the Catholic press.

71. *The Short Stories of H. G. Wells*. 1927 (later editions as *The Complete Short Stories of H. G. Wells*). Contains eleven stories (191 abs. pp.) not yet accounted for in this survey.

　　1. "The Time Machine and Other Stories." Stories 2, 3, 5, 6, and 8 were first collected in a 1911 omnibus, *The Country of the Blind and Other Stories*.

　　　　1:1 "The Time Machine." (*See* no. 1).

1:2 "The Empire of the Ants." (1905). A10. Biological science fiction. A new threat to man's predominance; cf. no. 7:7.

1:3. "A Vision of Judgment." (1899). A10. Fantasy. Sinner and saint at what is not actually the last judgment.

1:4. "The Land Ironclads." (1903). A20. Science fiction. Wells's chief claim to accuracy in technological prediction; *see* no. 49:2.

1:5. "The Beautiful Suit." (1909). A10. Mundane fantasy. A parable of innocence and experience.

1:6. "The Door in the Wall." (1906). A10. Unresolved fantasy. The classic story of the secret garden.

1:7. "The Pearl of Love." Written 1925 for A10. Mundane fantasy. A parable of the artistic process.

1:8. "The Country of the Blind." (1904). A10. Biological science fiction combining the lost-race and superman themes.

2. "The Stolen Bacillus and Other Incidents." (*See* no 4).

3. "The Plattner Story and Others." (*See* no 7).

4. "The Reconciliation." (1895). First collected in an 1897 omnibus, *Thirty Strange Stories*. Mundane melodrama.

5. "My First Aeroplane." (1910). A farcical science-fiction parable: childish man playing with a new and dangerous toy.

6. "Little Mother up the Morderberg." (1910). Mundane farce: a sequel to the preceding story.

7. "The Story of the Last Trump." A13. From no. 43.

8. "The Grisly Folk." (1921). Science fiction. The clash of true man and Neanderthal man; a fictionalization of no. 56:10:1.

9. "Tales of Space and Time." (*See* no. 12).

10. "Twelve Stories and a Dream." (*See* no. 19).

72. *Meanwhile: The Picture of a Lady.* 1927 (325 abs. pp.).

Novel. Eventually the constructive revolution; meanwhile, fascism in Italy and the general strike in England.

73. *The Works of H. G. Wells. Atlantic Edition.* Vol. 27. 1927. Contains three essays not previously collected (54 pp.).

   3. "What is Success? A Note on Lord Northcliffe." Of Wells's long acquaintanceship with the great press lord, of their working together at Crewe House (*see* no. 58), and of the difference between the official propaganda issuing from Crew House and the hate campaign waged against Germany in Northcliffe's newspapers.

   4. "The Gifts of the New Sciences." Like No. 38:25 in predicting that the great advances will be in biology, psychology, and eduction rather than in technology; less than prescient on atomic energy and the speed of travel.

   5. "The Ten Great Discoveries." First, the use of implements; second, the beginning of moral law and social restraint in the form of tabu; tenth, the realization that the world is one.

74. *The Way the World Is Going: Guesses and Forecasts of the Years Ahead.* 1928 (338 abs. pp.). One address and twenty-six newspaper articles, of which the following are perhaps of greatest interest.

   1. "Man Becomes a Different Animal. Delusions about Human Fixity." Of the "biological revolution now in progress."

   5. "Democracy Under Revision: A Lecture Delivered at the Sorbonne." 1927 pamphlet. Of the contrast between the indifference of the ordinary citizen-with-a-vote and the dedication of the members of such organizations as the Communist Party, the Fascist Party, and the Kuomintang, and of the similarities of these organizations to the New Republicans of nos. 15 and 18 and the Samurai of no. 21. (Chs. 2–4 cover much the same ground.)

   11. "The Present Uselessness and Danger of

Aeroplanes. A Problem in Organization." An instance of the failure of administrative units to adapt to the change in scale; cf. no. 18:12.

13. "Delusions about World Peace. The Price of Peace." 1927 pamphlet (as *Playing at Peace*). The price is the world state.

16. "The Silliest Film: Will Machinery Make Robots of Men?" A review of *Metropolis*, the Fritz Lang film, noting its similarity to no. 11 and the failure of its creators to learn anything from the developments of the last thirty years.

25. "The Man of Science and the Expressive Man. To Whom Does the Future Belong? Some Thoughts about Ivan Pavlov and George Bernard Shaw." This discussion of style and content is one of the major statements of Wells's artistic theory.

26. "The Future of the Novel. Difficulties of the Modern Novelist." Argues that the novel adapts its form to changes in its environment.

75. *The Open Conspiracy: Blueprints for a World Revolution.* 1928 (145 abs. pp.). 1931 (rev. as *What Are We to Do with Our Lives?*). The 1931 text, in which the revisions are more rhetorical than substantive, presents the final form of the third Wellsian manifesto (*see* nos. 18, 59, and 68). Abjuring anything so romantic as conspiratorial conspiracy; calling not for heroic action but only for the formation of study and propagandist groups, which would find their basic concepts in such books as nos. 56, 80, and 81, the manifesto must have struck many readers as less a call to world revolution than a device to sell books. Even so, today—forty years later—the basic concept seems eminently reasonable.

76. *Mr. Blettsworthy on Rampole Island. Being the Story of a Gentleman of Culture and Refinement who suffered Shipwreck and saw no Human Beings other than Cruel and Savage Cannibals for several years. How he became a Sacred*

Lunatic. How he did at last escape in a Strange Manner from the Horror and Barbarities of Rampole Island in time to fight in the Great War, and how afterwards he came near to returning to that Island for ever. With such Amusing and Edifying Matter concerning Manners, Customs, Beliefs, Warfare, Crime, and a Storm at Sea. Concluding with some Reflections upon Life in General and upon these Present Times in Particular. 1928 (328 abs. pp.). Novel: the second of the psychosis stories (*see* no. 68). Mundane comedy and satire in chs. 1, 2, and 4, but delusional fantasy in ch. 3, which presents a reversal of the situation in no. 20, the megatheria representing those swollen human institutions that have outlived their time but which refuse to die and thus clear the way for man's progress.

77. *The King Who Was a King: The Book of a Film.* 1929 (175 abs. pp.). Ruritanian romance; borderline science fiction. How a king outmaneuvers the foreign offices of the great powers and brings about a World Control for Calcomite (a science-fictional metal); cf. no. 61. (The film was never produced.)

78. *The Adventures of Tommy.* 1929 (42 abs. pp.). Cartoons with captions; a minor classic in children's books.

79. *The Autocracy of Mr. Parham: His Remarkable Adventures in this Changing World.* 1930 (321 abs. pp.). Science fiction in a delusional-fantasy frame. How Mr. Parham, philosopher of history and expert in geopolitics, is at a séance possessed by a visitant from Mars, the Master Spirit of Manhood and Dominion and Order, and thereafter proceeds to do for England what Mussolini has done, or talked about doing, for Italy.

80. *The Science of Life: A Summary of Contemporary Knowledge about Life and Its Possibilities.* With Julian S. Huxley and G. P. Wells. 1930 (2,700 abs. pp.). Has been issued in one-volume, three-volume, four-

volume, and nine-volume editions. Planned and organized by Wells, with about 70% of the writing by Huxley and about 25% by G. P. Wells. Like no. 56, the first comprehensive treatment of its subject. "Its effects are still manifest in the increased space allotted to biology in the educational curriculum, and the greater interest of the general public in biological facts and their consequences"—Julian Huxley, *Memories* (1970), ch. 12, which gives an account of the collaboration.

81. *The Work, Wealth, and Happiness of Mankind.* 1931 (in two volumes). 1932. Rev. ed.: U.K. 1934 (1,390 abs. pp.); U.S. 1936 (as *The Outline of Man's Work and Wealth*). In Wells's social, political, and philosophical thought, the culmination of all that precedes and the basic source of all that follows: most of his other non-fictional works might well be regarded as mere addenda to this one book. With nos. 56 and 80 forms what is often called the educational trilogy.

82. *After Democracy: Addresses and Papers on the Present World Situation.* 1932 (230 abs. pp.). Sixteen essays on politics, economics, morality, and the future, of which four had separate publication.

    3. "The Common-Sense of World Peace." 1929 pamphlet. The common sense of world peace demands a world state.

    5. "Imperialism and the Open Conspiracy." 1929 pamphlet. Laments that the concept of a self-sufficient empire with protective tariffs should be advocated by a director of Brunner Mond and Co. (*See* no. 69).

    6. "The World Change." One section of a 1930 pamphlet, *The Way to World Peace,* the remainder omitted as repeating ch. 3, as indeed it does, almost word for word.

    16. "What Should Be Done—Now." 1932 pam-

phlet. The economic crisis demands a controlled inflation, the expansion of public employment, the lowering of tariffs, and disarmament.

83. *The Bulpington of Blup: Adventures, Poses, Stresses, Conflicts, and Disaster in a Contemporary Brain.* 1932 (501 abs. pp.). Novel. This third of the psychosis stories (*see* no. 68) recounts the fantasy life and the real life of a literary intellectual.

84. *The Shape of Things to Come: The Ultimate Revolution.* 1933 (640 abs. pp.). Science fiction. Purportedly a schoolbook written in 2106, this history begins with the financial diasters of 1929 and moves through the depression years into a future extrapolated on the assumption that the nations will not be able to halt the steadily worsening economic and political disintegration. A decade of desultory warfare (the devitalized nations being unable to mount a war on the scale of 1914–18) is followed by a decade of plagues that halve the population of the world. With the world thus set free of its past, scientific and technical workers find it possible first to establish an Air Dictatorship and then to proceed to the building of utopia. For the film, *see* no. 87.

85. *Experiment in Autobiography: Discoveries and Conclusions of a Very Ordinary Brain (since 1866).* 1934 (1,033 abs. pp.). Covers his personal life through about 1900 and his professional life through the first half of 1934 (during which time he interviewed both Roosevelt and Stalin). Notable for the frankness of its strictly autobiographical parts and for the vividness of the numerous portraits of men prominent in literature or public life.

86. *The New America, the New World.* 1935 (60 abs. pp.). On the ways in which the friends and enemies of the New Deal are reacting to the world crisis.

87. *Things to Come: A Film Story Based on Material Contained*

in History of the Future "The Shape of Things to Come."
1935 (170 abs. pp.). In its first half, a drastically
simplified version of no. 84:2:9–12; in the second half,
a story of conflict in the utopian world of 2054 in
which the advocates of luxurious idleness try to
prevent the advocates of heroic endeavor from attempting a voyage to the moon.

88. *The Croquet Player*. 1936 (60 abs. pp.). Science fiction in
the form of a rationalized ghost story: the changed
environment is releasing and intensifying man's inherent aggression and cruelty.

89. *The Anatomy of Frustration: A Modern Synthesis.* 1936
(166 abs. pp.). Purportedly a review of a multivolume
work of the same name by a recently deceased
author—a work modeled on Burton and dealing with
the forces in human nature and modern life that
frustrate man in his collective effort to create a
rational world order, and the individual in his effort
to lead a worthwhile life. Compare the prig novels of
1911–1915.

90. *Man Who Could Work Miracles: A Film Story Based on
Materials in His Short Story. . . .* 1936 (106 abs. pp.).
Science fiction. An expanded version of no. 12:5,
together with a Prologue and an Epilogue in heaven
that make the misadventures of Mr. Fotheringay a test
case for the question whether man can safely be
trusted with such power as science is even now putting
into his hands.

91. *Star Begotten: A Biological Fantasia.* 1937 (151 abs. pp.).
Science fiction. The discovery among humanity of a
new human species and the search for the cause of its
origin. Compare no. 96.

92. *Brynhild; or, The Show of Things.* 1937 (264 abs. pp.).
Novel. Satire on the building of a literary reputation.

93. *The Camford Visitation.* 1937 (52 abs. pp.). Borderline
science fiction. The reactions of dons and students to
an invisible but highly vocal visitor from outer space

who lectures them on the shortcomings of mankind, especially as represented at Camford and Oxbridge.

94. *The Brothers*. 1938 (96 abs. pp.). Ruritanian romance. In a civil war the royalist and communist leaders discover not only that they are twin brothers, but also that they have, despite the contrast in their rhetoric, the same constructive principles.

95. *World Brain*. 1939 (154 abs. pp.). Ten addresses and articles on the establishment of a world encyclopædia center and on education in general. Includes Wells's presidential address to the education section of the British Association for the Advancement of Science, 1937, "The Informative Content of Education," and a 1936 pamphlet, "The Idea of a World Encyclopædia."

96. *Apropos of Dolores*. 1938 (344 abs. pp.). Novel. The story of a battle royal between man and wife; related to no. 91 by the presence of the biologist Foxfield and the concept of two human species. The Dolores of the title is said to be a portrait of Odette Keun; if so, the same lady is also represented by the Clementina of no. 69 and the Lolotte of Anthony West's *Heritage* (1955).

97. *The Holy Terror*. 1938 (575 abs. pp.). Science fiction. The life story of Rud Whitlow, who is paranoic as a child, heroic as the leader of the world revolution, and again paranoic as the Master Director of the World State. With respect to depression and war, the extrapolative assumptions here are the same as in no. 84, but in this case there is a well-organized Open Conspiracy ready to take advantage of the coming of war. This is the fourth of the psychosis stories (*see* no. 68); from no. 102:4:1:4 it is clear that the protagonist, though he may at times suggest Hitler or Wells himself, is modeled primarily on Stalin.

98. *The Fate of Homo Sapiens: An Unemotional Statement of the Things that Are Happening to Him Now, and of the Immediate Possibilities Confronting Him*. 1939 (280 abs.

pp. in U.S. as *The Fate of Man*). 1942 (*see* note on no.
100). Begins with a statement of the ecological crisis
and then surveys the "existing forces" that hold man
on the road to destruction and prevent him from
taking the road to utopia: Judaism, Catholicism,
Protestantism, Nazism, Totalitarianism, the British
oligarchy, Shintoism, the New Life movement, Imperialism, Communism, the American mentality. The
conclusion is that man will almost certainly fail to
adapt to his new environment and hence will pass out
of existence.

99. *Travels of a Republican Radical in Search of Hot Water*.
1939 (125 abs. pp.). Wells at his most cantankerous in
eight articles and one address, and at his noblest in a
second address, "The Honour and Dignity of the Free
Mind," which was prepared for delivery to the 1939
meeting of the P. E. N. Club, scheduled for Stockholm
in September, but canceled.

100. *The New World Order: Whether It Is Attainable, How It
Can Be Attained, and What Sort of World a World at Peace
Will Have to Be*. 1940 (142 abs. pp.). 1942 (*see* below).
This handbook for the constructive world revolution
was Wells's first response to the coming of the second
war; the same general ideas are developed more fully
and coherently in no. 108. NOTE: In *The Outlook for
Homo Sapiens: An Amalgamation and Modernization of
[98 and 100]* (1942), the Introduction and twenty-six
chapters of no. 98, with chs. 4–5 combined, appear as
chs. 1–26, and the twelve chapters of no. 100 as chs.
27–38. The only modernizations are a transitional
paragraph in ch. 27, the use in ch. 36 of a later version
of the Sankey Declaration (*see* no. 101), and the
addition of ch. 39, "Russia, the West, and World
Revolution."

101. *The Rights of Man; or What Are We Fighting For?* 1940
(93 abs. pp.). An account of the origin of the Sankey
Declaration, an exposition of its provisions, and an

argument for its immediate worldwide adoption. The version of the Declaration given here also appears in no. 103; an earlier version appears in no. 100, a later version in nos. 105 and 107, and the final version in nos. 108 and 111.

102. *Babes in the Darkling Wood.* 1940 (520 abs. pp.). Novel. This fifth of the psychosis stories (*see* no. 68) is in large part an exposition of "the new and entirely revolutionary philosophy of behaviourism" (ch. 0). The story relates how the young hero and heroine clash with their old-fashioned parents, what the hero experiences in Poland during the first days of the war, the facts of his mental breakdown and the failure of psychoanalysis to effect a cure, and the success of psychosynthesis. The Introduction is a defense of the novel of ideas as a literary form.

103. *The Common Sense of War and Peace: World Revolution or War Unending?* 1940 (124 abs. pp.). Material generally similar to that in no. 100.

104. *All Aboard for Ararat.* 1940 (90 abs. pp.). Fantasy. Having been so instructed by God, Noah Lammock, the well-known author, builds an ark in order to survive the flood of the ecological crisis.

105. *Guide to the New World: A Handbook of Constructive World Revolution.* 1941 (180 abs. pp.). Despite the title, this is simply a collection of fifty-two newspaper articles.

106. *You Can't Be Too Careful: A Sample of Life.* 1941 (386 abs. pp.). Novel. Wells's last book-length fiction is both a comedy of lower-middle-class life that caused some reviewers to applaud the old man for returning to his true forte, and a drama of the world crisis. It is the life story of Edward Albert Tewler, a representative specimen (as is every man) of *Homo Tewler*, which may survive long enough to become *Homo sapiens*, but probably will not.

107. *Science and the World-Mind.* 1942 (45 abs. pp.). Poses

the problem of the education of two billion people for
world unity.

108. *Phoenix: A Summary of the Inescapable Conditions of
World Organization.* 1942 (265 abs. pp.). A comprehensive summation of Wells's thinking on the ecological
crisis and the constructive revolution. Ch. 1:2, "The
Threefold Imperative," expresses more cogently than
ever before a set of concepts that had occupied him
since no. 59 in 1921. First, the abolition of distance,
which subjects every country to the danger of a
sudden blitzkrieg, makes imperative a world control
of transport and communication, especially in the air.
Second, the "stupendous enhancement of the power
of waste" makes imperative the establishment of a
world conservation authority. Third, the virtual disappearance of illiteracy and the danger posed by
masses of discontented young men makes imperative
the subordination of all states to a common fundamental law—a Rights of Man that includes the right of
every man to satisfactory employment.

109. *The Conquest of Time: Written to Replace His "First and
Last Things."* 1942 (88 abs. pp.). A compact exposition
of "the religion of the new man," with an appendix on
some theories of time. (Despite the intention indicated
in the subtitle and the Preface, the Rationalist Press
Association continued no. 29 as no. 1 in the Thinker's
Library and made this book no. 92.)

110. *Crux Ansata: An Indictment of the Roman Catholic Church.*
1943 (142 abs. pp.). Among other things, condemns
the Catholic Church for its failure to condemn
Nazism.

111. *'42 to '44: A Contemporary Memoir upon Human Be-
haviour During the Crisis of the World Revolution.* 1944
(360 abs. pp.).

　　　0. Preface. States that since this book is "strong meat
for babes" and may thus prove repellent to many who

follow his propaganda for the new world order, it will be published only as an expensive library volume. (It was published at 42s, about four times the ordinary price.)

1. "The Heritage of the Past. The Psychology of Cruelty." Considers, in fourteen sections, the possibility that man's addiction to cruelty may prove an insuperable barrier to the realization of a just world order and hence to his survival.

2. "How We Face the Future." Seventeen articles, mostly reprinted from periodicals, on stupidity and scoundrelism in high places.

3. "A Thesis on the Quality of Illusion in the Continuity of the Individual Life in the Higher Metazoa with Particular Reference to the Species *Homo sapiens.*" 1942 pamphlet. The thesis with which Wells, at eighty-five, won a doctorate from London University.

4. "A Memorandum on the Relation of Mathematics, Music, Moral and Aesthetic Values, Chess, and Similar Intellectual Elaborations to the Reality underlying Phenomena." In Wells's neonominalism, mathematics can not accurately reflect the ultimate reality.

5. "A Memorandum on Survival." On the survival or failure to survive of species in general and man in particular. Incorporates material also used in the 1945 edition of no. 63 and in no. 113.

112. *The Happy Turning: A Dream of Life.* 1945 (47 abs. pp.); *see* no. 113. Autobiographical fantasy: conversations with Jesus on disciples, a hymn of hate against sycamores (cf. the megatheria of no. 76), and a visit to Elysium.

113. *Mind at the End of Its Tether.* 1945 (35 abs. pp.); U.S. 1946 (with no. 112); U.K. 1968 (with no. 112, edited with an Introduction by G. P. Wells, as *The Last Books of*

H. G. Wells). Sections 1–3 announce that "the end of everything we call life is close at hand and cannot be evaded"; sections 5–8, not wholly consistent with this announcement, are from the 1945 edition of no. 63 and also, in part, from no. 111:5.

2   THE ATLANTIC EDITION

The Works of H. G. Wells. Atlantic Edition. 28 volumes. Printed in U.S. New York: Charles Scribner's Sons; London: T. Fisher Unwin, Ltd.; volumes 1–4, 1924; 4–14, 1925; 15–22, 1926; 22–28, 1927. There is a Preface to each volume, but only that to Al is noted in the following table.

Warren Wagar has said (in *Wagar) that for the study of the development of Wells's thought, the Atlantic Edition is valuable chiefly for its prefaces—a statement that has several times been echoed without the qualification. Any careful examination of the Atlantic Edition will show both that Wagar was correct and that the Atlantic Edition is still highly convenient in many respects, one being its inclusion of works difficult to locate elsewhere.

The prospectus for it announced that all its contents would be newly revised. With respect to the fictions and familiar essays, scholars are fortunate that Wells kept this promise only in a very desultory fashion. Although my investigation has not been thorough enough for unqualified statement, it has been extensive enough for me to feel safe in saying that here the revisions are not substantive but only stylistic in quite trivial ways, and that the Atlantic Edition is therefore a convenient source for all the novels and romances published through 1924 (marred only by the use of the 1910 version of no. 11 and the deletion of two chapters from no. 43, which some readers would regard as nonfiction) and for an adequate sample of the short stories and familiar essays in that it includes thirty-two of the sixty-two stories in no. 71 and twenty-two of the forty-three essays in no. 2 and no. 9.

Setting aside the two floor-game books (which might well have been included), the two 1893 textbooks (presumably of little interest to anyone), and *The Outline of History* (excluded for obvious reasons), scholars are left with what might be called Wells's controversial essays. Of the fifteen unified works of at least minimum book length (here set at 75 abs. pp.), seven are complete perhaps for a preface or an Epilogue, two all but complete, two drastically abridged, and four entirely omitted. Of the eighty-eight shorter essays published as substantial pamphlets or in the two collections (nos. 38, 67), thirty-four are reprinted, together with four essays not previously collected. Although many of the shorter pieces, especially those of no. 67, were surely dropped as simply not worth reprinting, it is quite obvious that the principal intent of the deletion, abridgment, and selection was to show the continuity in the development of the views held by Wells in 1924–1927 and at the same time to remove from consideration what he had come to regard as foolish aberrations. Even so, it must still be granted that Wells is quite frank and unembarrassed about such aberrations in the Prefaces, and that the Atlantic Edition all in all, gives the controversial essays a representation surely sufficient for all students other than those who want the full details of the various aberrations.

A1:00. A General Introduction to the Atlantic Edition.
    0. Preface to Volume 1
    1. *The Time Machine* (no. 1)
    2. *The Wonderful Visit* (no. 3)
    3. Other Early Fantastic Stories (nos. 7:12, 7:10, 4:2, 4:10, 4:11, 4:12, 4:14, 7:3, 7:6, 7:1, 7:11)
A2:1. *The Island of Dr. Moreau* (no. 5)
    2. *The Sleeper Awakes* (no. 11)

A3:1. *The Invisible Man* (no. 8)
   2. *The War of the Worlds* (no. 10)
   3. "A Dream of Armageddon" (no. 19:13)
A4:1. *Anticipations of the Reaction of Mechanical and Scientific Progress upon Human Life and Thought* (no. 15 [with 1914 Introduction appended])
   2. "Locomotion and Administration" (no. 18:12)
   3. "The Problem of the Birth Supply" (no. 18:2)
   4. "The Case for Republicanism" (no. 18:3 [first half only])
   5. "Thought in the Modern State" (no. 18:8 [last paragraph only])
   6. *The Discovery of the Future* (no. 16)
   7. *This Misery of Boots* (no. 26)
A5:1. *The Food of the Gods* (no. 20)
   2. *The Sea Lady* (no. 17)
A6:1. *The First Men in the Moon* (no. 14)
   2. *The Euphemia Papers* (22 essays from no. 9)
   3. "A Slip Under the Microscope" (no. 7:17)
   4. "Miss Winchelsea's Heart" (no. 19:12)
A7:1. *The Wheels of Chance* (no. 6)
   2. *Love and Mr. Lewisham* (no. 13)
A8:1. *Kipps* (no. 22)
A9:1. *A Modern Utopia* (no. 21)
   2. "Scepticism of the Instrument" (no. 21:Appendix)
   3. "The Contemporary Novel" (no. 38:9)
   4. "About Chesterton and Belloc" (no. 38:11)
   5. "The American Outlook" (no. 38:22)
   6. "The Ideal Citizen" (no. 38:24)
A10:1. *In the Days of the Comet* (no. 23)
   2-18. Seventeen Stories (nos. 7:9, 71:4, 12:5, 19:7, 19:2, 19:3, 19:8, 7:14, 19:4, 71:1:2, 12:1, 71:1:3, 12:2, 71:1:6, 71:1:8, 71:1:5, 71:1:7)
A11:1. *The Undying Fire* (no. 54)
   2. *First and Last Things* (no. 29)
   3. *God the Invisible King* (no. 50)

A12:1. *Tono-Bungay* (no. 30)
A13:1. *Ann Veronica* (no. 31)
    2. *Boon* (no. 43:1–5, 7–10)
A14:1. *The New Machiavelli* (no. 33)
A15:1. *Marriage* (no. 35)
A16:1. *The Wife of Sir Isaac Harman* (no. 40)
    2. *Socialism and the Family* (no. 25)
A17:1. *The History of Mr. Polly* (no. 32)
    2. *Bealby* (no. 44)
A18:1. *The Passionate Friends* (no. 37)
    2. "Divorce" (no. 38:15)
    3. "The Endowment of Motherhood" (no. 38:17)
    4. "The Great State" (no. 38:7)
A19:1. *The Research Magnificent* (no. 45)
A20:1. *The War in the Air* (no. 28)
    2. Other War Forebodings
        2:1. "The Land Ironclads" (no. 71:1–4)
        2:1–8. Seven essays (no. 38:1–5, 8, 23)
A21:1. *The World Set Free* (no. 39)
    2. Other War Papers
        2:1. *The Peace of the World* (no. 42)
        2:2. "The League of Free Nations" (no. 52:1–8)
        2:3. "A Memorandum on Peace Propaganda"
            (no. 58)
        2:4. "Democracy" (no. 52:9–11)
A22:1. *Mr. Britling* (no. 47)
A23:1. *Joan and Peter, I* (no. 53:1–11)
A24:1. *Joan and Peter, II* (no. 53:12–14)
    2. *The Story of a Great Schoolmaster* (no. 65)
A25:1. *The Soul of a Bishop* (no. 51)
    2. *The Secret Places of the Heart* (no. 62)
A26:1. *The Future in America* (no. 24)
    2. *War and the Future* (no. 49:0–2 [abridged])
    3. *Washington and the Riddle of Peace* (no. 61:1–11,
       13–16, 19, 22–23, 26–29)
    4. *Russia in the Shadows* (no. 57)

    5. *Articles Written in 1923–1924.* (no. 67:1, 4, 6, 8, 16,
       18, 26, 29, 32, 39, 47, 52, 54, 55)
A27:1. *History Is One* (no. 55)
    2. *A Short History of the World* (no. 63)
    3. "What is Success? A Note on Lord Northcliffe"
      (no. 73:3)
    4. "The Gifts of the New Sciences" (no. 73:4)
    5. "The Ten Great Discoveries" (no. 73:5)
    6. "The Human Adventure" (no. 38:26)
A28:1. *Men Like Gods* (no. 64)
    2. *The Dream* (no. 66)

NOTES

    1. Geoffrey H. Wells, *The Works of H. G. Wells 1887–1925: A Bibliography, Dictionary, and Subject-Index* (London: Routledge, 1926); The H. G. Wells Society, *H. G. Wells: A Comprehensive Bibliography* (Edgware, Middlesex, England: Michael Katanga, 1966; rev. ed. 1968). The former, whose author was not related to Wells, is a model of its kind, marred by fewer errors than one would expect; the latter, referred to below as *C.B.*, is a far less ambitious work in which the errors stand out more prominently.

    2. Bernard Bergonzi, "The Publication of *The Time Machine,* 1894–1895," in Thomas D. Clareson, ed., *Sf: The Other Side of Realism* (Bowling Green, Ohio: University Popular Press, 1971), pp. 204–215; reprinted from *Review of English Studies* 11 (1960): 42–51.

    3. Also omitted are two items (*C.B.:* 143 and 151) that I have not been able to locate and that are listed in *C.B.* without sufficient detail to enable me to determine whether they would qualify for the survey, or to satisfy me that they have actually been examined by the editors of *C.B.*

    4. Since the realistic is opposed not only to the fantastic but also to the idealistic, idyllic, romantic, sentimental, melodramatic, farcical, and so forth, I find the term *realism* quite unusable in discussing science fiction as a genre distinct from other genres—and much the same thing must be said for the term *naturalism*.

Contributors

TATYANA CHERNYSHEVA teaches at Irkutsk University, Irkutsk, U.S.S.R. A leading Soviet scholar on science fiction, she has published a number of essays on it in Russian.

DAVID YERKES HUGHES teaches at the University of Michigan, Ann Arbor. He has published several articles on Wells, and coedited with R. M. Philmus *H. G. Wells: Early Writings in Science and Science Fiction* (1974).

SAKYO KOMATSU worked as reporter, factory manager, and critic before becoming one of the best-known Japanese science-fiction writers and lecturers on futurology. He has published about thirty books of science fiction and essays. In 1971 he was chairman of the International Science Fiction Symposium in Japan.

RICHARD DALE MULLEN teaches at Indiana State University, Terre Haute. He has published a number of essays on science fiction, and is co-editor of *Science-Fiction Studies,* a well-known critical journal published in Terre Haute.

PATRICK PARRINDER teaches at Reading University, England. His publications include the books *H. G. Wells* (1970) and *H. G. Wells: The Critical Heritage* (1972), and essays on science fiction. He is an editorial consultant of *Science-Fiction Studies*.

ROBERT M. PHILMUS teaches at Concordia University, Montreal. His publications include *Into the Unknown* (1970) and *H. G. Wells: Early Writings in Science and Science Fiction* (1975—coeditor with D. Y. Hughes), and essays on science fiction. He is an editorial consultant of *Science-Fiction Studies*.

DARKO R. SUVIN teaches at McGill University, Montreal. His publications include *Od Luki jana do Lunjika* (1965), *Russian Science-Fiction 1956–1974* (1976), the anthology *Other Worlds, Other Seas* (1970, translated into four languages), *Pour une poétique de la science-fiction* (1977), and a number of essays on history and theory of science fiction. He is co-editor of *Science-Fiction Studies*.

J. P. VERNIER teaches at the Université de Rouen. His publications include *H. G. Wells et son temps* (1971) and essays on science fiction.

Index of H. G. Wells's Works

This index does not list titles from the two bibliographies at the end of the book, the collected edition, or books edited by others. Abbreviations from page 32 for two frequently quoted books are added in parentheses.

Index of Authors

This index does not list H. G. Wells, names in titles of articles or books, or names mentioned in the Acknowledgments.

275